Differentiating Math Instruction, K-8

Third Edition

Differentiating Math Instruction, K–8

Third Edition

*Common Core Mathematics in the
21st Century Classroom*

William N. Bender

CORWIN
A SAGE Company

CORWIN
A SAGE Company

FOR INFORMATION:

Corwin
A SAGE Company
2455 Teller Road
Thousand Oaks, California 91320
(800) 233-9936
www.corwin.com

SAGE Publications Ltd.
1 Oliver's Yard
55 City Road
London EC1Y 1SP
United Kingdom

SAGE Publications India Pvt. Ltd.
B 1/I 1 Mohan Cooperative Industrial Area
Mathura Road, New Delhi 110 044
India

SAGE Publications Asia-Pacific Pte. Ltd.
3 Church Street
#10-04 Samsung Hub
Singapore 049483

Acquisitions Editor: Jessica Allan
Associate Editor: Kimberly Greenberg
Editorial Assistant: Heidi Arndt
Permissions Editor: Karen Ehrmann
Marketing Manager: Maura Sullivan
Project Editor: Veronica Stapleton Hooper
Copy Editor: Terri Lee Paulsen
Typesetter: C&M Digitals (P) Ltd.
Proofreader: Dennis W. Webb
Indexer: Wendy Allex
Cover Designer: Karine Hovsepian

Printed in the United States of America

Library of Congress Cataloging-in-Publication Data

Bender, William N., author. [Differentiating math instruction] Differentiating math instruction, K-8 : common core mathematics in the 21st century classroom / William N. Bender. — Third edition.

pages cm

Revision of: Differentiating math instruction : strategies that work for K-8 classrooms! / William N. Bender. ?2009. Includes bibliographical references and index.

ISBN 978-1-4522-5545-3 (alk. paper)

1. Individualized instruction. 2. Mathematics—Study and teaching (Preschool) 3. Mathematics—Study and teaching (Elementary) 4. Mathematics—Study and teaching (Middle school) I. Title.

QA20.I53B46 2013

372.70973--dc23   2013025144

This book is printed on acid-free paper.

13 14 15 16 17 10 9 8 7 6 5 4 3 2 1

Contents

Acknowledgments

Corwin gratefully acknowledges the contributions of the following reviewers:

Marcia Carlson
Sixth-Grade Teacher
Crestview Elementary School
Clive, Iowa

Julie Duford
Fifth-Grade Math Teacher
Polson Middle School
Polson, Montana

Esther Eacho
Associate Faculty
Johns Hopkins University
Baltimore, Maryland

Debi Gartland
Professor of Special Education
Towson University, Department of Special Education
Towson, Maryland

Edward C. Nolan
Mathematics Supervisor, PreK to Grade 12
Montgomery Public Schools
Rockville, Maryland

Rachel Spenner
Sixth-Grade Teacher
Westridge Elementary
West Des Moines, Iowa

About the Author

 **Dr. William Bender** is an international leader in instructional tactics, with broad expertise in areas including project-based learning, technology in the classroom, differentiating instruction, response to intervention (RTI), as well as other areas dealing with general classroom instruction. In particular, Dr. Bender has written more books on response to intervention than any other author in the world, and two of these are best-selling books on that topic, and one was a 2010 finalist for the *Distinguished Achievement Award for Excellence in Educational Publishing.* By the summer of 2012, Dr. Bender had completed eight books and a professional development videotape on various aspects of RTI. He also served as a consultant to hundreds of districts and many states as they established their RTI plans. In the fall of 2010 he was selected to work with the Ministry of Education in Bermuda to establish their nation-wide RTI framework.

In addition to book development, Dr. Bender consistently receives positive reviews of his professional development workshops for educators at every level. He has an innate ability to use a combination of practical strategies and easy humor, to keep educators informed and engaged, eager to hear more. Dr. Bender's books and workshops provide research-proven, practical strategies, and convey this information in a humorous, motivating fashion.

Dr. Bender began his education career teaching in a junior high school resource classroom, working with adolescents with behavioral disorders and learning disabilities. He earned his PhD in special education from the University of North Carolina. As a professor of Education, he has taught in higher education around the nation including Bluefield State College, Rutgers University, and the University of Georgia. He is now consulting full time, writing several new professional development books. Dr. Bender has written over 60 research articles and 26 books in education, including his most recent books:

Cool Tech Tools for Lower Tech Teachers: 20 Tactics for Every Classroom

Project-Based Learning: Differentiating Instruction for the 21st Century

The Teaching Revolution: RTI, Technology, and Differentiation Transform Teaching for the 21st Century

Differentiating Instruction for Students With Learning Disabilities: New Best Practices for General and Special Educators (3rd ed.)

Response to Intervention in Math

Educators are invited to communicate directly with Dr. Bender if they wish at williamb@teachersworkshop.com. Educators may also follow Dr. Bender on Twitter (@williambender1), when he posts exclusively on educationally related content, his books or educational workshops, notices of other professional development (particularly free PD) opportunities, and other educational topics.

Introduction

This book was completely rewritten in 2012 and 2013, in order to address the ongoing transitions in mathematics education. From the author's perspective, the transitions in education today make this one of the most challenging tasks I've ever undertaken. Almost all of the states are moving toward implementation of response to intervention in mathematics and increased use of technology for instruction, and most are moving toward implementation of the Common Core State Standards in Mathematics, all at exactly the same time! Even in states such as Alaska or Texas that are not adopting the Common Core Standards, the transition to deeper conceptual levels of learning in mathematics has been emphasized. One example is the new Texas educational standards, which were initiated in 2011. In short, almost everything seems to be in transition in mathematics instruction today, regardless of where one teaches.

Further, the very concept of differentiated instruction is itself being redefined (see the discussion in Chapter 1), and I, among others, are interpreting many of the innovative instructional practices, such as the flipped math class and project-based learning, as different iterations of differentiated instruction (Bender, 2012a; 2012b). Like the changes mentioned above, this transition in the very fabric of differentiated instruction will impact how virtually all teachers teach mathematics.

In this context of change, I've made a concerted effort to pull these changes into a meaningful framework, and make these things interpretable from the practical point of view to mathematics teachers. Those teachers are in the vanguard of instruction and face nearly impossible demands on their time. Thus, the teachers on the front lines of mathematics instruction need a resource that provides research-proven, highly practical instructional ideas, without wasting a great deal of time on instructional theory, and this work is intended to meet that need.

BOOK AND CHAPTER ORGANIZATION

The current book has seven chapters, as described below. Each chapter focuses on one aspect of differentiated instruction, and most include a strong emphasis on technology in the classroom. Further, each chapter presents a continuing narrative in text, as well as additional information on various topics that did not seem to fit within the text itself. Generally that additional information is presented in numbered "boxes." Also, each chapter presents specific instructional strategies and tactics for the general education mathematics class, and those are called "Teaching Tips" and appear in number order. The book is intended to be digested as a whole, and I frequently refer to topics covered in previous chapters. For example, the case study RTI examples in Chapter 7 are based on instructional strategies described in previous chapters.

CHAPTER DESCRIPTIONS

Chapter 1: Differentiated Mathematics Instruction

This chapter is an introduction to the "New Differentiated Instruction" and also briefly introduces the Common Core Standards in Mathematics and the eight Standards for Mathematical Practice. The focus of Common Core Mathematics is described in terms of procedural fluency, conceptual understanding, and application of mathematical processes for problem solving in real-world contexts. Next, the chapter presents the original concept of differentiated instruction, and the brain-compatible research supportive of that concept, and then discusses five factors that have created a new understanding of differentiated instruction. The focus on multiple intelligences that originally characterized discussions of differentiated instruction has been de-emphasized somewhat, by introduction of other learning style/learning preferences perspectives, and a variety of brain-compatible instructional strategies in mathematics are presented.

Chapter 2: Differentiated Instructional Models: Lesson Modification and Learning Centers for Mathematics

While this is not a book on instructional theory, teachers do need to understand both the theory (as discussed in Chapter 1) and the practice of differentiated instruction in mathematics classes. This chapter focuses on the "how to do it" of differentiated instruction, by presenting two historic models for differentiation: modification of the traditional whole-group lesson plan, and learning centers for differentiating mathematics. In particular, learning centers in mathematics fluency, operations, measurement, and problem solving will be described as will a model by which learning centers become the primary basis for all mathematics instruction, rather than merely an "add-on" to the traditional math class.

Chapter 3: Flipped Mathematics Classes and Project-Based Learning: New Differentiated Instructional Models in Mathematics

This chapter is completely new, emphasizing once again the changes ongoing in mathematics education. Two new models for organizing mathematics instruction—each of which is interpreted herein as exemplars of differentiated instruction—are presented: the flipped mathematics class and project-based learning. Technology plays a key role in each of these instructional innovations and will be stressed in this chapter. Initially the flipped classroom will be described as turning the traditional lesson plan upside down, by requiring students to undertake initial instruction via self-study, and turning the math class into something resembling a math lab. The *Khan Academy* self-study mathematics curriculum will be described at length, along with specific guidelines on how teachers (referred to as coaches in that particular curriculum) may use that tool in mathematics classes. That is a curriculum focused on procedural competency rather than deeper conceptual understandings or applications of mathematics in problem-solving contexts. Of course, all students need deep conceptual understanding and application/problem-solving skills, but in spite of that limitation, this curricular option will be useful for many students. Next, project-based learning will be described at length, as the model for what happens in the differentiated math class, once students are receiving initial instruction in mathematics via self-study in the flipped classroom model.

Chapter 4: Strategies for Differentiating Early Math Instruction

Within the context of both the Common Core State Standards and the four models for differentiated instruction described in Chapters 2 and 3, this chapter presents a discussion of number sense in the primary grades, followed by discussion of differentiated instructional strategies. Technology tools such as animation (using Voki avatars), and educational games in mathematics to heighten interest in and motivation for mathematics, are described and recommended. Instructional tactics such as CRA, errorless learning, time delay, and classwide peer tutoring are also described at length as effective tactics for differentiation and for increasing students' enjoyment of mathematics. Finally, a differentiated lesson plan is presented, with specific recommendations of how a primary teacher might differentiate his or her class, with time allocations recommended for activities such as Khan Academy, guided math instruction, or computer-based gaming.

Chapter 5: Strategies for Differentiating Instruction in Grades 3 Through 6

This chapter presents strategies for differentiating instruction in the middle elementary grades. Initially, a constructivist perspective is described as a strong basis for developing deeper understanding of mathematics concepts, and that is followed by a discussion of scaffolded instruction in math. In addition, this chapter will include several new technology options for mathematics instruction, including using blogs and wikis in mathematics instruction to foster creative exploration of math concepts. Other strategies described include process mnemonics in math, guided visualization, using cue words in problem solving, and word problem maps. Again, a differentiated lesson plan is presented, with specific recommendations for elementary teachers and with time allocations recommended for various differentiated activities, building on the differentiated lesson plan presented in Chapter 4.

Chapter 6: Strategies for Differentiating Instruction in Grades 6 Through 8

This chapter focuses on differentiating mathematics instruction in the upper elementary and middle school grades. The chapter continues the technology emphasis, by focusing on collaborative social learning using social media tools such as Facebook, Twitter, and Ning for instruction. Next, Metacognitive Theory is presented as the basis for cognitive strategy instruction in mathematics, and a variety of cognitive strategies are presented, including RIDD, STAR, PASS, and schema-based instruction for problem solving.

Chapter 7: Differentiated Assessments and Response to Intervention

This chapter is totally new and begins with a brief description of the development of the Common Assessments associated with the Common Core, to be implemented in the 2014–2015 academic year. Next, the chapter presents an array of differentiated assessment strategies for the general education class, including standards-based assessments, criterion references assessment, CBM, authentic assessment, portfolio assessment, and rubric-based assessment for mathematics. Next, response to intervention in mathematics is discussed as an innovative interplay of both instruction and assessment, with a strong emphasis on universal screening in mathematics and progress monitoring for students in Tier 2 or Tier 3 math interventions. Finally two case studies for RTI in mathematics (third grade and sixth grade) are presented and discussed.

APPENDIX A: RECENTLY DEVELOPED OR WIDELY USED CURRICULA IN MATHEMATICS

Several additional interventions will be discussed here and related to various assessment demands discussed in the preceding chapters. This includes descriptions of the SAS Curricular Pathways, TransMath, Accelerated Math for Interventions, SuccessMaker Math, and Vmath. These are frequently used in both Tier 1 instruction and in Tier 2 or Tier 3 interventions in mathematics, and teachers should be aware of them.

THE INTENT OF THIS BOOK, AND A WORD OF THANKS

As an author and professional development facilitator, I'm proud that so many teachers have found earlier editions of this book useful and relevant. I meet many teachers each year who have used the teaching ideas from the book, and I continue to conduct scores of workshops yearly and have had the honor of working with thousands of teachers across the nation, the Caribbean, and in Canada.

In each of those workshops, I invariably learn some teaching idea or strategy that I usually share in the next book or workshop on this topic. Moreover, I stand in awe of the job mathematics teachers have done and continue to do, many of whom teach in very challenging situations. I've recently worked with rural schools from Tennessee to Michigan, Oregon, Washington, Ohio, Montana, and Bermuda, as well as inner city schools in Atlanta; Trenton, New Jersey; El Paso and San Antonio, Texas; and Manhattan, just to name a few. I've worked with teachers on Native American reservations from Albuquerque to Billings, Montana, and with charter schools in North Carolina as well as in the Pennsylvania oil country, and from the Silicon Valley to Detroit, to Maine.

In almost every situation I find a highly dedicated group of individuals seeking nothing more than to find new and innovative ways to excite students about learning mathematics. It has been, and continues to be, my honor to work with these teachers, and as this book moves into a virtually new, third edition, I want to say thanks to each of them, each of you, for ideas you share with me, and the excitement about teaching that I see in their, and in your eyes. For that reason, I'd like to dedicate this book to mathematics teachers everywhere. In this challenging field, we are teaching a topic focused on the very basic of understanding much of our universe, and few topics could ever be more important.

Also, I do invite teachers to communicate directly with me on this book topic if you so desire (williamb@teachersworkshop.com). Share a teaching idea, ask a question, or offer a comment, if you like. Give me a bit of time, but know that I do try to respond to them all. Also, you are welcome to follow me on Twitter (@williambender1), where I post exclusively on educational topics, free professional development opportunities, books in education I'm writing, mathematics strategies, technology tools for the classroom, or merely on great articles or blog entries on educational topics that I want to recommend for teachers. I hope these Twitter posts are a service to you.

Again, this book is dedicated to you, and thanks for the job you do in this important teaching field!

William N. Bender, PhD

Differentiated Mathematics Instruction

1

MATHEMATICS IN TRANSITION

Over the past two decades, our nation has witnessed an emerging emphasis on mathematics instruction, and as a result achievement in math among students in the United States has been increasing recently (Clarkson, Fawcett, Shannon-Smith, & Goldman, 2007; Doabler et al., 2012; Fuchs, Fuchs, Compton et al., 2007; Fuchs, Fuchs, Powell et al., 2008; Toppo, 2012). However, there are still significant concerns relative to mathematics performance, including the fact that students in the United States are no longer in the top students worldwide on mathematics achievement (National Mathematics Advisory Panel [NMAP], 2008). Further, a large percentage of students, perhaps as many as 68% of all students in the United States, are not ready for Algebra I when they enter the ninth grade. Also, there is a significant and persistent achievement gap between black and white students in mathematics, and this is highly problematic in terms of long-term school achievement for some minority students (Clarkson et al., 2007; NMAP, 2008). Finally, research has documented the fact that approximately 5% to 8% of school-age children may have a learning disability in mathematics (Mabbott & Bisanz, 2008), a disability rooted in a variety of factors such as poor calculation strategies, lack of automaticity in math facts, and poor working memory (Mabbott & Bisanz, 2008; Woodward, 2001, 2006).

> *As many as 68% of all students in the United States are not ready for Algebra I when they enter the ninth grade.*

These problems have resulted in more attention on mathematics instructional practice in recent years. In 2000, the National Council of Teachers of Mathematics published the revised mathematical instructional standards (NCTM, 2000). In 2008, the National Mathematics Advisory Panel (NMAP) published the report *Foundations for Success: The Final Report of the National Mathematics Advisory Panel* (NMAP, 2008). Finally, the Common Core Mathematics Standards (www.corestandards.org/Math) have now been published and are receiving increased attention as this book is being written in 2013. Those standards and the common assessments associated with them are scheduled for full implementation in 2014–2015. Finally, this increased emphasis on mathematics at the policy level has paralleled a growing body of research on effective mathematics instruction (Devlin, 2010; Doabler et al., 2012; Fuchs, Fuchs, Compton et al., 2007; Jordan, Kaplan, Locuniak, & Ramineni, 2007; S. P. Miller & Hudson, 2007; NMAP, 2008).

As a result of this increased attention, the emphasis within mathematics instruction has changed somewhat over the recent decades, and many of these changes are driven today by the shift to the Common Core State Standards in Mathematics. As of January 2013, 45 states have agreed to implement Common Core Standards in Mathematics, though some states are having second thoughts (Toppo, 2012). In those standards, students are expected to master a curriculum that has shifted away from computation, rote learning, and routine problem-practice activities toward an increased emphasis on reasoning, conceptual understanding, real-world problems, and connections between mathematical concepts (Toppo, 2012). The emphases in the Common Core reflect the interdependence of multiple aspects of mathematics, including procedural fluency, conceptual understanding, and the ability to apply mathematical processes in a problem-solving context.

The Common Core State Standards also emphasize a shift away from multiple-choice test questions to written responses to mathematical problems. Thus, much will be changing in mathematics instruction, and teachers today must employ the most effective and efficient instructional methods possible for increasing cognitive involvement of all students with the math curriculum. Because of these multiple emphases, teachers are searching for instructional ideas that will assist in this regard.

> *The emphasis within the Common Core State Standards in Mathematics reflects an interdependence of procedural fluency, conceptual understanding, and the ability to apply mathematical processes in a problem-solving context.*

DIFFERENTIATED INSTRUCTION IN MATHEMATICS

The concept of differentiated instruction can be of great benefit to teachers in developing and designing their mathematics instruction for students with varying ability levels in the elementary education classroom. Moreover, the emphasis on brain-compatible instruction, one founding principle of differentiated instruction, can now inform teachers concerning what specific instructional tactics may result in higher learning impact, as many of these techniques not only make learning more interesting, but also increase retention over the long term (Sousa, 2008, Sousa & Tomlinson, 2011; Tomlinson, 1999). While studies of how the human brain functions in reading tasks or math tasks have been undertaken for the past several decades, only within the last 15 years or so has this emerging biomedical research—often referred to as brain-compatible research—progressed enough to inform teachers concerning effective instructional strategies for the math curriculum (Geller & Smith, 2002; Gersten, Chard, Baker, & Lee, 2002; Sousa, 2008; Sousa & Tomlinson, 2011).

This chapter will initially present an overview of the Common Core State Standards initiative in mathematics, as a basis to discuss the changing emphases within mathematics instruction generally. Next, differentiated instruction is described as an effective instructional approach for mathematics. A brief history of differentiated instruction is followed by a description of changes that this concept has undergone over the last decade. Then, because differentiated instruction is heavily based in research on brain functioning, a discussion of research on how the brain learns mathematics is presented, coupled with instructional suggestions for increasing mathematics achievement using differentiated instruction. Finally, a discussion of how mathematics teachers might self-evaluate their instruction in order to increase differentiated instruction in their class is provided.

COMMON CORE STATE STANDARDS IN MATHEMATICS

As indicated above, 45 states have decided to adopt the Common Core State Standards in mathematics as of the spring of 2012 (Toppo, 2012). To date, only Texas, Alaska, Nebraska, Minnesota, and Virginia have not adopted these standards, meaning most teachers will be working within the context of the Common Core Standards. Clearly the Common Core State Standards in mathematics promise to significantly impact how mathematics instruction is undertaken over the next decade, as much more attention will be given to conceptual understanding of mathematics and applications of mathematics procedures for problem solving, as opposed to an emphasis on isolated math problems or procedural fluency in mathematics. Further, the current emphasis on memorization is likely to be replaced by the expectation that students be able to explain and justify their answers, and the mathematical procedures used to obtain them (Magee, 2013).

For that reason, teachers need some understanding of those standards might impact how teachers differentiate their instruction in math classes. In fact, various strategies in this book will be identified that focus on these different aspects of mathematics. For example, both scaffolded instruction (see Chapter 4) and project-based learning (see Chapter 3) emphasize conceptual understanding and applications of mathematical principles, whereas *Khan Academy* (in Chapter 4) or metacognitive learning strategies (in Chapter 5) generally tend to stress procedural processes in mathematics. Today, mathematics teachers need a wide array of instructional strategies, as all of these emphases are stressed within the Common Core (Magee, 2013).

> *The Common Core State Standards in mathematics promise to significantly impact how mathematics instruction is undertaken over the next decade.*

Initially, the Common Core State Standards were developed by the National Governors Association Center for Best Practices and the Council of Chief State School Officers in collaboration with teachers, school administrators, and curriculum experts, in order to provide a clear and consistent framework to prepare our children for higher education and/or the workforce (see www.corestandards .org/the-standards).

Standards were developed for grade levels from kindergarten through Grade 8, as well as for a variety of mathematics topics typically included within high school mathematics courses (e.g., algebra, geometry, functions, number and quantity, etc.). Feedback was solicited from many sources including various teacher organizations, higher education educators, civil rights groups, and advocates for students with disabilities. Following the initial round of feedback, the draft standards were opened for public comment, and nearly 10,000 responses were considered in preparing the final standards. The standards were finalized and released in June 2010. These standards represent, in participating states, the mathematics content that students are expected to learn. Further, the standards are intended to provide appropriate benchmarks for all students, regardless of where they live. They are described by the developing agency as clear and consistent, rigorous with an emphasis on higher-order skills, and evidence based.

Because these standards in mathematics were intended to represent a common core for instruction across states, in some cases there is little difference between the current state standards in mathematics and the Common Core Mathematics Standards. For example, the Common Core standards still call for fluency in addition and subtraction by the end of

Grade 3, and that is quite common in many existing state standards (Wurman & Wilson, 2012). In that sense, implementation of these standards may be more involved in some states than in others.

Still, implementation activities involving the Common Core are ongoing, and as of the spring of 2013, various organizations have partnered together for curriculum development and professional development activities. For example, in May 2012, universities and school districts from 30 states have partnered together to foster implementation of the Common Core State Standards in mathematics, though the scope of this partnership has yet to be determined (Sawchuk, 2012).

Mathematical Practices

However, there is some guidance on instruction in mathematics that might be impacted by these standards. The National Governors Association published, in conjunction with the standards in mathematics, a set of recommended performance skills as a general description of students' mathematics performance in order to guide mathematics instruction. A synopsis of these eight mathematical practices is provided in Box 1.1, and the complete descriptions are found at www.corestandards.org/Math/Practice.

BOX 1.1   STANDARDS FOR MATHEMATICAL PRACTICE

The standards for mathematical practice, as found on the Common Core State Standards website (www.corestandards.org/Math/Practice), describe the skills and expertise that students should demonstrate, and include a variety of areas such as problem solving, reasoning, communication, representation, strategic competence, conceptual understanding, and procedural fluency in mathematics. These are intended as an informative counterpoint to the standards themselves, and to compliment the standards by focusing on the goals of proficient mathematics for students at all grade levels.

1. **Students should make sense of problems and persevere in solving them.** Proficient students start by explaining to themselves the meaning of a problem and looking for first steps in problem solution. They analyze available information and make conjectures about the form and meaning of the solution, prior to planning a pathway to a solution. They consider analogous problems, and try special cases and simpler forms of the original problem in order to gain insight into its solution. They evaluate their progress and change their solution if necessary. Proficient students check their answers to problems using a different method.

(Continued)

(Continued)

2. **Students should reason abstractly and quantitatively.** Proficient students make sense of quantities and their relationships when working mathematical problems. They can both *decontextualize* (or abstract a given situation, represent it symbolically, and manipulate the representing symbols) and *contextualize* (pause during problem solution, as needed, in order to probe for meanings).

3. **Students should be able to construct viable arguments and critique the mathematics reasoning of others.** Mathematically proficient students understand and use stated assumptions, definitions, and previously established results in constructing mathematical arguments. They make conjectures, explore the accuracy of their conjectures, and analyze situations by breaking them into cases. These students can recognize and use counterexamples. They justify their conclusions and can communicate them to others, or respond to the counterarguments of others. Mathematically proficient students are also able to compare the effectiveness of two plausible arguments, and identify flawed arguments. Finally, students at all grades can listen or read the arguments of others, decide whether they make sense, and ask clarification questions.

4. **Students should model with mathematics.** Proficient students can apply the mathematics they know to solve everyday problems. This might involve writing an addition equation to describe a problem in the early years. In middle grades, students might apply proportional reasoning to plan a school event or analyze a local problem. By high school, a student might use geometry to solve a design problem at the school or in the community. Mathematically proficient students can apply what they know, and are comfortable making assumptions and approximations to simplify a complicated situation. They are able to identify important quantities in a practical situation and map their relationships using diagrams, two-way tables, graphs, flowcharts, and formulas.

5. **Students should use appropriate tools strategically.** Mathematically proficient students consider all available tools when working through a mathematical problem, including such tools as concrete models, rulers, a protractor, a calculator, a spreadsheet, a computer-based statistical package, or dynamic geometry software. Proficient students are sufficiently familiar with tools appropriate for their grade or course to make sound decisions about when each of these tools might be helpful. After using a tool, proficient students can detect possible errors by estimation. Mathematically proficient students at various grade levels are also able to use technological tools to explore and deepen their understanding of concepts.

6. **Students should focus on precision.** Proficient students communicate clearly and precisely in mathematical terms, using clear definitions in discussions and in their own reasoning. They state the meaning of the symbols they choose (e.g., equal sign, operations indications). They carefully specify units of measure, and label axes in diagrams or data charts. They calculate

accurately and efficiently, expressing numerical answers with an appropriate degree of precision.

7. **Students should look for and make use of patterns and mathematical structure.** Mathematically proficient students look closely to discern patterns or structures within the mathematics problems. For example, students in the elementary grades will see 7 × 8 equals the well-remembered 7 × 5 + 7 × 3, in preparation for learning about the distributive property.

8. **Students look for and express regularity in repeated reasoning.** Mathematically proficient students notice if calculations are repeated, and look both for general methods and for shortcuts. Upper elementary students might notice when dividing 25 by 11 that they are repeating the same calculations over and over again, and conclude they have a repeating decimal.

As they work to solve a problem, mathematically proficient students maintain oversight of the process, while attending to the details. They continually evaluate the reasonableness of their intermediate results.

Common Assessments

In addition to the Common Core Standards and the Standards for Mathematical Practice, two different teams at the national level are developing common assessments for the Common Core State Standards in mathematics and English/language arts (Shaughnessy, 2011). Once these different assessment frameworks are developed, it is anticipated that all participating states will choose which framework to implement, in addition to their Common Core instruction in mathematics. While that work is ongoing as of 2013, the implementation of these Common Core Assessments in mathematics is currently scheduled for the 2014–2015 academic year, and in each case, assessment is expected to reflect more complex problem-solving applications in mathematics rather than merely procedural fluency or solving isolated problems. These two assessment consortia and their proposed assessments are described a bit more in Chapter 7, the chapter focused on differentiated assessment. Also, additional information on these assessment plans is presented at the website of the National Council of Teachers of Mathematics (www.nctm.org/uploadedFiles/Research_News_and_Advocacy/Summing_Up/Articles/2011/AchieveCOMAPPARCC(1).pdf#search=%22Common Core Assessment Plans%22). As this discussion indicates, much work is ongoing as of 2013 in mathematics instruction, indicating an overall transition in the field.

Concerns About the Common Core Standards

As this description indicates, much is currently in transition in mathematics instruction. Also, the level of intensive work on the Standards, the Mathematical Practices, and the Common Assessments indicate a major national effort is underway, supportive of these standards. However, there are many who have raised concerns about the Common Core Standards, even prior to the implementation date of 2014 (Garelick, 2012; Loveless, 2012; Ujifusa, 2012; Wurman & Wilson, 2012). In early 2012, Tom Loveless published the report, *How Well Are American Students Learning?* as one of the Brown Center's Reports on American Education, published by the Brookings Institution (www.brookings.edu/~/media/Newsletters/0216_brown_education_loveless.PDF).

That Brown Center report was largely critical of the idea that setting rigorous academic standards enhances academic achievement, though that conclusion was based on academic achievement data related to previous state standards in various states, rather than the Common Core Standards themselves, as the Common Core Standards have yet to be implemented as of 2012. Still, that conclusion ignited a firestorm among educational leaders (Hess, 2012; Loveless, 2012). Specifically, Loveless (2012) argued that adoption of earlier state standards was not related to achievement scores on the National Assessment of Educational Progress from 2003 through 2009. Further, he concluded that there was little evidence that setting standards can close achievement gaps between groups (Loveless, 2012).

Independent of the debate on the impact of the Common Core on student achievement, other concerns with these standards have arisen, and several advocacy groups in education have gone on record as opposing these standards (Garelick, 2012; Ujifusa, 2012). The Common Core State Standards were intended to be more simple and streamlined than the standards adopted by the individual states previously, while demanding increased performance, but some have suggested that standards in mathematics for many states (e.g., California and Minnesota) were more rigorous than the Common Core State Standards (Wurman & Wilson, 2012). Others have suggested that the Common Core Math Standards place too much emphasis on "mental math" in an effort to have students conceptually understand the mathematics concepts prior to teaching procedurally, how to arrive at an answer (Garelick, 2012). Clearly, these critiques, if true, would defeat the purpose of the entire

> *The level of intensive work on the Standards, the Mathematical Practices, and the Common Assessments indicate a major national effort, but there are many who have raised concerns about the Common Core Standards.*

Common Core Standards effort, and needless to say, this major national effort is likely to cost millions of dollars across the nation.

In conclusion, it is not yet known how effective the implementation of the Common Core State Standards in Mathematics will be over the next decade. Further, it is not known if these standards are likely to impact students' achievement in mathematics, and, as shown above, some claim that this is not a likely outcome of the Common Core (Loveless, 2012). However, with both curricular standards and the common assessments associated with them as the focus of mathematics education in virtually all states, mathematics teachers in those states can expect considerable involvement with these standards and assessments in the near term. Thus, any description of differentiated instruction in mathematics must be framed in the context of the Common Core State Standards in Mathematics.

DIFFERENTIATED INSTRUCTION IN MATHEMATICS: CHANGING UNDERSTANDINGS

Origins of Differentiated Instruction

In the original conceptualization of differentiated instruction, Dr. Tomlinson encouraged teachers to offer a much wider array of instructional activities to students, based in part on the different learning styles, capabilities, and learning preferences shown by various students in the class (Tomlinson, 1999). Initially, she encouraged teachers to differentiate these instructional activities in a variety of dimensions, including the learning content, the learning process, and the learning product (Tomlinson, 1999, 2001, 2003).

Content: Teachers could differentiate in the class by focusing on providing different versions of the content to be learned or presenting the content in different ways.

Process: Teachers could vary the learning process by providing different levels of scaffolded guidance for different students.

Product: Teachers could vary the learning by accepting different products from students and thus allowing students to demonstrate their learning in different ways.

The main thrust of the differentiated instruction construct was that different students learn in different ways and that by increasing the variety and types of instructional activities provided in the class, teachers could ensure that students were provided with their best opportunity to learn the content, and thereby increase student engagement and, ultimately, academic achievement. Further, in addition to explaining how teachers could differentiated their instruction, Dr. Tomlinson drew from the work of Dr. Howard Gardner, and his theory of *Multiple Intelligences* as a basis for understanding how students might need to learn difficult content different ways (Tomlinson, 1999).

Dr. Gardner postulated that different students experienced the world and thus, learned in fundamentally different ways, and he referred to these as "intelligences," while indicating that these learning intelligences were relatively independent of each other (Gardner, 1983, 1993, 2006). Thus rather than one IQ or "intelligence" that could be summarized in a single IQ figure for a specific student, different students showed relative strengths and weaknesses in a variety of different intelligences. Originally, Dr. Gardner identified seven intelligences (the first seven listed in Box 1.2; Gardner, 1983). More recently, he identified several new intelligences that represent different ways a child may understand or demonstrate his or her knowledge in mathematics or other subject areas (Gardner, 1993, 2006).

BOX 1.2   MULTIPLE INTELLIGENCES

Linguistic: One's ability to use and manipulate language.

Bodily/Kinesthetic: One's sense of one's body in space, and one's ability to move one's body through space.

Logical/Mathematical: One's ability to understand logical propositions; one's "number sense."

Musical: One's ability to understand the structure of music as well as the rhythms, patterns that make up music.

Spatial: One's ability to interpret spatial relationships, or to cognitively manipulate spatial relationships.

Interpersonal: One's ability and skill at influencing others, reading subtle facial or bodily cues, and getting along with others.

Intrapersonal: One's sense of self, including awareness of one's self and satisfaction with one's self overall.

Naturalistic: One's ability to perceive relationships in the natural environment, to perceive categorical distinctions and various classifications, as well as the relationships between the classifications.

Moral: The very existence of this intelligence is still debated even among advocates of multiple intelligence theory and has not been confirmed by Dr. Gardner (1993, 2006). At various times referred to as "existential intelligence" or "spiritual intelligence," this intelligence describes individuals with a deep, individual sense of right and wrong, coupled with a concern for the rules and processes that govern human interaction. Examples would include individuals such as Dr. Martin Luther King and Gandhi.

Between 1990 and 2005 or so, this perspective on multiple intelligences had a profound impact on mathematics instruction in the United States and Canada, in part, because of Tomlinson's use of this concept in the original formulation of differentiated instruction (Hearne & Stone, 1995; Katz, Mirenda, & Auerbach, 2002). As one example, many mathematics textbooks presented instructional suggestions for students based on perceived strengths in one area or another, based on the multiple intelligences theory. Further, based on these intelligences, numerous instructional tactics have been suggested that focus instruction on one learning strength or another, and a sample of the types of teaching practices commonly recommended are presented in Teaching Tip 1.1.

> *This multiple intelligences theory has had a profound impact on mathematics instruction in the United States and Canada, in part, because of Tomlinson's use of this concept in the original formulation of differentiated instruction.*

Teaching Tip 1.1   Teaching Ideas Addressing Different Multiple Intelligences

Musical Teaching Ideas

Chanting of math facts is a good activity, and using rhythmic activities can greatly assist learning. Use the rhythm, "We will, we will rock you" and change the addition facts or multiplication facts (repeat that chant "One, two, three, rest" or "slap, slap, clap, rest" rhythm twice per fact and saying "one plus one is two; one plus two is three," and so on).

Other great tunes used by many teachers are the theme song from the old television show *The Addams Family* and "Row, Row, Row Your Boat."

As another alternative, teachers might identify several big ideas in a unit of instruction (e.g., place value in the ten's place), and have students write a "rap" about those ideas.

Spatial Teaching Ideas

Visual aids such as manipulatives or representations of concepts (e.g., fractional parts) will assist spatial learners because they can often see the relationships.

As one variant, teachers may challenge groups of students in the class to write "a picture example of this problem."

Interpersonal Teaching Ideas

Group work on math facts problems; have students debate mathematical intelligence points or concepts to each other. Every 15 minutes during math class, the teacher could say, "Turn to your partner and explain that concept to each other. See if you both understand it the same way."

(Continued)

(Continued)

Bodily/Kinesthetic Teaching Ideas

Movement along a number line on the floor during instruction on operations involving positive and negative integers is one example of a math movement activity.

Movement through an addition or subtraction math problem is another example. For the problem 6 + 8 = ____, the teacher should have 6 students stand on one side of the room and 8 stand on the other side, then have the groups move together. This can be adapted to teach a "counting on" tactic. Begin with the group of 6 kids (because that number came first in the problem) and, one at a time, have the other students join the group while the teacher demonstrates "counting on" (e.g., begin with the number 6, and when the first student joins, say, "7," and so on—thus "counting on" from 6).

Teachers might mount a large circle on the wall, from the floor to approximately head high. Have a student stand in front of the circle and use his or her body to divide the circle into fractions. Standing with hands by one's side, the body divides the circle into halves—head to foot. Holding one's arms out straight to each side divides the circle into fourths, etc.

Naturalistic Teaching Idea

Teachers could encourage students to explore the core of an apple, cutting it into fractional parts.

Intrapersonal Teaching Idea

For introspective students, journaling is recommended. Have these introspective children keep a daily journal of each experience in their home lives where they experience fractions (e.g., "I wanted more cake last night, so I ate 1/2 of the part that was left over.").

However, over the years, there has been considerable criticism of this theory, most of which stems from the lack of research support for this multiple intelligence construct (Bruer, 2006; Sousa, 2010). In fact, there is some discussion as to whether or not these different intelligences even exist (Bruer, 1999, 2006; Sousa & Tomlinson, 2011), and critics of this theory correctly point out that there is not widespread research support for this perspective.

Still, the fundamental thrust of this work has resulted in an effort by educators to develop a wider array of instructional activities that offer different types of learning options in the classroom, an end result that most educators agree has been positive for students (Gardner,

1993; Hearne & Stone, 1995; Katz et al., 2002). Further, the proponents of multiple intelligences research encourage teachers to view these intelligences merely as avenues for learning, rather than hard and fast cognitive capabilities (Hearne & Stone, 1995; Katz et al., 2002). From this perspective, students are viewed as having various strengths and weaknesses, and effective teachers must implement lessons that provide learning activities that address a wide variety of these intelligences in order to provide the best opportunity to learn for students with different strengths. Teachers are, therefore, encouraged to specifically plan their lesson activities with these intelligences in mind. Thus, over the course of an instructional unit involving math facts content, a teacher would endeavor to have some activities that involved each of these different intelligences.

THE NEW DIFFERENTIATED INSTRUCTION IN MATHEMATICS

With that brief history of differentiation in mind, the core construct of differentiated instruction still centers around increasing the array of different instruction options presented to students as educators respond to the wide diversity of learning needs within most classrooms today. Still, educators today have acknowledged that the very concept of differentiated instruction, like mathematics instruction generally, is in transition (Bender, 2012a; O'Meara, 2010; Richardson, 2012; Sousa & Tomlinson, 2011). Some authors have used the phrase "beyond differentiation" to discuss this transition (O'Meara, 2010; Richardson, 2012), while the author of this text has used the term *"The New Differentiated Instruction"* to summarize this transition in the concept of differentiated instruction. In fact, a variety of different factors have impacted the way differentiated instruction is currently described in most of the literature (see Bender, 2012a), and several other initiatives in education, initiatives that are independent of the differentiated instructional concept, have nevertheless impacted the implementation of differentiated instruction. At a minimum, five specific examples can be identified (Bender, 2012a; Richardson, 2012; Sousa & Tomlinson, 2011).

a) *The differentiated instructional concept has moved away from exclusive dependence on the multiple intelligences learning theory, and various alternative learning styles/learning preferences theories are now cited as a basis for differentiated instruction.*
b) *There is now an increased emphasis on neurosciences as a basis for differentiated instructional teaching suggestions.*

c) *There is now a broader set of variables described in the literature as areas in which teachers may differentiate instruction, beyond content, process, and product.*

d) *Instructional technology (e.g., smartphones, modern educational apps, Web 2.0 teaching tools), make differentiated instruction much more feasible, and easier to plan, as these technologies provide individual lessons that actively respond to learning variations from one student to another.*

e) *The response to intervention initiative has led to increased emphasis on differentiated instruction in mathematics in all general education mathematics classes* (Bender, 2012a).

> The very basis of differentiated instruction in mathematics has changed somewhat since 1999.

These factors have shifted the basis for differentiated instruction in both mathematics and reading classes to some degree (Bender, 2012a; O'Meara, 2010; Richardson, 2012). Thus, the concept of differentiated instruction has changed since the initial use of the term in 1999. Each of these factors is described below.

Learning Styles, Learning Preferences, Learning Profiles

As shown above, the original differentiated instructional concept was based to a large degree on the multiple intelligences theory of Dr. Howard Gardner (Gardner, 1983; Tomlinson, 1999). However, educators today look to a wider variety of learning styles and learning preferences than exclusively the multiple intelligences theory (Sousa & Tomlinson, 2011; Tomlinson, 2003, 2010; Tomlinson, Brimijoin, & Narvaez, 2008). In that sense, the basis for the concept of differentiated instruction has changed somewhat since 1999 (Bender & Waller, 2011a, 2012; Sousa & Tomlinson, 2011; Tomlinson, 2010; Tomlinson et al., 2008).

It is interesting to note that in some of the recent books and chapters on differentiated instruction the multiple intelligences theory is not mentioned at all (O'Meara, 2010; Tomlinson, 2010; Tomlinson et al., 2008), while other books mention multiple intelligences in the context of a wider variety of learning style theories or perspectives on differing learning profiles or variations in intellectual processing (Sousa & Tomlinson, 2011). This seems to indicate a shift toward more diverse perspectives on learning style and learning preferences, as well as increased attention to other student variations in interest and ability as the basis for forming differentiated instructional groups (Bender & Waller, 2011a; Sousa & Tomlinson, 2011). At least two alternative learning or intelligences

> Educators today look to a wider variety of learning styles and learning preferences than are typically presented within multiple intelligences theory.

approaches are considered as appropriate foundations for planning differentiated lesson activities.

For example, Robert Sternberg's triarchic theory of intelligence (1985, 2006) has been identified as one perspective that might inform how teachers create differentiated instructional groups within their classes (Sousa & Tomlinson, 2011). Sternberg suggests that students process information and ideas in one of three ways, as compared to the eight or nine intelligences presented by Gardner (1983). Sternberg described core intelligences as analytic, practical, or creative; these are briefly defined in Box 1.3. Again, this description of three "intelligences" has been specifically highlighted by Tomlinson recently as one basis for differentiated instructional planning (Sousa & Tomlinson, 2011).

BOX 1.3 ALTERNATIVE LEARNING STYLE THEORIES AS POSSIBLE FOUNDATIONS FOR DIFFERENTIATED INSTRUCTION

I. Sternberg's Triarchic Theory of Intelligence

Analytic Intelligence—This style emphasizes "part to whole" thinking and is typically strongly emphasized in many school tasks. A strength in this area aids in delving into the components or specific aspects of a task or concept and is heavily emphasized in mathematics curriculum.

Practical Intelligence—This sometimes described as contextual understanding, and emphasizes how students apply concepts or solve problems in real-world settings. A strength in this intelligence would allow a student to problem solve in one situation and subsequently apply their understandings in different situations.

Creative Intelligences—This can best be summarized as "out of the box" thinking. Rather than problem solving with an eye to real-world needs, the creative thinker tends to refocus or re-envision the environment such that novel solutions present themselves. This skill related specifically to abstract mathematical thinking as one important area within the mathematics curriculum.

II. Silver, Strong, and Perini's Learning Styles

Mastery Style—Students with this learning style proceed in a step-by-step fashion, focusing on practical implications of the content. Because many mathematics problems require this type of thinking, students with this learning preference typically do well in mathematics. These students are highly motivated by success, take pride in developing new understandings, and respond well to competitive and challenging learning tasks.

Understanding Style—Students with this style question the content, analyze the implications of it, and fit the pieces of a construct together. These students want to make sense of the mathematics content and are likely to see patterns prior to

(Continued)

(Continued)

other students. They generally respond well to puzzles, games, or discussions of controversy.

Self-Expressive Style—Students with this learning style demonstrate innovative thinking and imagination when undertaking a learning task. They long to be unique in their thinking and original in their approach to any task, seeking understanding that only they have reached. These students respond well to choices in their mathematics work, as well as creative assignments in the math curriculum.

Interpersonal Style—Students with this learning style learn best in the social context, exploring their own feelings or the feelings and understandings of others. These students thrive in cooperative learning mathematical tasks and are highly emotive in sharing their feelings.

Another conceptualization of students' mental processing styles has been proposed by Silver, Strong, and Perini (2000) as a basis for differentiating instruction in the classroom. These researchers advocated consideration of four learning styles that impact the motivation shown by learners, and within that context these authors recommend specific types of differentiated instructional tasks for various learners (Silver & Perini, 2010; Varlas, 2010). Box 1.3 presents the four learning styles identified by Silver et al. (2000) and suggestions for the types of learning tasks that might work for various learners in the mathematics classroom.

In addition to discussing different learning style preferences as the basis for differentiated instruction, even the definitions of the terms used in the literature seem to be somewhat clouded. I have chosen in this book to use the terms *learning style, learning preference,* and *learning profiles,* as if they are roughly synonymous, since most educators, at least in the experience of this author, consider multiple intelligences as one perspective in the broader learning style literature. Other theorists, however, might argue against such usage, considering learning styles to be fundamentally different from innate cognitive abilities or intelligences. For others, learning styles or preferences may represent choices students tend to make regarding their preferred learning environment (lighter versus darker lighting in the classroom, or completing only one task at a time versus doing many tasks simultaneously; see Sousa & Tomlinson, 2011). In contrast, the term *intelligences* may be limited to mental processing styles that are relatively independent of the environment, such as the multiple intelligences in Dr. Gardner's original multiple intelligences theory (1983, 2006).

In the extreme, some educators and theorists have advocated elimination of any consideration of learning styles or learning preferences altogether, since the evidence on learning does not yet support the concept that instructional activities based on differences in learning style or learning preferences result in increased academic achievement (Bruer, 1999, 2006). In fact, research on learning has not yet shown that students learn in fundamentally different ways or by using different neural networks for similar learning tasks (Sousa & Tomlinson, 2011).

However, more recently Sousa (2010) reported on a growing consensus on this question, as well as the broader question of differentiated instruction generally. Today, terms such as *learning preferences* or *learning profiles* are used (Sousa & Tomlinson, 2011). Also, teachers across the United States have been, and continue to be, encouraged to differentiate instruction in order to better meet students' learning needs. Berkeley, Bender, Peaster, and Saunters (2009), in a recent survey of state policy on response to intervention, demonstrated that virtually every state stressed differentiated instruction as the basis for general education classes in their respective response to intervention models.

Next, most educators today do believe that students learn mathematics in a variety of distinctive ways and that attention to these learning preferences will positively impact student engagement with the math content, and ultimately student achievement in mathematics (O'Meara, 2010; Silver & Perini, 2010; Sousa, 2010; Sternberg, 2006; Tomlinson et al., 2008). Thus, discussions of differentiated instruction today focus more broadly on differences in general learning profiles or preferences, and individualized or small-group learning center instruction for either heterogeneous or homogeneous groups based on these learning preferences. One might well say that, in contrast to 1999, the differentiated instructional paradigm is now free from dependency on only one theory of intelligence (Sousa & Tomlinson, 2011).

Brain Physiology for Learning Mathematics

> *Most educators today believe students learn in a variety of ways and that attention to these differences in learning style and learning preferences will positively impact student engagement with the math content, and ultimately student achievement.*

The shift in emphasis to a broader perspective on learning profiles and learning preferences has been paralleled by increased emphasis on how brains learn mathematics (Devlin, 2010; Sousa, 2008). It should be noted that much of the work on the physiology of learning processes has been completed since the original articulation of the differentiated instruction construct in 1999 (Tomlinson, 1999). Further, this research has clear implications for differentiating instruction in both reading and

Much of the work on the physiology and neurochemistry of learning mathematics has been undertaken since the original differentiated instructional concept was described.

mathematics (Bender, 2009; Devlin, 2010; Sousa, 2010; Sousa & Tomlinson, 2011).

Often referred to as brain-compatible learning, this research is now providing a more solid basis for differentiated instructional recommendations than did the multiple intelligences theory in isolation (Bender & Waller, 2011a; Sousa & Tomlinson, 2011). More information on this brain-compatible research, and the differentiated instructional suggestions stemming from that research, is presented later in this chapter.

Broader Inclusion of Ways to Differentiate Instruction

Next, differentiated instruction today is more broadly focused than the original differentiation concept (Sousa & Tomlinson, 2011; Tomlinson, 2010). Initially, differentiated instruction focused on the three areas presented above (i.e., content, process, and product; Tomlinson, 1999), and differentiated instruction groups in the classroom were to be based on the various multiple intelligences in order to strengthen student learning in those three specific areas. However, today while differentiated instruction still stresses these three areas, other areas have been identified as ways that teachers might differentiate instruction, including respect for the learner; a powerful, engaging curriculum; flexible groupings for academic tasks based on student interest; student readiness; as well as learning preferences, ongoing assessment, and a positive learning environment (Sousa & Tomlinson, 2011). As these areas continue to increase, the concept of differentiated instruction continues to broaden over time.

Technology for Differentiating Mathematics Instruction

There is no area within education that is changing as rapidly as technology for teaching, and this trend has, and will continue to, impact differentiated instruction (Bender & Waller, 2011a, 2011b). While differentiated instruction has always emphasized consideration of students' learning styles, strengths, and the formation of instruction groups based on those variables, the increased availability of technology today will allow teachers to deliver differentiated instructional activities for every single student. Tech strategies using Web 2.0 tools (tech programs that allow students to collaboratively create and publish information, rather than merely function as consumers of information), wikis, social networking, and computerized curricula or variations in lesson plan organization can all play a significant role in the differentiated instructional activities offered in the mathematics class. In one sense, placing individual students in an appropriate, engaging, well-designed, and individualized computer-based curricula might be envisioned as the epitome of differentiated instruction, since such well-designed curricula do deliver individualized instruction that is highly targeted to students' individual needs and based on their individual academic levels.

In many modern computer programs, educators can vary the amount of stimulation that the program delivers to the student during the lesson, how questions might be answered, or how new content is presented, thus addressing some of the factors associated with various learning styles and preferences. These might include variations in the level of problem presentation; variations in the amount of color, or noise, or animation used; or variations in the level of instructional assistance provided by the program. Even the timing may be varied in modern computer-based curricula (i.e., the rate of presentation of the questions, etc.).

All of these possible variations allow educators to tailor the computer-based instructional presentation to students with various learning styles, and thus, this can be considered highly differentiated instruction (Bender & Waller, 2011b). While some computer-based instructional programs have offered many of these variations for at least 25 years, today most programs do, and teachers are becoming adept at using these options to provide differentiated instructional assignments for their students. Thus, computer- and Internet-based instruction today holds much more potential for allowing teachers to differentiate instruction than was the case in 1999.

However, technology is impacting instruction in many ways today that go far beyond merely effective computer-based instructional programs, and rather than students working individually on computer programs, modern instructional technologies are fostering truly innovative collaborative study options. For example, various social networking options (e.g., Facebook, Twitter, or Ning), use of wikis or class blogs for instructional collaborations, and collaborative creation of content offer options for delivering highly differentiated instruction in virtually any classroom, without students working exclusively in isolation (W. M. Ferriter & Garry, 2010; Richardson & Mancabelli, 2011). Further, the more recently developed (and developing) networking technologies can aid the differentiated effort as well, as students choose their role in various learning projects in their effort to create their own learning content (Bender & Waller, 2011a).

> *Computer- and Internet-based instruction today holds much more potential for allowing teachers to differentiate instruction than was the case in 1999.*

Students are demonstrating, via their nonschool behaviors, that they love social networking, and as educators grow in their understanding of how these social networking tools may be used in education, many opportunities for increased differentiation of instruction are likely to result. Today's students expect and respond to nothing less than the stimulation they have grown used to in today's digital, media-rich, highly interactive, and technological world, and teachers must structure their mathematics instruction to approximate that modern world in order to reach today's students. Thus, using brain-compatible teaching ideas, coupled with modern technologies to engage our students, is now critical. Teachers must create differentiated learning activities in mathematics that emulate the high-tech world of our students, and on that basis instruction is much more likely to be more effective (Bender & Waller, 2011b). For this reason, various technological instructional options will be discussed in each subsequent chapter of this book.

The Response to Intervention Initiative in Mathematics

Another instructional innovation that has transformed, and continues to transform, education today is the response to intervention (RTI) initiative. RTI represents a mandate to deliver multitiered levels of supplemental instruction for students in the classroom, in order to assure that students' instructional needs are met with the exact level of instructional intensity necessary to assure students' individual success (Bender, 2009; Bender & Crane, 2011). Most states adopted a three-tier model of RTI, in which the basic tier (Tier 1 instruction) represents instruction available for all students in the general education mathematics class. This would include all whole group instruction, and all differentiation efforts undertaken by the general education teacher during the mathematics period. Tier 2 is a more intensive level of mathematics instruction for struggling students that takes place outside of the general math class. It is anticipated that perhaps 20% of students might require this level of intensive, supplemental mathematics instruction. Tier 3, in the RTI paradigm, is very intensive supplemental instruction for students who did not succeed in Tier 2.

While the RTI initiative was originally applied in the area of reading, many states now require RTI efforts in mathematics as well (Bender & Crane, 2011). However, the provision of supplemental, intensive instruction in mathematics will be required much less often if a wider variety of instruction needs in math are met in general education via an increase in differentiated instruction. That is why, in many states, the differentiated instructional paradigm was "written into" or required by the various state plans as the basis for all Tier 1 mathematics instruction within the RTI initiative (Berkeley et al., 2009). More detail on the impact of RTI on differentiated instruction in mathematics is presented in Chapter 7, Differentiated Assessment and RTI Strategies for Mathematics.

Efficacy of Differentiated Instruction in Mathematics

It is somewhat surprising that research supportive of differentiated instruction is still somewhat limited. While research has challenged the original learning style instructional approaches (Bruer, 1999, 2006), there has not been a concerted research effort investigating the efficacy of highly differentiated classrooms compared to more traditional classrooms. Further, as of 2012, there has been no systematic empirical research on differentiated instruction in mathematics, and, in an educational world of "show me the data," this lack of empirical research for differentiated instruction in mathematics is somewhat surprising. In particular, more than a decade of time has now passed since differentiated instruction was introduced in 1999 (Tomlinson, 1999), and one may well ask, where is the supportive research?

There is some anecdotal evidence of the efficacy of differentiation, suggestive of the positive impact of differentiated instruction on student achievement in mathematics and/or reading (Doidge, 2007; King & Gurian, 2006; Merzenich, 2001; Merzenich, Tallal, Peterson, Miller, & Jenkins, 1999; Silver & Perini, 2010; Sousa, 2008; Sternberg, 2006; Tomlinson, 2010; Tomlinson et al., 2008). For example, Tomlinson and her coauthors (2008) presented evidence of academic improvement in mathematics at two schools as a result of implementation of differentiated instructional practices. Conway Elementary School and Colchester High School were described as two ordinary schools in different districts of the United States (Tomlinson et al., 2008). Data were collected from statewide assessment scores in mathematics and other subject areas, and the results are presented in terms of percentages of students demonstrating advanced or proficient scores on mathematics for several years prior to the implementation of differentiated instruction and for several years after implementation. Data at Conway Elementary School, in Conway, Missouri, indicated that decidedly more students were achieving at the proficient level and/or the advanced level in mathematics, after a three-year implementation of differentiated instructional practices. When compared to other students in the state during the same time period, the data showed a decided increase in mathematics achievement at Conway and not significant change across other schools in the state (Tomlinson et al., 2008). Percentages of students achieving "proficient" or "advanced" jumped from an average of 64% prior to implementing differentiated instruction, to an average of 80% for the three years after implementation of differentiated instruction in the math classes.

Data for Colchester High School were also indicative of the positive impact of differentiated instruction in mathematics. Those data presented the number of students passing the statewide assessments in reading, writing, and mathematics. These assessment results from Colchester High compare scores on three specific areas in mathematics, and in each area the percentage of students passing increased by an average of 26% after the school implemented differentiated instruction.

Conclusion: The New Differentiated Instruction

These factors discussed above have resulted in a new understanding of differentiated instruction in mathematics. The increased emphasis on the physiology of learning, the broader basis for differentiating instruction, the use of modern instructional technologies for teaching, and differentiated instruction within the RTI paradigm have all merged to create a new differentiated instructional paradigm (Bender, 2012a), and this book represents the initial discussion of that new differentiated instruction in mathematics. Further, there is now some evidence on the efficacy of differentiated instruction for improving mathematics achievement, and this suggests that teachers should consider differentiated instruction as a cornerstone for general education instruction in mathematics.

With that noted, this new differentiated instruction does represent a challenge to many new teachers and even to some veteran teachers, as does any significant paradigm shift. With teachers now expected to split their classes into smaller differentiated groups, those groups are likely to be quite fluid, and management of instructional processes in such classes can represent a challenge. Teachers should consider serving as resources for each other, as they struggle to teach in these new and innovative ways. In fact, because the mathematics curriculum is somewhat different from other subject areas in that it is not wholly dependent on reading skill, mathematics teachers have often served as resource or collaborative teachers for others within the mathematics department. Such collaborations, creative sharing of ideas and techniques, can broaden every teacher's insight into how to differentiate the mathematics class.

THE MATHEMATICAL BRAIN

As noted above, the ongoing research on how human brains function undergirds the concept of differentiated instruction (Sousa & Tomlinson,

2011). Because of the evolving nature of this brain-compatible research, the next section presents more information on how brains function in the mathematics classroom, as well as suggestions for teachers resulting from that research. As noted above, the new differentiated instruction is largely based on the research from the neurosciences on how brains function (King & Gurian, 2006; Sousa, 2008, 2010; Sousa & Tomlinson, 2011), and there has been a great deal of progress in our understanding on brain functioning in mathematics. This section presents the current insights from this research from the perspective of the teacher in the mathematics classroom.

Regions of the Mathematical Brain

Studies have demonstrated that mathematics involves many mental processes including reasoning, concept formation, mental processing speed, long-term and working memory, and attention (Devlin, 2010; Mabbott & Bisanz, 2008; Seethaler & Fuchs, 2006). Like most complex thought processes, there are a number of brain areas or different brain regions involved in mathematical processing (Sousa, 2008, 2010). First of all, language is important in math performance, including students' "private speech" patterns, which are used to instruct oneself in mathematical problem completion (Ostad & Sorensen, 2007; Seethaler & Fuchs, 2006). Thus, areas of the brain associated with language such as Broca's area, the angular gyrus, and Wernicke's area are involved in mathematics since they are involved heavily in language (Sousa, 2001).

The frontal lobe and parietal lobe of the cerebrum (i.e., the areas of the brain that are responsible for higher-order thinking skills) are highly involved in mathematical understanding. The visual cortex is also involved, since students need to see most math problems, and the involvement of the visual cortex may be more complex than merely seeing the problem. Sousa (2001) suggested that the involvement of the visual cortex in almost all mathematical thinking indicates that math requires one to visualize mathematics problems. Further, this would seem to be supported by studies over the years that have reported correlations between a child's mathematical ability and visualization capabilities (Seethaler & Fuchs, 2006; Sousa, 2008).

Mathematics is a highly complex skill that rests on many other brain functions as well. While reading is a complex skill that can be mastered relatively independently of other skills, mathematics is not. Whereas a child does not need to learn mathematics (or any other subject) in order to learn reading, the child does need to learn reading in order to master mathematics, since so much of math involves reading mathematical equations or word problems. Even having students do a set of vertical or horizontal math facts problems requires the students to read the numerals within the problems (Barton, Heidema, & Jordan, 2002). Thus, reading is highly involved in most mathematical work in the public school classroom, and understanding the complex reading process may help show how complex math can be. Sousa (2001) presented a model of the "reading brain" that may be helpful here (see Figure 1.1).

As shown in Figure 1.1, four areas within the brain are primarily responsible for reading. First, the visual cortex takes in the stimulus of several squiggle lines on a page; for example, consider the equation:

$$6 + 3 = \underline{\hspace{2cm}}.$$

Initially this equation, like all reading content, is "perceived" by the visual cortex. Next, this stimulus is sent simultaneously to both the angular gyrus, which is the area of the brain that decodes sounds and processes in written language, and to Wernicke's area—the area of the brain that is involved in comprehension of language. Next, Broca's area becomes involved; this brain area searches for meaning in the context of the numeral and its relation to other numerals presented in the problem. At this point, the frontal lobe and parietal lobe of the cerebrum become involved in "thinking through" the problem. These

Figure 1.1 The Brain

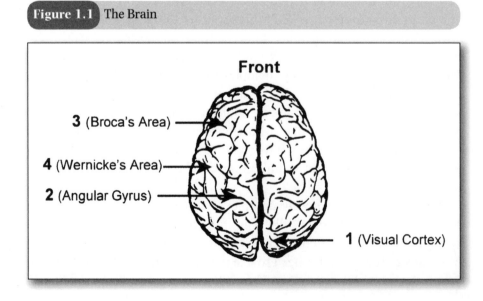

areas "imagine" the number problem and may even plan a strategy for solving it, such as;

> Hold up six fingers, and count them, then hold up three more fingers and "count on," beginning with seven. Then say the answer.

As this example demonstrates, mathematical thinking is a highly complex process that involves a number of areas within the human brain, including at a minimum the frontal lobe, the parietal lobe, the visual cortex, and the angular gyrus, Werkicke's area, and Broca's area. Other areas beyond these may also be involved in the mechanics of thinking through mathematical problems, and only further research will allow us to understand how complex mathematical problems truly are, or how many brain regions are involved in mathematical understanding.

Gender Differences and Maturation

Research has recently examined how young boys and young girls may differ in brain functioning and how such differences might impact mathematics and other learning tasks (Sousa & Tomlinson, 2011). In fact, recent research has documented that during math, different brain areas are activated in young girls compared to young boys (Keller & Menon, 2009). Of course, teachers have often noted that young girls mature a bit earlier than boys, particularly in areas such as linguistic skill and fine motor control. Further, these are exactly the skills that early schooling depends upon for reading and writing, and when girls excelled in schools it was often assumed that girls simply matured faster overall.

That concept is now being challenged. It is not correct to assert that young girls mature faster than young boys, but rather, girls and boys mature faster in various areas. Brain research has now documented that while young girls' brains do mature faster in the several areas noted above, young boys seem to mature faster in certain other areas, including spatial and visual abilities. This may explain why young boys seem to do better in mathematics than young girls (Strauss, 2003). At a minimum, it is not correct to assume that girls mature faster in all areas or in some overall way compared to young boys. Rather, the specific abilities associated with gender must be more carefully studied. With those maturation differences noted, there are a number of established learning differences between young girls and boys, and many of these may impact the efficacy of various instructional tactics (King & Gurian, 2006; Sousa, 2008). These are noted in Box 1.4.

BOX 1.4 BRAIN-BASED GENDER DIFFERENCES IN THE MATHEMATICS CLASS

Girls are . . .

- *more sensitive to sound than boys;*
- *more likely to be sensitive to bright colors;*
- *more likely to listen to the teacher;*
- *more able to describe their emotional state or feelings than boys;*
- *more likely to seek teacher approval (e.g., complete homework, participate in class);*

  —more likely to learn better in collaborative tasks (Sousa & Tomlinson, 2011).

In contrast, boys are . . .

- *more attuned to motion than girls;*
- *more likely to succeed in movement or action-based instructional tasks;*
- *more likely to engage in risky behaviors than girls;*
- *more likely to learn better in competitive tasks;*
- *more likely to succeed in stressful circumstances;*
- *more adept at spatial tasks, and some number-based tasks* (Sousa & Tomlinson, 2011).

One, Two, Three, Many. . . . Hardwired Numbers

A number of researchers have studied the normal maturation process of the developing brain in infancy and early childhood and have inquired about basic math skill. This research seems to suggest that only minimal math skills are hardwired into the brain during the normal maturation process (Devlin, 2010; Geller & Smith, 2002; Sousa, 2008, 2010). These simple number recognition skills, like the development of language skills, would seem to be associated with normal maturation of young brains and central nervous systems rather than with schooling or preschool learning experiences.

In survival terms, this is quite understandable. Our ancestors' brains learned early in our evolutionary history to distinguish rapidly between one tiger that might be attacking and two tigers attacking in a coordinated attack plan, because the numbers and location of the tigers would suggest the best escape route or the best direction to run. In that sense, basic numeration (numbers one, two, and perhaps three), became hardwired into our brains. However, counting past the lowest numbers (i.e., numeration higher than 2 or 3), however, was not a selective survival skill, since that many tigers presumably left no viable escape route. Thus, our brains, at a very young age, seem to be able to reflexively interpret the lowest numbers (i.e., 1, 2, and perhaps 3) and even to understand the numeration sequence of these numbers, but it cannot distinguish higher numbers without some instruction. Therefore, one way to understand the brain's response to observed objects in a set can be summed up in the phrase, "One, two, three, many . . . "

From the perspective of the math teacher, this means that instruction in math will be built almost entirely on prerequisite learned skills rather than on maturational-based knowledge. Thus, the importance of mastery of prerequisite skills prior to moving on to higher-level skills in mathematics cannot be overstated.

The Priorities of the Emotional Brain

Because of the research completed within the past 15 years, educators have realized that emotional intent and attitudes play a much larger role in learning than previously thought (Clarkson et al., 2007; Sousa, 2008, 2010). The recent report of the National Mathematics Advisory Panel (2008), for example, emphasized the importance of social, affective, and motivational support for mathematics. We now know that much of the information taken into the brain by the senses is first processed in the midbrain or the "emotional" region within the brain. Further, this emotional brain often serves as a filter through which stimuli must pass prior to being "considered" by the cerebrum (i.e., the forebrain and parietal lobe—or the "thinking" areas of the brain). Thus, a negative emotional response to a stimuli or particular type of task—such as a math problem—can in and of itself set up a lack of higher brain function involvement with the problem. In short, higher levels of stress for some students within the mathematics class tend to make their brains less efficient.

Research has shown that brains perform at their best when they are highly motivated and involved and experiencing "manageable" stress (Goleman, 2006), rather than acute, high levels of stress. Thus, to the degree that students fear mathematics, their brains are less likely to be engaged in mathematics. Should a student experience too much stress (e.g., when presented with a mathematics problem he or she cannot do), cognitive energy is shunted into the emotional centers of the brain, and the cerebrum or "cognitive area" of the brain actually demonstrates reduced brain activity. Thus, higher-order thinking—which takes place in the cerebrum—decreases when students are overstressed in the mathematics classroom. Further, many teachers of mathematics have actually seen this phenomenon in the classroom. How often have teachers noticed that students seem to "freeze up" from time to time in mathematics?

Research has frequently shown that many students perceive mathematics quite negatively or even fear math (Kortering, deBottencourt, & Braziel, 2005; Montague, 1997; NMAP, 2008). In one recent survey of high school students, 55% of students with learning disabilities identified mathematics as their least favorite subject, and the next subject on the list was English, which was identified as least favorite by only 16% of the subjects. Clearly, mathematics is either feared, or disliked, or both by many students. Of course, such fears often provide a significant emotional barrier that may well preclude successful learning in mathematics. For this reason, attending to a student's attitudes toward math and a student's motivation in learning math are critically important. In fact, this author, in working with mathematics teachers in various workshops, stresses that math teachers have a "higher hurdle to jump" than teachers in other subjects in that teachers of mathematics have to work harder to alleviate the stress often associated with mathematics.

In contrast, positive emotional experiences associated with mathematics will tend to foster higher motivation to actively engage in math. In order to foster positive emotional experiences in mathematics, teachers can try a number of tactics. First, teachers might find ways to use "math-play" activities to make mathematics less threatening. Scaffolded instruction can also offer support in mathematics that can, over time, offset the negative feelings many students have toward mathematics. Teaching Tip 1.2 presents additional instructional tactics that teachers in mathematics might use to foster more positive emotional associations for mathematics exercises. Also, in order to make mathematics less emotionally threatening, many educator are exploring mathematics games, and that topic is discussed in depth in Chapter 4.

Teaching Tip 1.2   Strategies to Foster Positive Emotional Associations With Mathematics

Begin Class With Fun Counting Activities

Even young children can typically count to 10, and choral counting out loud emphasizes counting without the embarrassment of being wrong. For example, the teacher might say, "Let's count together how many objects are on this shelf in the front of the class." The class would then count the objects in unison out loud (which decreases the chance of embarrassment if a child does not know his or her numbers). Then the teacher might say, "Who can find another shelf in the class with the same number of objects?' After a few days of counting, pair the counting with written numbers on the dry erase board.

"Catch the Teacher" Games

Teachers may occasionally wish to make mistakes and have students point out these counting mistakes. This is a tactic that can work for students in a variety of grade levels. For example, teachers may skip numbers or repeat numbers while counting and instruct the students to quietly raise their hands if they hear a mistake. Students must then describe the mistake that the teacher made (Griffin, Sarama, & Clements, 2003).

Teach With Edibles

For younger kids, using an individual supply of edibles (fruits such as raisins work well here) can make using manipulative counters more fun! Use edibles as the counters, and after each correct problem, the student can eat one of the counters. The child's lesson is finished when the edibles in his or her pile are gone, and that student will have experienced mathematics in a novel and fun way!

The "Right Answer, Different Question" Tactic

Every math teacher has had the experience of asking questions of students, calling on someone, and having the student give a wrong answer. This is often embarrassing for the student who answered the question incorrectly and may lead to negative emotional reactions to mathematics (Clarkson et al., 2007). In that situation, teachers should immediately use the "right answer, different question" tactic. When given a wrong answer by a student, teachers merely state, "There are no wrong answers, just answers to different questions." The teacher might then switch to an example, emphasizing the same content, for which the student answer is correct.

Here's an example. Imagine instructing students on double-digit addition with regrouping, using the problem $64 + 28 = $ _____. Some excited student—a student who only last week learned double-digit addition without regrouping—may well answer "82!" Rather than immediately correcting him, the teacher could say something like, "I like that answer, but it really answers another question better. Let's figure out what question it answers. Who can help with that?"

At that point, rather than continuing with the problem above, the teacher should elicit answers from the class about how the problem above could be modified to result in an answer of 82. For example, one could change each digit in the ones place above, resulting in a problem of $61 + 21 = $ _____, or even $60 + 22 = $ ___. Teachers should stay with this line of discussion for a minute or so, having students generate several possible answers. To finish, the teacher should

(Continued)

(Continued)

have the student who answered "82" come write his or her answer in the blank at the end of one of the new problems. That way, that answer is not wrong—it is just the answer to a different problem. Note that good instruction is taking place, even during the minute or so that the class is generating new problems. Further, this tactic reduces the negative emotions that are sometimes associated with math, and students become more inclined to participate in class questions. Note that once the teacher has finished the activity above, he or she should have the class return to the original problem.

Use Peer Buddies

Either during initial instruction, or after students have been exposed to a new concept, when some students are doing reteaching work, the teacher may wish to have students do math problems together as peer buddies. This addresses the "interpersonal" learning style and typically involves having two or more students work together on the same set of problems. This can alleviate the discomfort associated with mathematics for many students, since it is more fun to work together and each student can "assist" the other.

Teach Teams of Students

Another interpersonal instructional idea that makes mathematics less threatening is to have all initial work done by teams of students that can help each other. The teacher begins by dividing the class into teams. At a signal from the teacher, one member of each team runs to the team's chart to write a relevant fact on the chart about the topic. The other team members should make certain the fact is correct. At the next signal, the next team member writes down another fact. This activity involves movement and cooperation among team members, as well as competition between the teams, and is a good activity for students with strength in interpersonal learning. This will also tend to make mathematics instruction much more fun.

Cross Out Some of the Problems

This approach to practice work can assist children who have attention problems, as well as mathematics anxiety. On a page of math problems, the teacher may instruct the student to merely cross out up to half of the problems, and work the others. This can often help those students who find that looking at an entire page of math problems quite daunting. Also, for students with negative emotional reactions to math, crossing out some of the problems may make the work seem much more possible.

Set Goals Using Personal Learning Timelines

When students see that they are reaching their mathematics learning goals, they will have a more positive experience in mathematics. Each student should keep a timeline, illustrated with pictures of the types of problems he or she was working on at various dates during the year. This can be quite motivating for students, who see their progress in mathematics. These personal learning goals and timelines should also be shared with parents at various points in the school year. Coupling these timelines with a math portfolio can assist students to see their own progress in math over time, and will be likely to enhance the students' sense of accomplishment.

Source: Bender (2009).

Brains as Prioritizing Filters and Pattern Seekers

In the same fashion as the midbrain, or the "emotional brain," filters out information, many other brain areas function as filters, and any of these filters may prohibit learning in mathematics. When we consider the amazing number of stimuli to which our five senses are exposed every second, we can readily understand why the brain requires a variety of filtering mechanisms. Yet as teachers, we must make certain that the concepts we wish to teach get past the brain's filters that nature has provided. There are several effective ways to do that. First, using novelty in teaching is critical. Tactics such as color coding or novel presentations of new information can greatly assist students in focusing on the mathematical content to be mastered. These tactics will assist every learner in mastering mathematics.

Perhaps more important is the teacher's presentation of the material. One brain function that allows the brain to filter information involves the brain's search for patterns, broad concepts, or organizing principles (Devlin, 2010; NMAP, 2008). Such broad concepts allow the brain to categorize and classify knowledge, and thus provide a type of "brain shorthand" by which concepts may be classified and mentally stored.

Many researchers are stressing instruction based on teaching patterns in mathematics, and terms such as *big ideas,* or *essential questions* are frequently used for this emphasis within the mathematics curriculum (Dehaene, 2010; Devlin, 2010). These would include increased instructional emphasis on ideas such as the base-ten number system and concepts based on that system such as place value; expanded notation; commutative, associative, and distributive properties; and so on (Harniss, Carnine, Silbert, & Dixon, 2002; NMAP, 2008). Of course, this parallels the emphasis within the Common Core Standards in Mathematics, which stresses patterns in mathematics instruction (see item 7, in Box 1.1, Standards for Mathematical Practice).

In order to get past the filtering function of children's brains, teachers should address explicitly and repeatedly the patterns and big ideas in each mathematics unit. Further, teachers should assist students in making connections between these big ideas across instructional units, in order to foster deep conceptual understanding in mathematics (NMAP, 2008). With appropriate instruction based on these critical concepts, almost all learners can master the basic mathematics curriculum content in the primary and elementary grades.

Number Sense

Over the last decade, a number of researchers have stressed the concept of "number sense" (Devlin, 2010; Gersten & Chard, 1999; Griffin et al., 2003; N. C. Jordan, 2007; N. C. Jordan et al., 2007; NMAP, 2008; Sousa, 2008; Whitenack, Knipping, Loesing, Kim, & Beetsma, 2002). Number sense may be best understood as a student's conceptual understanding of basic number and numeration concepts such as counting, or recognizing how many objects are present in a set, and how a number may be used to represent that set of objects (N. C. Jordan, 2007; Sousa, 2008). The concept of number sense also involves recognizing that patterns make up the sequence of numbers. Gersten and Chard (1999) defined number sense as "fluidity and flexibility" with numbers. Number sense in the early years allows a child to make judgments of magnitude, comparison, mental computation, and estimations (Devlin, 2010; Seethaler & Fuchs, 2006; Sousa, 2008).

For example, students with number sense can translate real-world quantities and the mathematical world of numbers and numerical expressions (N. C. Jordan, 2007). Young students are often quite capable of expressing the numbers in several different ways. They can show eight fingers by holding up five on one hand and three on the other, or when asked to show the same number another way, they can hold up four on one hand and four on the other. Students with a highly developed number sense know that five objects are more than two objects; they recognize the relative size of the numbers though they may not know the actual difference between the two numbers (Devlin, 2010).

In contrast, younger students without number sense may be able to count and recognize the figure that symbolizes a particular number, and they may be able to write or point to the numeral "5," but they do not comprehend the actual meaning of the number (Devlin, 2010; N. C. Jordan, 2007). They cannot yet tell if seven is more than five, or less than five. While many children can count, children without number sense do not seem to have the concept of what the numbers mean or of the fact that numbers may be used to represent objects in a set (N. C. Jordan, 2007). These problems may stem from a lack of understanding of one-to-one correspondence or simply from lacking the insight that higher numbers represent more "things" in a set.

However, number sense is not limited to prekindergarten or primary skill levels, and the concept of number sense is quite important for teachers at all levels of mathematics. For older children, deficits in many mathematical skills may stem from the types of number sense problems noted above. For example, students in the elementary and middle grades should realize that both 2/3 and 5/8 are larger numbers than 1/4, because of the numerator/denominator relationship (e.g., when the numerator is larger than half the value of the denominator or it is almost as large as the denominator, the fraction is more than 1/2). Without such recognition, students in the middle grades will show deficits in their understanding of fractions, and that deficit might permeate throughout the mathematics curriculum.

Gersten and Chard (1999) suggest that number sense is necessary, but not sufficient for mastering problem-solving skills at all levels. Children must learn number sense in order to interpret mathematical problems in the real world, but they must also learn simple operations in order to begin mastery of problem solving. With this growing importance associated with number sense, it is unfortunate that few math curricula provide instructional tasks that address this critical phase in mathematics achievement. Strategies for developing number sense are presented in Chapters 4 and 5, with an emphasis on the age-appropriate tactics for different students.

> *Number sense is not limited to prekindergarten or primary skill levels, and the concept of number sense is quite important for teachers at all levels of mathematics.*

Summary of Research on the Mathematical Brain

With this emerging understanding of how brains function in learning mathematics, some preliminary conclusions can be provided for teachers. The following list of brain-compatible instructional guidelines is a general list of instructional suggestions, compiled from a variety of sources, and should provide you with food for thought on how you teach mathematics (King & Gurian, 2006; Sousa, 2008; Sousa & Tomlinson, 2010; Tate, 2005). Of course, these should be viewed merely as general guidelines, and different students will certainly require different approaches to instruction, based on their academic skill level, as well as their particular learning styles and preferences.

Teaching Tip 1.3   Tactics for Brain-Compatible Mathematics Instruction

Create a safe, comfortable class environment. Brains filter stimuli on several levels, and one involves safety, while another involves emotional comfort. First, the brain selectively focuses on stimuli that might threaten safety, often to the exclusion of other stimuli. A second priority involves emotional safety and a sense of well-being. Only as a last priority does the brain process information for new, nonthreatening learning tasks (Sousa, 2001). Thus, students who are threatened emotionally by past failures in mathematics typically invest less cognitive energy in learning new mathematics concepts.

Clearly, students must feel safe and comfortable in order to be prepared to focus on new material in math (Sousa & Tomlinson, 2011), and teachers should intentionally construct various games and fun activities around math to alleviate some of the emotional discomfort students might feel in this subject. Also, in mathematics (as in any subject), a positive personal relationship with the teacher is critically important. Only in that context will students turn their attention to mastering new mathematical content.

Use comfortable furniture and lighting. Teachers should make their class as warm and inviting as possible. Teachers may wish to bring in house furniture (e.g., sofa or a couple of chairs) to set up group study areas. Lamps can be used to provide more "home-like" lighting.

Teach with strong, novel visual stimuli. Although teachers have known that novel visual stimuli often enhance learning in mathematics, this commonsense insight has been confirmed by the brain-compatible instructional literature (Sousa, 2008). Therefore, teachers should use color enhancements, size, and shape enhancements, and technology-based presentations (i.e., YouTube videos on a particular type of math problem, or graphics to represent math content). The human brain and central nervous system are specifically attuned to seek out novelty and movement differences in stimuli (Sousa, 2001, 2006), so teachers should use this whenever possible. Further, when different colors or movement presentations highlight important concepts, the teacher should point that out directly and explicitly to maximize learning. From the perspective of differentiated instruction, these instructional modifications represent modifications of the learning processes for students with various learning challenges.

Encourage frequent student responses. Students will learn much more when they are required to participate by producing something. When regular work is required, students are generally much more engaged in the process of learning. While requiring some mathematics during a lesson is a good idea, that is not the only way to encourage students to participate in the content. Students' responses might include a requirement to "hold a discussion on this mathematics problem with your peer buddy," rather than completion of problems on a worksheet.

Use chanting, rhymes, and music in teaching math. Because music and rhythms are processed in a different area of the brain from language, pairing mathematical concepts to a musical melody, or a rhythmic chant, can enhance learning (Tate, 2005). Most adults, on reflection, can remember the song that was frequently used to memorize the ABCs—the tune to "Twinkle, Twinkle, Little Star"—and many students used that same song for other memory tasks in the higher grades—the periodic table or division math facts. Again, teachers have used this insight for a number of decades, but the emerging research on the human brain has documented the basis for enhanced learning when music and rhythms are used to enhance memory for the academic content (Tate, 2005). Here is an example for teaching components of a circle, using the rhythm of the song, "We Will Rock You." Students should slap their desks to emphasize the "We will, we will, rock you!" rhythm, while chanting:

This is circumference, all around the side

This is radius, the middle to the side

This is diameter, all the way through

All of that's a circle, I'll show it to you!

Teach with bodily movements that represent mathematics content. Have you ever wondered why motor skills such as swimming seem to be retained for life, even without routine practice, whereas use of a foreign language quickly atrophies if it is not practiced? Brain research has shown that motor skills represent a deeper form of learning than merely cerebral learning, which is why movement is now recommended as a highly effective teaching tool in math as in most subject areas, even in the upper grades (Sousa, 2010; Sousa & Tomlinson, 2011). Mathematical content associated with movement, once learned, is remembered much longer than math skills that do not involve a motor response, and this suggests that whenever possible, teachers should pair factual memory tasks with physical movements.

Here is an example of a movement activity that emphasizes mathematics content. While having some of the students use the chant above on components of a circle, the teacher might have other students "act out" those components of a circle. Each line of the chant above could be enacted by several students, as follows:

"This is circumference . . . " Have eight students walk in a circle, and then turn to face the center, as that line ends.

"This is the radius . . . " Have another line of three students bisect the circle with the first student stopping right in the middle.

"This is diameter . . . " Beginning 90% around from the "radius" line of students, have another line of five student bisect the circle, and extend all the way across, perpendicular to the radius.

(Continued)

(Continued)

While this chant and movement activity may seem somewhat immature to some teachers, particularly at the higher grades, I must emphasize that the brain research is showing that movement does enhance retention of content (Sousa, 2010). I suggest that on every day of instruction, teachers should develop some movement-based activity to represent concepts. For every graph or chart, teachers should find creative ways to represent the sections of the chart with bodily movements (touching the head, shaking the fingers, etc.). Alternatively, teachers may stand students in the positions of various math problems and then move them through the problem. Such movement-based examples take only a couple of minutes, and these can be fun, novel exercises for teaching. If such an exercise is repeated five or six times on different days while the class studies circles, this will result in increased long-term retention for that mathematical content.

Offer student choices. One way to make students more comfortable in mathematics is to provide them with choices. In fact, many educators today emphasize the importance of student choice in the activities they undertake (Larmer, Ross, & Mergendoller, 2009; Sousa & Tomlinson, 2011). In short, if teachers want their students to make reasonable and informed choices when they are not in the context of the school, teachers must offer choices within the classroom, and coach students in making informed choices. Such choices may involve the options for demonstrating competence or understanding a set of facts or other choices among assignments on a particular topic, and in a highly differentiated classroom, students will be offered many choices and are likely to use their own understanding of their learning styles and preferences to make such choices.

Use social networking for learning mathematics. It has often been noted by veteran teachers that having students explain new information to other students can enhance learning, and the new social networking craze provides the opportunity to extend such social exchanges well beyond the classroom. Further, the frequency with which most students today participate in social networking indicates a general preference for social learning opportunities within the classroom (Bender & Waller, 2011a), and mathematics teachers should take advantage of this. Teachers might get in the habit of presenting some information in shorter time frames and then requiring that students discuss that information together, thus enhancing the opportunity for social networking on the mathematics content.

Offer water and fruits if possible. Research has shown that brains require certain fuels—oxygen, glucose, and water—to perform at peak efficiency (Sousa, 2001, p. 20). Up to one-fourth of the blood pumped in our bodies with each heartbeat is headed for the brain and central nervous system, and water is critical for even blood flow. Furthermore, water is essential for the movement of neuron signals through the brain (Sousa, 2006). Finally, we now know that fruits are an excellent source of glucose for the brain, and research has shown that eating a moderate amount of fruit can boost performance and accuracy of word memory (Sousa, 2001, 2006). Thus, in brain-compatible classrooms, individual water bottles are usually present on the desks for students to take a sip whenever they need to. Some teachers even offer light fruits as snacks, if these can be obtained from the cafeteria at school.

Teach less to teach more. The National Mathematics Advisory Panel (2008) recommended streamlining the math curricula throughout the grade levels, in part because we now understand that from the perspective of a child's brain, less is more! Students with math problems will usually master more content if exposed to less content. Teachers should adapt content in the math curriculum based on the needs and learning profiles of the students. Generally, it is much more advisable to truly develop understanding of a few problems rather than assign many problems. Also, some students may not be as successful as others in mastering problems in the same time frame. Fewer problems that are similar in structure that allow students to develop deeper understanding are preferable to many problems of varying types.

Teach patterns and "big ideas" in mathematics. Teachers should assist students in searching for and emphasizing the big ideas in math that cut across problem types (Harniss et al., 2002). We now know that brains seek patterns, or "shorthand ways of understanding," and our teaching should explicitly address these ideas. Using the patterns of counting by threes or fives can help with multiplication math facts. If possible, present patterns or steps in problem solution as an outline that remains posted on the wall for the entire unit. Use math patterns as classroom "games" with fluid, fun, "quick check" questions fired out to the class at various points in the day (Fuson & Wearne, 1997; NMAP, 2008).

Teach math facts to a high level of automaticity. Research has demonstrated the critical importance of automaticity in math facts as one critical basis for increased achievement in higher mathematics (NMAP, 2008; Woodward, 2006). Students can proceed successfully in math only after the math facts are learned at a high level. The use of chants, music, and other novel teaching tactics will enhance memory for facts. These techniques are quite enjoyable and will assist students who learn better via using their strengths in musical intelligence.

Teach algorithms explicitly. Have students identify word problems that do and do not involve the same algorithms. Teachers should model both examples and nonexamples of the new concept or algorithm. Further, teachers should emphasize concepts when correcting student work, and in this fashion assist students in developing a deep understanding of the concept. Research has clearly shown that merely informing students of their correctness or errors shows no positive effects on student learning (Gersten et al., 2002), so teachers should always strive to develop understandings, as encouraged by the Common Core Standards in Mathematics.

Scaffold the students' practice. Teachers should use real-world examples and provide scaffolded assistance to students throughout the learning process (various examples of scaffolding are presented later in this text). Applications of

(Continued)

(Continued)

constructs should be emphasized in varying levels of complexity, using various authentic instructional and authentic assessment techniques. Teachers should make connections between students' prior knowledge and new concepts using real-world examples, as emphasized in the Common Core Standards in Mathematics. Also, use students to teach each other, to summarize main points, and to tutor each other in new concepts in short (e.g., five-minute) tutoring lessons. These types of activities will enhance student motivation to learn math as well as stress interpersonal learning activities.

Understand the fear and explore the beauty. Many students fear mathematics (Montague, 1997) because they may remember early failures, and this negative "affective response" to mathematics can be quite debilitating. Teachers should intentionally plan activities that assist students in developing a more positive response to mathematics (Montague, 1997). For example, teachers may offer error-free learning practices or buddy-learning activities that may remove some embarrassment from periodic failures. Also, many students study math for years without having a Gestalt or excitement-in-learning experience. Showing the beauty of math patterns can be quite satisfying for a naturalistic-oriented person. It is the patterns, the constructs, the logical progression of algorithms that make math like music—a symphony to share with students. Effective math teachers seek ways to share that beauty daily in the mathematics class.

SHEMR: High-Impact Mathematics Instruction

This author has often summarized the brain research using the acronym SHEMR (which can be pronounced *She' mer*). Remembering this simple acronym can assist teachers in developing a repertoire of instructional skills that are likely to enhance mathematical learning, and make number sense and mathematical play a characteristic of the classroom. These activities tend to stress procedural processes in mathematics more so than deeper conceptual understanding, and many activities are presented throughout this text, based on the components of this acronym. These types of instructional activities are based on the recent research on how brains function (Sousa, 2008). I use the phrase "high-impact teaching" since these instructional activities tend to involve more brain regions than merely linguistically based rote learning exercises in the math class. However, these techniques should not become merely "rote learning" activities in the classroom. Rather, when using all of these brain-compatible techniques, teachers must always discuss after the activity, the conceptual meaning that undergirds the songs, chants, or movements.

The letters in the acronym SHEMR represent:

S   **Songs,** rhythms, chants for learning

H   **Humor** to teach content

E   **Emotional impact** of the content

M   **Movement-based** content instruction

R   **Repetition** of these memory enhancement techniques

Songs should be used across the grade levels to enhance memory for academic content (Tate, 2005), and use of this tactic can ease the fear some students have for mathematics. While teachers of young students have frequently used songs and chants for teaching, the use of songs, rhythms, and chants do help students memorize mathematics content, so this tactic is now recommended across the public school grade levels. Teachers should develop a song or chant that captures the essential concepts or big ideas (no more than six or eight such concepts) in every instructional unit in math. The song should not be too long, and teachers can even have a small group of students write that song. Students should then be required to sing that song every day during the unit to reinforce those essential concepts. This type of activity makes learning both novel and more interesting, and even upper elementary grade students typically enjoy this instructional innovation.

Humor should be used to help alleviate stress in the math class, as well as to activate the brains in the class. A humorous story (perhaps a poem, or chant) can often be used to summarize the important aspects of a particular type of mathematics problem. Humor activates regions of the human brain that are not otherwise involved in learning, and thus is likely to increase retention for the content. Further, a bit of well-timed humor can help alleviate much of the discomfort some students experience in mathematics, and this will make mathematics seem much less threatening.

As noted previously, the emotional associations that a student makes with mathematics content can have either a positive or a negative impact. Positive learning experiences in math will greatly enhance learning since these connections will enhance motivation for most students. Again, teachers in mathematics typically have a higher standard to reach to make students comfortable in this subject area, but with the use of the techniques described in this text, teachers can generate positive associations with mathematics for most students.

The brain research has now demonstrated that movement is an important teaching tool and can greatly enhance the students' fun in learning mathematics content (Sousa, 2008, 2010). Because movement is considered by the brain as a survival skill, any mathematical content associated repetitively with movement will be learned more quickly and retained longer. Several movement examples have already been presented, and Teaching Tip 1.4 presents several additional ideas for using movement for mathematics instruction in the elementary grades.

Teaching Tip 1.4　Ideas for Using Movement for Mathematics Instruction

Number Lines on the Floor

Teachers have long used personal number lines, which were typically placed on students' desks. Having a large number line on the floor can make numeration exercise into movement exercises. For younger students, floor number lines can be the basis of addition and subtraction problems, and for older students adding positive and negative integers on a number line on the floor allows students to move through the problem, whereas a worksheet does not.

A Movement for Bar Graphs

Students placed in lines can be used to teach bar graphs (2 students in one line, four in the next, seven in the next, etc.). In fact, many different types of graphs can be represented by students standing in relative position to each other.

Skip Counting Using Floor Number Lines

Much of telling time involves increments of five minutes, so students need to be able to skip-count by fives. To facilitate that, teachers can create a large number line across the floor with every multiple of five printed in red and other numbers printed in black or blue. Students can then move down the line counting, and the same principle applies when counting by 2s or 10s or other numbers.

A Clock Face Movement for Teaching Time

Teachers should prepare a large clock face (perhaps six feet in diameter) on the floor, using masking tape to make the circle, and placing digits 1 through 12 in the appropriate spots. A meter stick may be used as the minute hand and a ruler as the hour hand. Students, working in teams of two or three, should be required to display various times on the large clock by moving the hands as necessary; they may be told, "Make the clock say 1:20." In order to assure involvement of all students, each student should hold a small clock face and individually complete the same task while a team of students is working on the large clock face. Teachers may couple this activity with a song on telling time (sung to the tune of "The Wheels on the Bus Go Round and Round").

The short hand says its number first,

Number first, number first.

The short hand says its number first,

When we're telling time

The long hand is tall and counts by five,

Counts by five, counts by five.

The long hand is tall and counts by five,

When we're telling time.

Finally, repetition is emphasized in the brain-compatible instructional literature, but rather than merely practice mathematics on worksheets, repetition is most effective when it involves repetition of one or more of the brain-compatible teaching exercises discussed above—the exact types of activities as those emphasized in SHEMR. Those mathematics activities are more likely to result in long-term retention of mathematical concepts. Specifically, repetition of problem completion on a mathematics worksheet is not likely to be as effective as having students work out a movement to represent problem solution.

As a general guideline, if a mnemonic is available for content instruction in mathematics, and it is not too long or time consuming, students should repeat that mnemonic a minimum of three times each time they repeat it, and should repeat it at least every day during an instructional unit. This level of repetition is quite likely to result in long-term retention, and students across the grade range enjoy this type of learning activity.

In using SHEMR, teachers should begin each unit of instruction by seeking from four to six fundamental facts or concepts that may be considered the essential content for that unit—the "big ideas" in the unit. Then, teachers should develop a high-impact learning

> *If a mnemonic is available for content instruction in mathematics, students should repeat that mnemonic a minimum of three times each time they repeat it, and should repeat it at least every day during an instructional unit.*

tactic (i.e., one of the SHEMR tactics—a song, chant, movement, humor-ous story, or emotion-invoking example) to teach those facts and/or sum-marize those fundamental concepts. Rather than creating this SHEMR-based teaching tactic yourself, teachers may also choose to merely enumerate these concepts, present them to a small group of stu-dents and have those student generate a SHEMR-based teaching tactic to emphasize that content. That exercise can then be used daily to teach and reinforce those concepts, and repetition of that tactic is likely to result in long-term retention of those basic facts and concepts.

Of course, this should not be interpreted to mean that only those facts/concepts will be learned in the unit. Rather, when students master the essential concepts or facts using these high-impact learning tactics, they can then use that knowledge as a basis for learning other factual material.

WHAT'S NEXT?

With this background on differentiated instruction and the brain-compati-ble instruction research, as well as the current transitions in both mathe-matics instruction generally, the next chapter focuses on several of the traditional models for differentiated instruction. Specifically, the modifica-tion of a traditional mathematics lesson and the use of learning centers as a basis for differentiated instruction in mathematics are described.

Differentiated Instructional Models

2

Lesson Modification and Learning Centers for Mathematics

As discussed in Chapter 1, differentiated instruction involves more than mere application of effective teaching ideas that address a wider variety of learning styles and preferences. In fact, differentiated instruction represents a rather drastic paradigm shift that fundamentally changes the way teachers teach mathematics (and other subjects) across the elementary school grades, resulting in increased student engagement with the learning tasks. Coupled with this refocusing in mathematics instruction is the recent national emphasis on documenting students' response to targeted interventions in mathematics (Bender & Crane, 2011). These two initiatives in education promise to refocus how teachers plan and deliver the mathematics lesson to the highly diverse students in today's classrooms.

> *Differentiated instruction represents a rather drastic paradigm shift that fundamentally changes the way teachers teach mathematics, resulting in increased student engagement with the learning tasks.*

This chapter focuses initially on how differentiation affected lesson delivery in mathematics, by presenting two traditional models of differentiated instruction: modification of the traditional lesson plan and using learning centers for differentiating instruction in mathematics. Since Tomlinson's original work in differentiated instruction (1999), these two traditional differentiated instructional models have dominated the discussion of differentiation in mathematics, and they provide an excellent basis for understanding the nuts and bolts of differentiated instruction.

DIFFERENTIATED INSTRUCTION MODEL ONE: MODIFY THE TRADITIONAL MATHEMATICS LESSON

Teachers who wish to develop a differentiated classroom for mathematics instruction must begin in the lesson-planning phase, and the initial model for differentiating instruction rested on modification of the traditional, whole group lesson plan. For at least the past 30 years in education, lesson planning has been based on a body of research that was known as the "effective schools" research of the 1970s (Bender, 2012a). Other names for this research movement include "direct instruction," "mastery learning," and "effective teacher behaviors." All of these involve highly developed, whole group lesson plans that were designed to maximize instruction time or "engaged" time in which the student was cognitively engaged with the content. In some examples of direct instruction, scripted lessons were used in which teachers literally read a prepared script while teaching. (See Bender, 2012a, for a discussion of effective teaching behaviors and direct instruction.)

For our purposes, we'll use the term *whole group lesson* to represent this traditional instructional approach. Today, our lesson planning and even our way of thinking about mathematics instruction stems from this body of research, and most teacher manuals in most mathematics curricula specifically emphasize this direct instructional, whole group lesson plan.

Of course, to understand this whole group lesson plan we must consider the classroom setting on which this instructional approach was based, as well as the research from that classroom setting. Specifically, researchers of the 1960s and 1970s based their work on the types of classrooms and the types of students who were then prevalent in the public schools. For example, if a teacher taught in Grade 5 in the early 1970s, he or she could realistically assume that most of the students in that class were working on mathematics somewhere near that grade level, perhaps from grade levels 3 through 6 or so, and in that type of class, whole group instruction worked. In other words, while there were some differences in the children's mathematics skills, there was a fairly narrow level of academic diversity within the class. Further, much of the effective schools research took place in classrooms prior to the full implementation of Public Law 94–142 (the Education for All Handicapped Children Act, later re-codified as the Individuals with

Disabilities Act); thus, many students with special needs were excluded from much of this research.

In contrast, in today's fifth-grade class it is quite likely that students' achievement levels in mathematics range from grade level 1 up through grade levels 10 or 11. Today's teachers face wide variance in mathematics achievement among students in the classroom, and it seems logical to inquire how well a traditional whole group lesson, designed and intended for a rather homogeneous class, might work in a highly diverse classroom. In fact, the levels of academic diversity noted in the typical classroom today in the 21st century are much higher than in the 1970s, when the whole group lesson was developed. However, even with this increase in the range of academic skills, educators have not effectively reconceptualized how teachers should conduct mathematics lessons to meet the demands of this level of diversity. Tomlinson's (1999, 2001) initial work on differentiated instruction provided an initial option for teaching that is relatively free from the whole group lesson format of the 1970s.

However, even today's modern mathematics curricula have highly developed lesson plans that employ the whole group lesson model, as witnessed by the fact that whole group instruction is almost always presented as the basis for teaching in most instructor's manuals in mathematics. Yet, if the range of the students' mathematics skills in today's classrooms has changed, it may be time to adjust our thinking about how to structure our lessons and lesson-planning activities, in order to free ourselves from the whole group lesson. Again, Tomlinson's (1999) work on the differentiated classroom represents a fairly drastic paradigm change in how teachers should conduct mathematics instruction. Thus, the lesson-planning job in mathematics becomes an exercise in planning the activities for various groups of students in the class who do not need to follow the traditional whole group lesson or who need an alternative lesson format.

> *If a teacher taught in Grade 5 in the early 1970s, he or she could realistically assume that most of the students in that class were working on mathematics somewhere near that grade level, and in that type of class, whole group instruction worked.*

Teaching Phases in the Whole Group Mathematics Lesson

The traditional whole group lesson is often described as a series of instructional phases that were originally referred to as the "direct instruction" steps. These phases of

> *Even today's modern mathematics curricula employ the whole group lesson model, as witnessed by the fact that whole group instruction is almost always presented as the basis for teaching in most instructor's manuals in mathematics.*

learning, as enumerated in the effective schools research of the 1970s, have become the steps in the typical lesson plan in schools today. Presented in Box 2.1 are the usual steps in direct instruction, and the types of instructional activities involved in each phase of instruction. While the terms may change from one mathematics curriculum to another (some math curricula use the phrase "activate their understanding" rather than "orientation to the lesson," for example), teachers have planned their instruction for the past 30 years around these phases of the whole group lesson.

BOX 2.1 STEPS IN A DIRECT INTRODUCTION LESSON

Orientation to the Lesson	Teacher gains students' attention and relates today's lesson to content previously studied. Teacher uses essential questions to activate students' thinking.
Initial Instruction	Teacher leads completion of several sample problems, models problem completion, and points out difficult aspects of problem.
Teacher-Guided Practice	Students complete problems in class. Teacher monitors each student's success, and assists students independently. Students might discuss problems with each other.
Independent Practice	Students complete sample problems independently, as either class work or homework.
Check	Teacher checks student performance on independent work.
Reteach as Necessary	Teacher reteaches content to the group that did not get it.

Source: Bender (2009).

The fundamental assumptions behind the direct instruction lesson format were that all students would complete the same instructional activities, following the main line of this lesson plan, and that this sequence would facilitate learning for all students. As noted above, this assumed a relatively narrow range of academic diversity, and all educators today realize that this assumption is no longer valid. This whole group lesson plan also assumed that all students could and would learn in the same general fashion.

Problems With the Whole Group Mathematics Lesson

As Tomlinson (1999) stated so succinctly, the increasing diversity of students, of learning styles, and of learning needs in the general education mathematics classes has effectively outgrown these assumptions on which the whole group lesson was based. In today's typical fifth-grade classroom, the broad range of academic diversity makes it impossible for a teacher to teach mathematics effectively using only one instructional format.

> *The fundamental assumptions behind the direct instruction lesson format were that all students would complete the same instructional activities, following the main line of this lesson plan, and that this sequence would facilitate learning for all students.*

In fact, the direct instructional format has never truly worked for many students within a class. In an average sized mathematics class (say perhaps 22 to 25 students), there would be a number of advanced and/or gifted students, as well as many students functioning below grade level. For the advanced students in those mathematics classes, the whole group instructional plan often led to abject boredom, since many advanced or gifted students may already have mastered that specific type of mathematics problem prior to the teacher's initial instruction. Given the cyclic nature of mathematics curricula (i.e., the returning to various topics in subsequent years), many gifted students know the content of a given mathematics unit prior to the teacher even teaching it! Thus, those students would, most likely, be off-task very quickly after the whole group lesson began. They might even begin to disrupt others in the class.

For students with less ability in the typical mathematics classroom, this model of instruction often failed to engage them because they frequently lacked the prerequisite skills necessary for a given lesson. Consequently, many of those students demonstrated either off-task or disruptive behaviors, since they are bored with material that they cannot learn and are not engaged with the lesson activities. Therefore, as a result of teachers' attempting to follow this whole group lesson, based on one lesson activities for all students, many students in the typical mathematics class were bored and often misbehaved. Of course managing those problems took the teacher's time away from delivery of the lesson.

Clearly, for today's diverse group of students, we will need to modify this whole group instructional lesson considerably in order to differentiate the lesson. Thereby, teachers can both increase the variety of activities in this class, and increase student engagement with the mathematics content. While various theorists have provided such models of curriculum and lesson reorganization, Tomlinson's (1999) differentiated instructional model seems to offer the most effective option.

> *For today's diverse group of students, we will need to modify this whole group instructional lesson considerably in order to differentiate the lesson.*

Differentiated Modification of the Mathematics Lesson

This author has used the phrase *Guess, Assess, and Tear Out* to summarize how teachers might modify the traditional lesson after each phase of the lesson, to form differentiated groups for different activities within the mathematics class. In using the Guess, Assess, and Tear Out idea, the teacher would begin the lesson-planning process with the first step as suggested by the traditional, whole group lesson described above—orientation to the lesson. However, after each instructional step in the traditional lesson, the teacher would form a differentiated group for an alternative learning task, by doing three things:

1. **Guess** which students have the concept,

2. **Assess** those several students with one or two quick questions, and

3. **Tear Out** of the class a small instructional group of those students who will perform an alternative instructional activity.

In this modification of the whole group lesson, the terms *guess* and *assess* are self-explanatory. The teacher is (based on his or her judgment and previous experience with the students) guessing which students may have grasped the concept. Next, the teacher will quickly assess them informally, perhaps with a question such as, "Do you understand this idea?"

The final term above requires a bit more explanation. I've used the term *tear out* deliberately, since forming more than one instructional group in a classroom very early in the lesson is quite difficult for many teachers. While teachers have been using instructional groups for many years during the independent practice phase of the whole group lesson, in a differentiated class the differentiated groups will be formed much earlier in the lesson. In fact, during a differentiated class, teachers will form instructional groups even before they have presented the initial instruction in the topic to the class! Further, teachers will form many more instructional groups than traditional whole group lessons called for.

Because most of today's teachers were trained in the whole group teaching model, the modification of this standard lesson plan in order to differentiate the mathematics activities in the classroom may be one of the most challenging aspects of the model. In short, one of the most difficult things to encourage teachers to do is to form multiple instructional groups that will be less supervised by the teacher, since using three or four groups of students in the classroom means that teachers must assume that students can learn from each other without as much instructional supervision. This idea requires some degree of faith on the part of teachers, many of whom have not been prepared for this type of teaching.

> *Using three or four groups of students in the classroom means that teachers must assume that students can learn from each other without as much instructional supervision.*

Also, students as well as teachers are generally not well prepared for this type of instruction. While learning collaboratively from one's peers during the performance of an assigned task is certainly one requirement in the modern workplace, the whole group teaching model is rather authoritarian and doesn't provide ample opportunity for such peer mediated learning. Thus, providing students with increased opportunities to learn content from each other in settings that are somewhat less supervised by the teacher can result in enhanced instruction for a modern world. However, both teachers and students will need some experimental learning in order to function well within this differentiated instruction model. Perhaps a concrete example will demonstrate this concept.

A Differentiated Instruction Lesson Example

In order to demonstrate the Guess, Assess, and Tear Out differentiation approach, we might imagine the following instructional lesson in Ms. Adrian's third-grade math class. The class includes 22 students, 5 of whom are special education students, and 2 of those students have attention deficit disorders coupled with high levels of hyperactivity. The class also includes 3 gifted students, who are functioning at a fourth-grade level in mathematics. In schools today, this would seem to be a typical class. In this scenario, Ms. Adrian is teaching a mathematics lesson concerning the aggregation of data, the creation of a tally table, and the eventual formulation of a frequency table summarizing those data.

As an advance organizer of the Guess, Assess, and Tear Out technique, Teaching Tip 2.1 below shows a comparison of the traditional whole group lesson and a modified lesson plan for the same lesson. Note the whole group lesson activities for each phase in the lesson (the main line of instruction) appear on the left of the chart, and the types of "tear out" activities for the differentiated lesson as suggested by the Guess, Assess, and Tear Out tactic are noted on the right-hand side of the chart.

Teaching Tip 2.1   Modifying the Traditional Whole Group Mathematics Lesson

Whole Group Lesson	Differentiated Instruction; Guess, Assess, and Tear Out Activities
Orientation	
Cover tally tables and frequency tables	After the introduction, break out one group (Omega Group) to create a tally table on the floor, then rejoin main group
Initial Instruction	
Teach tally tables and frequency tables	Tear out a second group (Beta Group, using examples from the test); Beta Group is to use the tally table on the floor for some sample problems
Teacher-Guided Practice	
Have mainline group complete practice worksheet	Have Omega and Beta groups evaluate each other's work
Tear out another group if necessary	
Independent Practice	
Have students complete the independent practice	Omega and Beta groups move into other enrichment activities
Check	
Have Omega and Beta groups describe their activities to the entire class; continue to check comprehension	
Reteach	
Reteach the concepts to a smaller group of kids who haven't mastered it	Use members of Omega and Beta groups to "buddy up" with students who need help

Source: Bender (2009).

To begin this lesson with an attention-grabbing orientation activity, Ms. Adrian might ask her students to identify their favorite type of dinosaur, since most students enjoy that topic. She would hold up a picture of one of the three most recognizable types of dinosaurs and have a student at the dry erase board begin to tally how many students like the *Triceratops*, the *Stegosaurus*, or the *Tyrannosaurus rex*. Once the tally marks are added in the second column, she has completed a tally table. Then, once she has tally marks on the dry erase board, she may then say something like, "Can we summarize these data so they make sense?" Ms. Adrian may ask for suggestions from the class, but she will eventually show a completed frequency table that looks something like Table 2.1.

Table 2.1 Information on Dinosaurs

Dinosaur Picture	Tally Count	Frequency
	///// ///// //	12
	////	4
	///// //	7

After this brief orientation activity, the traditional whole group lesson would suggest that Ms. Adrian begin to teach about tally tables, and ultimately frequency tables, using several similar examples. The differentiated lesson plan on the right-hand side of Teaching Tip 2.1, however, presents another approach. For example, it is possible that, after the orientation to the lesson, and prior to initial instruction, some of the advanced students have already mastered the concept. During the orientation phase of the lesson, several students may have looked ahead in the text and seen several examples of how to tally data in table form. They may even have generated a frequency table from the tally data, and thus, they know the lesson content prior to the teacher even teaching it. In short, even before the lesson is taught some students may already have grasped the idea and may need a more challenging lesson.

At this point, the Guess, Assess, and Tear Out technique offers an alternative for effective differentiation of the mathematics lesson. After the orientation to the lesson, rather than beginning the initial instruction for everyone in the class as a whole group, Ms. Adrian should use the Guess, Assess, and Tear Out tactic. Prior to any actual teacher-led instruction, it is possible—in fact, it is likely in most heterogeneous classes in today's schools—that Ms. Adrian could identify some students who have already mastered the basic concept. In other words, some of the more advanced students do not even need to be taught the lesson. Ms. Adrian would identify three to five students by educated guess and a quick assessment question or two directed to the group. Questions such as "Do you think you could structure a tally table to collect data, and then transfer those data to a frequency table?" For three or four of the students who indicate they could, she should tear out these students and provide some group work as an alternative instructional activity. Further, she could place one or two students who didn't grasp the content in that group, under the assumption that they could learn the content from other students in the tear-out group. Let's follow the next part of the lesson for a moment from the perspective of that tear-out group, by exploring the group's tiered activity assignment.

The Omega Group

We'll call the first tear-out group the Omega Group. These are students in the first group torn out of the mainline of instruction in the whole group lesson. Of course, you may use any terms you like to name these groups, as long as the names for the groups are nonsequential and thus do not indicate a qualitative judgment on the skills or the intellect of the group. For the first activity of the Omega Group, Ms. Adrian may hand them a preselected assignment sheet for a group work activity involving structuring such a frequency table. These students would be instructed to move to a separate section of the room to begin their group project.

In a differentiated lesson, the good news is that teachers usually don't have to create these alternative activities and assignments; these group project alternatives are usually described in the teacher's manual as "enrichment" activities or "reteaching" activities. Thus, Ms. Adrian does not have to create this activity—she merely selects it. She will then provide a brief set of directions for that assignment as well as any necessary materials to the

Omega Group. For the directions, she may merely copy an activity out of the math text with instruction along the lines of the following:

> This activity requires some floor space (15' by 15') and a roll of masking tape. Students will place masking tape on the floor to develop an outline for a frequency table. The rows will represent choices of students' favorite singers (teachers should select five specific pictures of individual singers of different styles of music in advance from various popular music magazines). One column will be used for a count of individuals who like a particular singer, and another column will be used to write the digit number of persons who like a particular singer.

Based on this set of instructions, the students in the Omega Group should be provided with a roll of masking tape, and then should do this activity in one corner of the room.

Given that the next instruction phase—the teacher-directed phase—typically takes 10 to 15 minutes, the group activity for Omega Group should be planned with that time frame in mind. Also, teachers should select an alternative activity that involves one or more of the learning styles that have not been involved in the lesson, and place students in that group who exhibit that learning style of preference. For example, in the activity above, the Omega Group is instructed to use masking tape and structure a frequency table on the floor. This grid will consist of a series of boxes in which students may stand as their preferences are noted. The Omega Group students would have to jointly plan what the tally table should look like, how big the boxes are going to be in order to hold various groups of students, and how the categories in the tally table should be organized. This would be an effective activity for students adept in social learning, as well as movement-oriented learners.

In a differentiated lesson, teachers usually don't have to create these alternative activities and assignments; these group project alternatives are usually described in the teacher's manual as "enrichment" activities.

In this activity, the box on the left is the "category" box, where pictures of singers may be placed in order to identify the specific category. That box need be only large enough to accommodate the pictures. In contrast, the box in the middle must be large enough for a number of students to stand in, as they stand by their preferences. The box on the right end will hold only a digit that summarizes the data in the middle box, so it can be somewhat smaller. The point is that the Omega Group has to figure all of this out—including the number of categories and the relative size of the boxes—while working as a group. The group would be required to place these boxes on the floor using the masking tape, for subsequent classroom use. Thus, this involves a variety of learning styles and preferences, including interpersonal learning, spatial learning, analytic learning, and bodily/kinesthetic learning.

Further, these students—the advanced or gifted students, and the more challenged students—are exactly the students who are likely to become unengaged with the lesson content in the traditional whole group lesson. However in the differentiated assignment, they are collaboratively engaged with the structure of a tally table and a frequency table, the exact content Ms. Adrian wants them to learn. In that sense, creating this differentiated group has increased the engagement of these students with the mathematics content, which in turn leads to increased academic achievement overall.

Of course, given the considerations in designing this floor grid, it is always possible for the Omega Group to make a mistake in their work. For example, while the Omega Group may develop a five-by-three grid, they may forget to consider the relative size of the boxes. Specifically, rather than merely a set of tally marks—as in the earlier example on the dry erase board—the grid on the floor must include a second column of boxes that are large enough to hold a number of students. Thus, the challenge of making this grid is a more complicated activity than merely copying the example developed within the lesson orientation. Still, because of the collaborative nature of this work, such mistakes are likely to be identified by members of the group. In that sense, this activity is more intellectually demanding than the lesson activities offered to the mainline instructional group.

The Mainline Instruction Group

It is relatively easy in this classroom scenario to note the differentiation of lesson demands. After only a 2- or 3-minute orientation to the lesson and prior to having "taught" the lesson, Ms. Adrian has two groups of students in her class—the Omega Group and the mainline group (i.e., the group of students who were not torn out for the differentiated activity). As the Omega Group does its work, Ms. Adrian will engage in traditional teacher-led initial instruction as she normally would for the mainline students. She may use a variety of activities from the instructor's manual, but she should make certain that a variety of activities are offered, and that her instruction addresses a variety of learning styles and preferences, and is at least as interesting as the work done by the Omega Group. For example, after she models how to formulate a tally table to summarize data, and transfers those data into a frequency table, she may have students work as peer buddies to do another sample problem on data aggregation and then explain their solution of the second problem to the mainline group within the class.

In order to further understand differentiated lesson planning, we should also consider what Ms. Adrian's teaching might look like. In a mathematics class of 22 students, if she selected 6 students for the Omega Group, only 16 students would remain in the mainline group during the initial instruction, and they would be more homogeneously grouped. Consequently, Ms. Adrian's instruction is likely to improve because:

- Ms. Adrian would be teaching a more focused, homogeneous group.
- Ms. Adrian would be less distracted by the gifted or advanced students who might be bored had they remained in the mainline group.
- Ms. Adrian is more likely to make eye contact more frequently with 16 students than with 22 students.
- Ms. Adrian is likely to have a better sense of the level of understanding of each member of this group.
- Ms. Adrian's examples during this teaching phase are more likely to be on target for these students than if she were working with the entire class.

In each of these ways, Ms. Adrian's instruction has become more focused and responsive to students' needs in this differentiated lesson given that she is working with a smaller group of students. This is the strength of differentiated instruction—it is strategically targeted instruction aimed more explicitly at the learning needs of each individual student in the math class, and increases the engagement of almost all of the students in both the tear-out group and the mainline instructional group.

Changing Instructional Phases in the Lesson

After 15 minutes or so, Ms. Adrian will have completed the lesson orientation and the initial instructional phases for the mainline students. Also, the Omega Group will have completed its work in designing the frequency table grid on the floor. Again, the teacher should use the Guess, Assess, and Tear Out tactic. With a few judicious questions, the teacher can again identify a second group of perhaps five or six other students in the mainline group that now understand the data aggregation concept and do not need the next direct instruction phase of teacher-guided practice. We'll call this group the Beta Group. Again, Ms. Adrian would select this group from the mainline instructional group and provide an alternative assignment. Throughout this process, Ms. Adrian can choose to form homogeneous groups of students at approximately the same academic level, or she may form heterogeneous groups and assign a task in which the students learn the content from each other, as they complete their work.

For example, this group may be provided the assignment to work with the Omega Group to "test out" the large frequency table grid that has been developed. The Beta Group could be given two or three frequency table assignments based on student preferences for (1) colors of tennis shoes worn in the class, (2) favorite musician, or (3) favorite national leader. Using those tasks, the students in the combined two groups may be assigned to develop frequency tables for each by standing beside their favorite choice. Thus, it would be perfectly appropriate to use them to work with the Beta Group to develop these activities for later classroom use. Alternatively, at this point in the lesson, the Omega Group might be assigned a different task, or they might be required to rejoin the mainline instructional group.

Again, we should consider what is happening in Ms. Adrian's class at this point in the lesson. First, note that Ms. Adrian's class will be quite differentiated only five minutes or so after the lesson begins. Specifically, after she oriented the students to the whole group lesson, she tore out the Omega Group, and again, after the initial instruction phase, she tore out the Beta Group. Thus, in 15 minutes or so after the beginning of the lesson, several students in the Omega Group were doing a second tear-out assignment, the Beta Group was testing the grid on the floor with several sample problems, and the mainline instructional group, which by then included only 11 students or so, were receiving instruction from Ms. Adrian. Again, Ms. Adrian's instruction was increasingly focused on the needs of the students in the mainline group. Thus, those students received additional, intensive instruction from Ms. Adrian. In that sense, differentiated instruction in this mathematics lesson would result in highly focused instruction and students that were highly engaged in the learning tasks.

Guidelines for Differentiated Lesson Planning

With these several modifications in mind, we can now identify the general guidelines for modifying a direct instructional lesson and transforming it into a differentiated lesson in math. I do wish to emphasize that these are merely guidelines, and that every teacher should, based on his or her understanding of the individuals in the class as well as the demands of the subject content, adapt these to the specific needs of the students. These guidelines are presented in Teaching Tip 2.2.

Teaching Tip 2.2   Guidelines for Differentiated Mathematics Lessons

Subdivide the class early and often. The teacher in a differentiated class should provide many tear-out activities. In fact, teachers employing differentiated instruction will sub-divide their class much earlier in the lesson than is usual in the direct instruction model, and will do so much more frequently. For this reason, the Guess, Assess, and Tear Out tactic offers the most effective, differentiated instructional option for students at all levels of ability in the class. When teaching within a differentiated instructional lesson, teachers should tear out either a homogeneous or heterogeneous group of students for an alternative instructional activity after each phase in the traditional lesson plan. In the latter case, teachers should select some students who have grasped the concept and some who haven't, by exercising judgment concerning who can work effectively in a group and who can or will work together.

Never plan one lesson activity when you need two or three! The academic diversity in today's elementary classes often necessitates the presentation of the same content in multiple ways, so I suggest that each time a teacher plans one activity, he or she plans at least one more and sub-divides the class, with some students doing one and some doing the other. While creative teachers can always generate interesting instructional ideas, many ideas can be found in today's teacher's manuals for math curricula. These are typically included as "enrichment" or "alternative teaching" ideas. In most cases, teachers merely need to select these activities from the curriculum ideas presented.

Use the tear-out activities more than once in the unit. In the example in Ms. Adrian's class, the Omega Group was the first to develop a frequency table on the floor. On subsequent days within that unit of instruction, other students in other groups may also be challenged with that activity. Further, it is perfectly acceptable for a particular student to be included in several groups doing the same activity. That would merely be a good example of a repetitive instruction technique!

Modify alternative activities to address different learning styles and preferences. Ms. Adrian, in using the grid activity in her class, provided an activity that emphasized several intelligences, including spatial, logical/mathematical, and interpersonal. Can this activity be modified and subsequently used to involve other intelligences? If the assignment were to blindfold a student, and have him or her provide verbal directions for the formulation of the grid on the floor without watching the process, could linguistic intelligence be strengthened?

Use what you have in your local community! In math instruction, as well as many other subjects, using examples in the students' community can involve students more and motivate them to complete the math. For example, in farming communities, tying math problems to local crop sales can be quite effective. For students in urban areas, describing math problems in terms of the types of clothes

(Continued)

(Continued)

or tennis shoes that are in vogue can motivate students more than simply using whatever math problems are on the page. If students live near a major historical park, teachers should consider math examples that could be tied to that local resource (e.g., How many patriots fought at the Battle of Trenton versus how many British mercenaries?). Teachers in every field should use examples from the community whenever possible.

One interesting type of assignment for some tear-out groups is to rewrite each of the word problems in a particular unit using some local example. The others in the class can then use those problems for their practice work. This results in more "authentic" learning than some of the math problems presented in the standard math texts.

Tie students in emotionally. We now know that, prior to learning, the student must sense emotional safety in the learning environment. Further, if teachers can tie the math content to an emotional hook, students will become more involved in the content. Discussions of math in terms of the number of students who can go on a school trip might be one illustration of this idea. Here are two more examples:

Grade 3 Problem: "We have 4 buses for the third-grade trip, and each will carry 25 students and 4 supervisory adults. If 22 adults volunteer to go on the trip, how many students can go?"

Grade 6 Problem: "We have 4 buses, each of which will take 25 students and 4 adults. If students were selected for the class trip based on their math grades, and 96% of a total student math population of 115 students scored high enough to go, would we have to leave eligible students or adult volunteers behind?"

If students have parents in the military, a number of math problems on variable troop strength in a particular engagement might be used. I noted this personally while working in the schools in Clarkesville, Tennessee, since that city is adjacent to the military base that houses the 101st Airborne Division—a division that had recently been deployed overseas.

Use differentiated instruction for inclusive classes in mathematics. The overall fit between inclusion and differentiated instruction is almost perfect. Teachers should jointly plan to use differentiated lessons in inclusion classes, and with more than one teacher present in the room, one adult or another can work with the tear-out groups.

Continue some whole class lessons. I encourage teachers not to attempt differentiated lessons each and every day. While lectures seem ineffective with many students today, other traditional whole group lessons do work wonderfully, including group project activities, whole class discussions of video- or media-based examples, student presentations, and collaborative student research. These instructional activities should always be an important component of learning in the elementary classroom.

One question I am frequently asked is how often should teachers differentiate? I usually tell teachers to aim for a highly differentiated lesson structure perhaps three days each week, and on the alternate days utilize more traditional instructional procedures, such as those mentioned above. I believe that this will provide an appropriate mix of activities and will create an effective classroom learning environment where the needs of all students can be met. I also find that teachers respond to this suggestion positively; while teachers have a difficult time seeing themselves teaching three or four groups of students in different tasks during each 15-minute segment each day of the week, they can see themselves doing this two or three days each week and using other effective whole group tactics on the other days.

Teachers should "test the waters" of differentiated instruction tentatively. Once a teacher decides to attempt differentiated instruction, he or she should try this approach in a successful class—a classroom that seems to be working well. The teacher should also initially do this in an area of math that students know well. This will effectively increase the teacher's comfort zone, and will be more likely to result in a pleasant differentiated instructional teaching experience than trying this new teaching paradigm in a challenging class. Also, testing this idea in a class that is not presenting challenges is more likely to result in initial student success. After that, teachers can attempt to differentiate in other, more challenging classes. Moreover, teachers who have moved into this slowly and have seen it work as both they and the students grow to understand this instructional system have stated that teaching is simply much more fun this way!

Identify practical ways to make differentiated groups work. Various teachers have suggested some simple, practical guidelines to make differentiation work in their classes. While these may not be critically important in every situation, teachers may wish to consider these additional suggestions:

Be careful how heterogeneous groups are selected for differentiation. Teachers should take care not to embarrass students who may not know the content when forming the first differentiated group.

Move furniture as necessary to visually monitor the tear-out groups. When a differentiated group is doing a movement-based activity in the front of the room, where the extra room space might be located, the teacher should move to the opposite side of the room, and have students that will continue to work with the teacher move their desks into a semicircle facing away from the differentiated group. Those students are thus more likely to pay attention to the teacher, and the teacher will be in a position to both teach the mainline instruction group and visually monitor the differentiated group.

(Continued)

(Continued)

Provide informal "coaching" to students with overt behavior problems. Such coaching will often enable students to function successfully in differentiated groups. As an example, one teacher decided that one student who often displayed anger (e.g., cursing at other students) could be included if the teacher provided that student with an "opt out" strategy. In short, she waited until the angry student asked "Why don't I ever get to go and work over there?" The angry student was told the following. "I would love to put you working with that group, but I know that sometimes you get upset with other students and then you might call the other student "stupid" or something. Of course, that's never wise, since the other students don't like to be called names. Here's what we'll do. Today, I'll put you over there, but if you find yourself getting angry, just raise your hand and I'll call back over to the group I'm working with and have you help me demonstrate that activity with them!" This informal coaching and the opt-out strategy, conducted over a series of days, was enough to get that angry student to a place where he could be included in a less supervised, tear-out group, and work in that group.

Empower the students that do not know the content. Experienced teachers can readily see that in differentiated groups, the students who know the content might do the work, and ignore the students who do not know the content. Thus, the teacher should "empower" the students who do not know the content. In the text example involving the formation of the tear-out group to develop the grid on the floor using masking tape, the teacher should give the tape to a student who does not know the content, thus facilitating group interaction. In short, the other students will need to interact with that student, and, ideally, teach him about why the grid should be formed in a certain way.

Results of Differentiated Lessons

Teachers who have chosen to move into differentiation for instruction in mathematics have generally found that many of the anxieties they had about such instruction did not materialize. For example, many teachers are initially concerned about the issue of management of so many different instructional groups within the classroom. Of course, every class includes some students who, at least initially, should not be selected for tear-out activities since their behavior patterns necessitate close teacher supervision. However, teachers typically find that after the class as a whole gets accustomed to this learning format, even those behaviorally challenged kids can participate meaningfully in tear-out activities.

Also, because the training of most teachers in schools today was formulated on the whole group instructional model, some teachers cannot bring themselves to believe that learning will take place in the tear-out groups. In fact, some teachers view these unsupervised groups as disaster waiting to happen. Nevertheless, I've had teachers state repeatedly that once they moved to a differentiated instructional format, they found that students do learn from each other in the tear-out groups, and that this lesson plan resulted in increased student engagement and increased student learning overall.

All teachers are under pressure today to address the Common Core State Standards in Mathematics, and this differentiated lesson format will result in improved instruction in mathematics compared to whole class, traditional instruction. Teachers, however, must exercise some judgment in initial group formulation. Box 2.2 below lists the typical results reported by teachers once they begin the transition to a truly differentiated classroom using this differentiated model.

> *All teachers are under pressure today to address the Common Core State Standards in Mathematics, and this differentiated lesson format will result in improved instruction in mathematics compared to whole class, traditional instruction.*

BOX 2.2   TYPICAL RESULTS OF DIFFERENTIATED INSTRUCTION LESSONS

Use of More Varied Instructional Activities

Teachers often report that they are using a wider variety of instructional activities in differentiated classes than they did in whole group lessons.

Increased Involvement of Advanced Students

The advanced kids in this procedure will be more challenged and thus less likely to get bored and engage in problem behaviors.

Varied Behavior Management Concerns

Management of an increased number of instructional groups will be a concern, and the teacher should move into differentiation slowly for this reason. Students who would otherwise be bored with traditional lessons will be more engaged in this instructional model, however, and it is hoped these behavior management results will effectively even things out for the teacher in the differentiated lesson.

Improved Instruction for Those Who Need It

As the mainline group gets smaller, the instruction for that group is likely to improve, since the teacher is concentrating on a smaller group. Thus, the teacher

(Continued)

(Continued)

is providing increased support for the students who really need the help on a particular lesson.

Provision of the Best Instruction for Everyone

Differentiated instruction encourages teachers to offer the most effective enrichment/instruction to kids across the ability spectrum. Teachers must make the mainline group activities as varied, as novel, and as exciting as any of the alternative assignments for the tear-out groups.

Effective Use as a Model for Inclusive Instruction

Teachers can readily see the comfortable fit between the use of multiple tear-out groups, formed to be heterogeneous, and the demands of the inclusive classroom. Differentiated instruction provides one of the most effective models for inclusion currently available.

Teachers Become Used to Teaching This Way

Once teachers try this instructional model, particularly if they test this model in an academic area within their comfort zone, they typically find that they enjoy this type of teaching. While all teachers differentiate to some degree, teachers who devote themselves to this approach often state that they would not like to return to teaching in a traditional fashion. In fact, teaching a differentiated lesson is simply more fun.

Source: Bender (2009).

A DIFFERENTIATED INSTRUCTION OVERVIEW: WHAT IT IS AND WHAT IT ISN'T

With the guidelines for differentiation of instruction in mind, we can now take a broader look at the overall concept. When I first began to investigate differentiated instruction, I was somewhat confused as to what it really was. I have since learned that such confusion is quite common. Specifically, in many books I have read and in many workshops I attended I found that a wide variety of great teaching ideas were presented, but I found no "central theme" on what differentiated instruction was. While I always enjoy acquiring novel teaching ideas, I left many such workshops wondering if "differentiated instruction" was merely an array of "good teaching ideas." I had not grasped the essential element or elements of the concept.

More recently, I have come to understand that differentiation is more than merely an innovative set of brain-compatible teaching tactics.

Differentiated instruction is, in reality, a new way of conceptualizing the structure of learning in the classroom context. Teachers in the 21st century should no longer believe that children make up a "class" of third graders or a "class" of sixth graders. Rather, teachers teach individuals, and, in today's classrooms, teachers must be willing to free themselves from the confines of the traditional whole group lesson plan, since that approach is clearly inappropriate for most classrooms today. Teachers today are facilitators of learning, rather than "content delivery" specialists, and the shift to a more differentiated type of mathematics instruction parallels other recent changes in the teacher's role, from lecturer to instructional guide and facilitator.

In that sense, differentiated instruction represents a real paradigm shift for teachers who have been trained to think of instruction as a group phenomenon—as in the direct instructional model described earlier. Teachers must now shift their thinking to lesson planning for individual children, and they must consider the emerging information on the wide variety of ways that children learn (e.g., learning styles, differing attention levels, varied capabilities, different academic levels, different learning preferences). Only from such a perspective can teachers hope to meet the wide variety of needs in today's classrooms.

> *Differentiated instruction represents a real paradigm shift for teachers who have been trained to think of instruction as a group phenomenon; teachers must now shift their thinking to lesson planning for individual children.*

Of course, I have now come to realize that many teachers are differentiating their mathematics instruction without realizing it. Indeed, many teachers have been "differentiating" their classrooms for many years. The academic diversity found in today's classes simply demands it! In fact, the diversity in today's classes suggests that in order to survive as teachers, educators must be about the business of novel and innovative teaching to diverse groups of students within the class. For these math teachers, the construct of the differentiated lesson plan will merely mean that they develop their different instructional activities more deliberately, more strategically. These teachers will then deliver a more diversified lesson within the mathematics class, having initially planned to address these diverse learning needs.

With that noted, there are alternative models for differentiating instruction. I typically present the modification of the whole class lesson first, because teachers relate most easily to the traditional lesson plan. However, a variety of alternatives exist for differentiating mathematics instruction, including the following model, learning centers in the mathematics class.

LEARNING CENTERS FOR MATHEMATICS: DIFFERENTIATION MODEL TWO

Another traditional model for differentiating instruction is the learning center (or learning stations, a term which is more frequently used in the upper grades, middle and high school). Many mathematics classrooms currently include learning centers, and in most such classes, the learning centers are used to provide adjunct educational activities in mathematics that supplement ongoing instructional units in the classroom. That is to say, in most classrooms today, learning centers or learning stations are not the primary method of instructional delivery. In those classes, learning centers would be used by some students at the same time as the teacher leads other students in other instructional activities in a given instructional unit, and the activities within the learning center are typically considered supplemental activities within that instructional unit.

However, if learning centers are intended to be the primary method of differentiating instruction in the math class, the learning centers should be established such that virtually all instruction can be delivered in the context of the learning centers. Of course, both types of learning centers work well, but we'll discuss the second type of classroom here, classrooms in which the learning centers are the primary model for differentiating instruction.

> If learning centers are intended to be the primary method of differentiating instruction in the math class, the learning centers should be established such that virtually all instruction can be delivered in the context of the learning centers.

In order to envision this differentiated instructional approach, teachers might imagine a classroom in which no whole group lessons are planned. Rather, students are divided into groups based on academic levels and learning styles, and receive their instruction in a variety of learning centers, and most of the student groups would visit and work within most of the learning centers each day. The teacher, in this context, becomes an instructional facilitator rather than a content delivery agent, as in the traditional whole class lesson.

When learning centers are used as the primary model of instructional delivery, the learning centers should be developed to allow for modifications and adaptability within the mathematics classroom (Bender, 2009). For primary and elementary mathematics, a variety of learning centers might be established including learning centers focused on:

Numeration and Operations

Measurement

Problem-Solving Applications

Special Projects

Computer Center

Guided Mathematics Instruction

Assignments Within the Learning Centers

In each case, the learning center would be a designated location in the room where a table full of activities would be located that addressed that topic. A sign should be placed on the wall above the table, with the title of the learning center on it. In each learning center, teachers should provide some instructions for the students working there. Many teachers post "activity cards" on the wall in each learning center that instruct the students in different groups on the activities that must be accomplished to receive credit for completing the work in that center. Some learning centers include small dry erase boards on which assignments may be written.

Each center usually includes a storage box of some type, with 10 to 15 file folders in the box. Each file folder should be labeled with the name of the center, a sequenced number, and the title of a specific activity (e.g., Linear Equations, Level One, or Whole Group Operations in Addition/Subtraction With Regrouping). Each folder might include a worksheet, instructions to conduct an activity, a manipulative activity, or directions for partner or team-based activities. Further, each activity in each center should be developed to require approximately 15 to 20 minutes. Students should be specifically taught to go to the correct learning center, and get into the correct folder for the assigned activity, and initially teachers will need to check to see that students have, in fact, pulled out the right activity.

To make these learning centers accessible for students with learning disabilities, teachers should keep the instructions for these activities simple and clear, and by varying the instructions, assigned for different groups in the same learning center. For example, a single math class may have various levels of assignments present on these activity cards and instruct some students to complete the "Level 1" activities while others complete "Level 2" or "Level 3" activities. Again, such differentiated instruction must be provided to meet the needs of students with learning disabilities or other diverse learning needs.

Learning centers or learning stations provide an excellent opportunity to make virtually all types of assignments, including assignments for small groups of students. Students typically enjoy the creative activity of developing instructional content on their own, with some teacher guidance. For example, the teacher might present a list of concepts or points for the small group to use, and request that the group make up a chant, song, or movement emphasizing those points. Teaching Tip 2.3 presents an example of a brain-friendly change and movement that can be used to teach the parts of a circle.

Teaching Tip 2.3   A Brain-Compatible Song for Teaching Operations With Positive/Negative Integers

Once a group is provided with the basic guidelines on how to complete operations with positive and negative integers, the small group might be assigned to develop a song, movement, or chant to teach that content. One fifth-grade teacher reported that her students created a nice little song to guide them in addition of positive and negative integers. This is sung to the tune of "Row, Row, Row Your Boat."

Same sign, add and keep,

Different sign subtract!

Take the sign of the highest number

Then you'll be exact!

Multiply and divide

It's an easy thought!

Same signs are positive

Different signs are not!

Content of the Learning Centers

As the categories above suggest, most of the mathematics curriculum can be addressed under one learning center or another. For example, in the numeration and operations center, a variety of activities might be included that focus on numeration (at a grade level appropriate for that classroom) and operations. Activities can include a variety of manipulatives, worksheets, or "peer buddy" work outlines, games that teach operations, and/or computer activities to foster basic numeration and operations understandings.

The materials that should be included in each learning center should be obtained on a continuous basis and subsequently labeled and organized in a way to facilitate the student's retrieval of appropriate materials. In particular, students with various disabilities should be taught *how* to obtain their own work materials from the learning center because this will assist them in the development of organization skills as well as instill an ability to focus on the specific task at hand. In that sense, the learning centers must be a model of efficient organization of materials.

Activities in the learning centers vary widely. In most cases, educational games may be identified for the centers and various manipulatives might be available. Most learning centers include materials to develop art projects in various subject areas, and posters might be in the centers for various subjects (e.g., a times table chart in the mathematics center, or a chart presenting the PEMDAS order of operations guidelines). Most teachers also develop sets of worksheets that may be used, either individually or by small groups of students, and place these worksheets in the learning centers as well. Also, teachers should seek out the media specialist and inquire whether materials in mathematics are available for long- or short-term loan to a particular class. In many cases, with special permission, the teacher may be able to check out materials for use for a week, a multiweek instructional unit, or a month. Teachers will also want some materials for lower-level students—including lower-level readers—to use. This will enable almost all students to obtain assignments from the learning center.

In the measurement learning center, teachers should place assignments and appropriate manipulatives to allow the students to focus on the Common Core Math standards for that particular grade level. However, teachers should make certain that appropriate measurement activities are included such that even the more gifted or accelerated learners can be assigned meaningful, challenging work.

In the computer center, six or seven computers may be placed along one wall, each of which is programmed with appropriate computer software for mathematics instruction. Then, a group of six or seven students might go to the computer center in the room, and there, each student can access a mathematics software program that is specifically targeted to his or her mathematics needs and individual skill level. Vmath and SuccessMaker Math are computer-delivered mathematics instructional packages that deliver individually targeted instruction via computer, thus leaving the teacher free to instruct other students in other learning centers (see Appendix A for descriptions of other programs in mathematics).

In the guided mathematics instruction center, small-group guided instruction is provided by the teacher. Typically, once groups have begun their work in other learning centers, the teacher calls one group to the work table for targeted, direct instruction that is teacher directed. In that case, those students would receive 15 to 20 minutes of teacher-led, targeted instruction that addresses their specific needs.

Organization of Learning Centers

In this model of differentiated instruction, teachers should use students' individual learning styles, along with their academic achievement levels in either reading or mathematics, to divide the class into four relatively homogeneous groups (Bender & Waller, 2011b). Each group should be assigned to a specific learning center for 15- to 20-minute timeslots. At the end of each 15-minute segment, teachers would instruct all students to check their work and save it. Then each homogeneous group of students would move to the next center and begin the work in that location, as per assignments previously developed by the teacher for that specific group.

In that fashion, the teacher can move from center to center helping students individually and facilitating instruction, rather than deliver a traditional whole group lesson for all members of the class. Alternatively, as students begin their work in the learning centers, teachers might call one group to work directly with the teacher on a direct instruction program in mathematics.

In this example, imagine beginning a fifth-grade mathematics class by the teacher saying the following:

> *Welcome to mathematics class everyone. Today, I want Group A to work in the Computer Center. You guys have already taken the placement assessment, so get into the series of problems we decided would be next for each of you individually. Group B should come to work with me at my worktable. Group C will begin in the Measurement Center, and your assignment is on the dry erase board in that center. That leaves only Group D, and I want you guys to go to the Special Projects Center and finish up the teamwork project you began there last week. You'll have about 20 minutes and then we'll change centers. I'll give you a two-minute warning just before we make that change. Please move to your center and begin your work now.*

DIFFERENTIATED INSTRUCTIONAL OPTIONS WITHIN THE LEARNING CENTER MODEL

When students are working in learning centers, the options for differentiated instruction are virtually endless. By varying assignments that different groups do in the learning centers, a wide variety of instruction can be offered, addressing a wide variety of academic levels, learning styles, and preferences. Further, teachers can likewise vary how much teacher-led instruction students receive. For example, for advanced groups, teachers may choose to let them spend two 20-minute periods completing a team-based project in the special projects center, since more advanced students may require less teacher-led instruction than other groups. That group may only work at the teacher's work desk two or three times each week, rather than daily. Instead, those higher-functioning groups may benefit more from individualized instruction, delivered via computer program, and thus, they may spend two 20-minute sessions a day in the Computer Center.

For lower-level groups, teachers may choose to work with them somewhat longer each day at the teacher's worktable. By keeping the lower-functioning students at the teacher's worktable for two 20-minute segments daily, those lower-functioning kids are receiving much more individualized, teacher-led instruction than would others in the class.

As teachers implement response to intervention programs in mathematics around the nation, this learning center model for differentiation has proven to be a very flexible instructional alternative for the mathematics class. As noted previously, in virtually every mathematics class, some of the students will need more teacher-led instruction than other groups, and those groups may need an RTI, Tier 2 mathematics intervention (Response to Intervention, or RTI, is described in more detail in Chapter 7). Delivering this intensive intervention for several students will, in turn, require additional teacher time, and by having all students work in learning centers, teachers can more easily address that need. In this example, a mathematics teacher can deliver a Tier 2 intervention for one homogeneous group of students by merely working with that instructional group for an extra 20-minute period each day at the teacher's worktable.

Advantages of Learning Centers for Differentiating Common Core Instruction

In using learning centers in the mathematics class, as the differentiated instructional model, teachers can see how they will rarely, if ever, lead whole group lessons again! In this learning center differentiated instruction model, the teacher becomes a planner and facilitator for everyone's mathematics instruction, while working more intimately with every student in the teacher-led small groups daily or several times each week.

As teachers move into Common Core Mathematics instruction, we will be increasingly confronted with the expectation that we aim instruction at deeper understanding of critical mathematical content. Virtually all discussions of Common Core Mathematics include emphasis on deeper understanding, transfer of knowledge, and

> *In using learning centers as the differentiated instructional model, teachers can see how they will rarely, if ever, lead whole group lessons again!*

problem solving, and those in-depth mathematics insights are generally better stressed in small-group work of working with students individually, rather than whole class lessons. In that sense, the learning center approach for differentiating mathematics instruction fits nicely with the move into Common Core Mathematics instruction.

Further, in the learning center differentiation approach described above, each student would receive both small-group instruction from the teacher, and highly targeted, individualized instruction, via the computer for a 15- or 20-minute period daily. In fact, students taught in this fashion are likely to receive higher-quality instruction overall than they would in a whole group mathematics lesson, since so much instruction in this approach is directly targeted to their specific needs. Again, this approach to differentiation seems to fit well within the emphasis on deeper understanding embedded within Common Core instruction in mathematics.

Next, learning centers place more of the responsibility for learning on the students than traditional instruction, and this is likely to increase student engagement with the learning task. Of course, one aspect of the Common Core in mathematics is a strong emphasis on student engagement with conceptual issues and problem solving, and the learning center approach is likely to foster that deeper conceptual insight, as students become more involved in and responsible for their own lessons. As long as the teaching/learning process is based on a view of students as passive learners (i.e., the targets of whole group lessons, lectures, or discussions led by the teacher), only limited learning is likely to take place, particularly among struggling students. However, a learning center approach makes students responsible for their own learning activities, and this is likely to foster both greater achievement and deeper understanding.

> *The learning center approach for differentiating mathematics instruction fits nicely with the move into Common Core Mathematics instruction.*

Next, in technology-rich classrooms, software-based guided mathematics lessons tend to be exactly focused at the individual mathematics levels of particular students, and the same can be said of the intensive work with the teacher at the teacher's worktable. This would suggest that this approach meets the needs of today's diverse students in most general education mathematics classes better than traditional, whole group instruction.

Finally, a learning center approach is adaptable to many topics in mathematics including problem solving, operations, fluency, and so on. Computer centers are excellent options for individualized mathematics instruction, and even interdisciplinary studies (e.g., mathematics and science activities) can be undertaken in the context of such computer centers. In fact, the Computer Center, if equipped with appropriate software, can easily serve as a learning center in many other subject areas as well.

WHAT'S NEXT?

This chapter has presented two of the original models for differentiated instruction in mathematics, modification of the whole group lesson plan and using learning centers rather than whole group instruction. These tried and true approaches will be of benefit to most teachers as they begin their journey into highly differentiated mathematics instruction, and given the emphasis within the Common Core on deep understanding, information transfer, and problem solving, these two models for differentiating instruction will serve most teachers well.

However, over the last decade, several new, more innovative differentiated instruction models have evolved, including the flipped classroom and project-based learning. Each of these innovative approaches to differentiated instruction promises to replace the traditional whole group lesson in the mathematics class, and these more recent instructional models are discussed in the next chapter.

Flipped Mathematics Classes and Project-Based Learning 3

New Differentiated Instructional Models in Mathematics

As noted previously, the transition to Common Core Mathematics is underway in 46 states (Toppo, 2012), and even in states that have chosen not to undertake the Common Core State Standards, there is a broader emphasis in mathematics instruction overall to stress deeper understandings, problem solving, and transfer of knowledge. This has led to several innovative instructional approaches that are utilized in classes today, including flipped mathematics classes and project-based learning.

While educators should always experiment with newly devised instructional practices, no instructional innovation alone is likely to lead to increased academic achievement, unless the newly developed instructional technique results in more instructional time for teachers to spend guiding the learning of individual students or instructing small groups in mathematics. Fortunately, both the flipped classroom and project-based learning have that effect—the teacher spends more time with individuals and small groups as they complete their mathematics work. Further, because these innovative instructional practices modify, rather drastically, the traditional whole group lesson plan, each of these innovations is best understood as another model for differentiating instruction within the mathematics class.

Of course, project-based learning has been around for several decades, whereas the flipped mathematics class is quite recent, having only appeared widely in the literature in the 2009–2011 time frame. Still, these instructional innovations are being implemented in many mathematics classes across the United States and Canada, as well as elsewhere around the world, and each provides many opportunities for teachers to differentiate the instructional

> *No instructional innovation alone is likely to lead to increased academic achievement, unless the newly developed instructional technique results in more instructional time for teachers to spend guiding the learning of individual students or instructing small groups in mathematics.*

activities in the class, and thus meet the needs of individual students much more effectively. In this chapter, we'll discuss the flipped classroom initially, since this is directly related to the traditional lesson plan previously discussed. Next, project-based learning is described as another option for differentiating instruction in mathematics.

FLIPPING THE MATHEMATICS CLASS TO INCREASE DIFFERENTIATION

As early as 2006, two high school chemistry teachers in Colorado, Jonathan Bergmann and Aaron Sams, began to explore ways to maximize the efficacy of their teaching by using instructional time within a different framework. While teacher-led initial instruction (phase 2 of the traditional mathematics lesson—see Box 2.1 in the previous chapter) has been a mainstay of instructional planning for decades, these teachers realized that time spent assisting individual students, troubleshooting students' understanding of specific problems, or directing small-group instruction is much more beneficial for students than initial instructional time (Bergmann & Sams, 2012). In contrast, teachers delivering initial instruction, typically lecture-type content or demonstrations of problems to the whole class, is not one of the most effective instructional behaviors, in terms of directly impacting students' understanding of mathematics (Green, 2012; Maton, 2011; Sparks, 2011; Toppo, 2011). Therefore, these innovative teachers began to use recorded, media-based presentations to "export" that teacher-led instructional time, thus making the initial instruction phase of learning a "homework" assignment. In that sense, the initial instruction (which is the second phase of the traditional whole group lesson, as presented previously in Box 2.1) becomes homework, and the teacher can then spend more time in the class, working with students individually or in small groups as students practice their mathematics. In that sense, the order of learning has been

> *In a flipped classroom, students are required to use web resources as homework and teach themselves new mathematics problems, while the class time is used for interesting laboratory explorations or practice activities using the new math content.*

flipped—with initial instruction done as homework, and homework (i.e., practice on the math concepts) done as classwork! This is, in essence, the flipped classroom model.

As these two teachers, Bergmann and Sams, experimented with flipping their classes, they noted that this benefits not only the average and above-average students in the class, but students at all ability levels (Bergmann & Sams, 2012). By flipping the class instruction in this fashion, teachers spend more in-class time working directly with students at all ability levels.

This growing trend toward flipped math classes has led to a fundamentally different method of instruction. Teachers today are assigning initial instruction on a brand-new topic as independent study work to be completed at home, and students use video demonstrations and various websites for learning that new type of mathematics problem (Bender & Waller, 2013; G. Cook, 2011; Green, 2012; Maton, 2011). In some cases, teachers videotape their own content in brief (5- to 10-minute segments), and then make those videos available to students via a school or class website. In other cases, teachers locate video demonstrations developed by others in mathematics on the Internet and assign those. Students then use those video demonstrations to learn the new content outside of class time. Then, with more time for individual mathematics practice in the mathematics class, the class often turns into a mathematics lab, with the teacher spending more time with individual students and/or working with small groups of students. The class time might also be used for interesting laboratory explorations or practice activities using the new content. While there are a variety of other ways to "flip" one's traditional lesson organization (Bergmann & Sams, 2012), the idea above is the model most commonly described in the literature as the flipped classroom.

Modern technology has increased this trend. With the advent of high-quality web-based teaching resources, teachers have determined that many demonstration videos for specific types of mathematics problems are available on the Internet (Edick, 2012). A large number of video demonstrations and instructional examples can be accessed and used by teachers and students alike, using open-source websites such as YouTube and TeacherTube (Edick, 2012), and many math websites include instructional videos and/or gaming activities that demonstrate specific types of math problems. Box 3.1 includes some of the sources of videos that teachers frequently use for instruction.

BOX 3.1 WEBSITE SOURCES FOR INSTRUCTIONAL VIDEOS IN MATHEMATICS

Tutor-USA.com—This site has a variety of free mathematics videos, as well as printable mathematics worksheets (tutor-usa.com/videos). This is also a great resource for teachers and/or home-schooling parents to use.

Math TV—This is the channel of a veteran mathematics teacher and author, Mr. Pat McKeague (www.mathtv.com/about). A wide variety of videos, mathematics lessons, and worksheets are provided here on a fee-for-service basis, and teachers can sign up for a newsletter from this channel on mathematics topics.

Mathademics—This site offers mathematics tutorials on topics such as number sense, arithmetic, fractions, decimals, algebra, math functions, and geometry (mathademics.wikispaces.com/ or www.youtube.com/user/Mathademics).

The Video Math Tutor—This website provides a rather extensive set of instructional videos, some ranging up to 30 minutes long, on various mathematics problems. These are free, along with downloadable written materials for each lesson video. The site also provides brain teasers and calculator tips (www.videomathtutor.com/).

Math Train—This website provides a variety of instructional videos that were developed by students at Lincoln Middle School in Santa Monica, California (Mathtrain.tv/index.php). It may be useful to share with your students, simply to let them know what other students are accomplishing in mathematics.

PatrickJMT Free Math Videos—This YouTube channel has more than 100,000 subscribers and is considered one of the best math channels on YouTube (patrickjmt .com or www.youtube.com/user/patrickJMT). It has videos on many different higher-level mathematics topics such as calculus, derivatives, differential equations, limits, integrals, and more.

Several authors have suggested that the flipped class instructional model provides an excellent option for differentiating mathematics instruction by allowing the teacher more instructional time to meet the needs of every student in highly diverse mathematics (Bender, 2012a; Bergmann & Sams, 2012). Clearly, the flipped classroom can be interpreted within the current paradigms of differentiated instructional pedagogy, because this instructional process will increase the time that teachers can devote to individual student's needs—thus differentiating the lesson.

To get a sense of how teachers and students respond to flipping the classroom, I recommend teachers view a brief video on a flipped fifth-grade mathematics class at Lake Elmo Elementary school in Lake Elmo, Minnesota (see the video at: www.eschoolnews.com/2012/02/09/

Teachers have determined that many demonstration videos for specific types of mathematics problems are available on the Internet.

a-first-hand-look-inside-a-flipped-classroom/). I further recommend that every mathematics teacher review that video, and consider how flipping his or her class might make more time available for small-group or one-to-one instruction in mathematics.

Efficacy of Flipped Math Classes

The flipped class model of instruction is quite recent, having been implemented only since 2006. Further, this instructional approach has been discussed in the national educational literature only since 2009 or 2010 (Bender & Waller, 2013; Bergmann & Sams, 2012). Thus, no long-term research studies exist to date that demonstrate the efficacy of this approach. However, there is a growing body of anecdotal research attesting to the positive impact of flipping the mathematics class, and many educators review that research when they explore flipping their mathematics classes (Bergmann & Sams, 2012; Green, 2012).

In one recent example, Green (2012), the principal of Clintondale High School, reported on flipping the instruction in all classes, schoolwide. Clintondale is a school in a financially challenged district in Detroit, and when considering how to improve learning overall, the entire faculty decided to flip their classes. Principal Green reported that, prior to flipping the classes, the failure rates were "through the roof" at Clintondale High. Thus, the faculty was motivated to undertake a significant school reform effort and decided to flip their classes as a part of that reform effort.

Teachers began this school restructuring effort by videotaping their own lessons on new content, and they then posted those videos to the school website. Students were required to access that content as the initial instructional phase of the lesson prior to class, whenever they began a new unit of instruction. The class period then became a laboratory for practice with that content, in which students could request specific help on the content, as they practiced and applied that new knowledge. In this school, the students responded quite positively to this flipped classroom approach in mathematics, as demonstrated by the data. After 18 months, Principal Green reported failure rates in mathematics dropped from 44% to 13%, with similar reductions in failure in science, reading, and social studies. These improvements demonstrate that flipping the mathematics classes had a very positive impact on student achievement in mathematics in that school across the grade levels.

While more rigorous research is currently in process on the flipped classroom, this body of anecdotal evidence supportive of flipping the mathematics class continues to grow. In addition to the example above, a great deal of other evidence, most of which is anecdotal in nature, suggests extremely positive results from this flipped classroom approach to instruction (G. Cook, 2011; Maton, 2011; Stansbury, 2012a). Again, all mathematics teachers should consider this differentiated instructional option for their class, as it seems to engage the students much more deeply with the mathematics content, certainly one goal of the Common Core Mathematics Standards.

KHAN ACADEMY!

While flipping the mathematics class has been, and can certainly be, based on self-recorded mathematics demonstrations, one major factor in the development of this trend toward flipped classrooms in mathematics is the development of Khan Academy (www.khanacademy.org). Khan Academy is an online mathematics curriculum that ranges from math facts and kindergarten operations (1 + 1 = 2) up through calculus. The content was, initially, developed by Mr. Sal Khan and, because of recent support of the Bill and Melinda Gates Foundation, as well as other industry support, this curriculum and all the associated videos are available free for anyone to use, worldwide! While various other curricula areas are covered (e.g., physics, biology, astronomy, chemistry), the mathematics portions of this curriculum are the most extensive and cover virtually all topics in the Common Core State Standards in Mathematics, though there is less emphasis on problems solving in general, than on basic operations.

This author is a strong advocate of Khan Academy for virtually all teachers in mathematics across the grade levels, and use of Khan Academy for flipping the mathematic classes does seem to be something of a trend. For example, in a first-of-a-kind statewide initiative, the state of Idaho recently announced a pilot program in which selected schools would be allowed to implement the use of the Khan Academy curriculum (Dvorak, 2013). Forty-seven Idaho schools have been selected, from among 75 that applied, and those selected schools will pilot the curriculum in mathematics, physics, and history classes. While over 40 individual schools in California, as well as many in other states, have previously partnered with Khan Academy, Idaho has become the first statewide effort to pilot this curriculum. In Idaho, Khan Academy will be applied using the flipped classroom instructional model.

What Is Khan Academy?

Khan Academy is a cloud-based curriculum with no initial software to download. Rather, the entire curriculum is accessible via the Internet and can be considered as an anytime-anywhere learning tool for students worldwide (Dvorak, 2013; Sparks, 2011; Toppo, 2011; Watters, 2011a).

> *Khan Academy is a cloud-based, stand-alone mathematics curriculum that represents an anytime-anywhere tech tool, and it is free for anyone, worldwide.*

It is self-directed, such that students can study this curricular content alone if necessary. However, students are encouraged to work under the supervision of a "coach," who may be a mentor, a mathematics teacher, a parent, or anyone else. In fact, many mathematics teachers, from kindergarten up, are beginning to use Khan Academy in their classrooms, and this author recommends that all mathematics teachers consider using Khan Academy to supplement their current mathematics curriculum.

In essence, there are three main components to Khan Academy:

- Online, game-based mathematics exercises,
- Online library of video demonstrations associated the exercises, and
- Online individual knowledge map showing each individual student's achievement over time, on the math exercises.

First, the Khan Academy website above presents thousands of online learning exercises and game-based activities in mathematics. When a student begins with a specific type of problem, a number of examples are presented. If the student succeeds on that series of problems, a merit badge is awarded to the student by the software program. The badge of achievement appears on the student's individual Knowledge Map (described below). This simple reinforcement appears much more significant than many teachers (including this author) might initially suspect, and in fact, this intrinsic reinforcement has resulted in many students choosing to work on mathematics beyond their own grade level!

If a student does not succeed on each example of a specific type of mathematics problem, the student is referred to a specific 8- to 10-minute video featuring an in-depth explanation of that particular type of problem. In those videos, students see an interactive whiteboard where the various steps of the problem appear, as a "voice" guides the students through the problem by explaining the necessary steps. For example, level one, linear equations such as $3x + 5 = 23$ are presented, and multiple steps are modeled on the board, as students are guided toward the solution to the problem. While the steps are discussed, the narrator's voice (which in most instances is Mr. Khan himself) explains the reasons for various steps and mathematics operations. Thus, this curriculum can function, for many students, as initial instruction on that type of mathematics problem. In fact, this is the component of Khan Academy that has helped foster the flipped classroom instructional procedure in mathematics classes. By 2012, over 3,500 videos were included on the Khan website as demonstrations of different problems. Each video is a single chunk of topical information, emphasizing only one type of problem, and none are over 10 minutes in length.

Generally, students will access the website, try some practice exercises for a particular type of problem, and then, if necessary, watch a demonstration video on that type of problem (Dvorak, 2013; Toppo, 2011; Watters, 2011a). Throughout the exercises, students are highly motivated by the gaming basis of this curricular support program.

The final component of Khan Academy is the individual student's Knowledge Map. In some ways, the Knowledge Map may be the core of the entire program. While teachers can use the videos or math exercises independently, full implementation of Khan Academy involves having all students set up within Khan Academy with a personal Knowledge Map. This map is an individualized progress monitoring tool that tracks each individual student's progress in relation to the whole mathematics curriculum. The Knowledge Map will also remind students when they might need a review of certain content. Anecdotal evidence suggests that students typically find receiving their achievement badges on the Knowledge Map quite motivating. Students (or their coaches) can determine from the Knowledge Map what the student has completed, what concepts have been mastered, and what the student's next emphasis needs to be.

It is not an overstatement to say that the Knowledge Map, as both a progress tracking and motivational tool, is the core of this program for individual students. As soon as students begin their work, they will begin to earn merit badges and points for learning specific content. The more students challenge themselves, the more they achieve, and the more badges they earn. While some badges can be earned in five minutes by successful completion of only a few exercises, other badges take many months or even years to earn. Some badges represent success in mathematics content for an entire year's worth of study (e.g., Algebra I).

The Knowledge Map within Khan Academy is an individualized student progress monitoring tool that tracks each individual student's progress in relation to the whole curriculum.

However, other documentation is also available for teachers with Khan Academy. For example, a class profile lets mathematics teachers glance at the dashboard, which is a classwide summary of students' performance in mathematics. Teachers can then determine what content to emphasize in the math lab the following day. While some students will need mini-lessons from the teacher on particular types of problems, others will not, so this class profile can help the teacher differentiate the mathematics instruction on a daily basis.

Also, students' performance data are presented as an X/Y axis chart showing individual student growth over time. Using these documentation tools, teachers or parents will know immediately if a particular student is having difficulty with any particular content, and they can then assign other videos on that content, or work through a video with the student. Further, all of these data are saved over time, such that teachers can review students' progress, and make determinations about students' rates of progress relative to stated goals.

Concerns With Khan Academy

However, there are a number of valid criticisms of this instructional tool. First, while the gaming aspect of this tech tool is highly motivational, the pedagogy is somewhat dated. For example, the video segments are not highly developed, nor do they provide highly developed graphic demonstrations that can greatly enhance mathematical understanding. In the video demonstrations, the student sees a mathematics problem completed on an interactive whiteboard, while a disembodied "teacher's" voice discusses the steps to follow to solve the problem. Of course, this modeling of problem solution represents an excellent example of 20th century teaching, as opposed to 21st century teaching, since this basically involves the students seeing a mathematics problem completed on the board while a teacher describes the steps.

Another concern involves the level of the explanation in the videos. These step-by-step descriptions are clearly aimed at normally achieving students, and of course, that is exactly as it should be, given the overall goal of anytime, anywhere learning that serves as the basis for Khan Academy. However, these step-by-step instructions are aimed as a level that is probably too high for some students with difficulties in mathematics, such as students with learning disabilities and/or other learning challenges. Many such students will need more in-depth, one-to-one instruction from the teacher to understand the step-by-step process for a given type of mathematics problem.

Next, the videos in Khan Academy tend to stress algorithms, and procedural understandings, rather than deep conceptual understanding. Teachers using this tool will have to carefully consider how these videos may be integrated into their math classes, within the framework of an individual lesson or a unit of instruction. Further, teachers should make every effort to go beyond the videos, and stress the concepts behind them.

In the flipped classroom model, if the videos are used as homework, the teacher should plan on stressing the underlying concepts during the next class session. In that fashion, this tool can greatly enrich student understanding, even at the conceptual level.

Finally, even with these problems noted, every teacher who is teaching mathematics should investigate the possible use of Khan Academy, since this curriculum does seem to strengthen procedural understanding in math and can enrich mathematical insight at the conceptual level. Further, teachers might use this curriculum and consider flipping the instruction in the math class. Teaching Tip 3.1 presents a series of specific steps.

Teaching Tip 3.1   Getting Started With Khan Academy

Explore Khan Academy Content

The first step in using Khan Academy is to become very familiar with the Khan Academy content. The website itself (www.khanacademy.org) presents many tools for coaches to use as they guide students through Khan Academy learning experiences. I urge teachers to watch several of the instructional videos (as well as videos about Khan Academy that are on that website), and then practice with several of the mathematics exercises. Teachers must consider the fit between Khan Academy coverage of content and terminology, and the terminology used in the Common Core State Standards and/or your state's mathematics curriculum. Also teachers should consider their potential use of the Knowledge Map for each of their students.

Get Signed In

Many schools have chosen to block web-based content, and unfortunately, this sometimes involves instructional content like Khan Academy. Teachers should consider the school's Internet usage policies and make certain your administrators are kept in the loop relative to use of this resource. I also recommend that teachers carefully investigate how teachers sign students into Khan Academy. Ultimately teachers should register their entire class, including students who have no computer or Internet access at home.

Use Khan as an In-Class Tool First

While Khan Academy is structured as a stand-alone teaching tool, having students access and use it in the classroom is recommended, since teachers can troubleshoot any access issues with their students. Teachers generally indicate that they find it beneficial to teach students how to use this resource prior to flipping the class, and many use Khan Academy as a reference tool to supplement class activities at first,

(Continued)

(Continued)

until students get used to it. For example, at Hapeville Charter Middle School in Atlanta, Georgia, the mathematics faculty began using Khan Academy videos as demonstrations tools. When a student asked a question on a mathematics process, several teachers began by referring them to Khan Academy for a demonstration of the mathematics problem. Once the students went through one or several of the videos, those students can explain that mathematical process to the class. Viewing these videos is also a great partner activity in class.

Share Uses of Khan Academy With Parents

In general, it is always a good idea to keep parents in the loop, and teachers should let parents know of Khan Academy as a teaching tool in mathematics. Parental permission would not typically be necessary, but providing parents with this information is advisable for several reasons. One reason that some parents are reluctant to assist or even monitor their child's homework is that they may not know the content, and they don't want their child to view them as uneducated. With Khan Academy, that worry can be alleviated, as the mathematics exercises and instructional videos can be used by child and parent together while working through a mathematics problem.

In a recent workshop for educators, this author shared Khan Academy with a group of middle school teachers. One teacher reported that he was definitely planning to use Khan Academy to assist his own adolescent in algebra. He indicated that he'd been reluctant to do so, since his own background in that subject was not strong. However, with Khan Academy as a backup, that parent is now working with his own son in a subject that his son found difficult.

It is clear from anecdotal reports that Khan Academy opens many doors for parents and child to work together on school work, but this is much more likely when the teacher, using Khan Academy, encourages it. Sending a letter or e-mail home about this curriculum and suggesting that parents and students work through this together can often get parents involved in the process.

Use the Knowledge Map

The Knowledge Map within Khan Academy is an organizational tool to let students and their parents know what the students should study next. As students demonstrate their ability in certain mathematics content, the Knowledge Map awards them a "badge," and then suggests the next area for them to study. Thus, the individual Knowledge Map empowers students as independent learners, and anecdotal reports indicate that some students have moved far beyond their own grade placement in mathematics (Green, 2012; Toppo, 2011). Clearly, the Knowledge Map and the possibility of earning the merit badges is quite motivating for many students. For students who do excel, additional classroom or schoolwide recognition is always recommended.

Assign as a Pre-Instructional Assignment

At some point, after students have demonstrated their ability to use Khan Academy in the classroom, teachers should begin to assign a specific type of problem from their curriculum as homework, prior to having covered that content in class. Of course, this is likely to work for some students and not for others. While many students can begin with Khan Academy with no in-class practice (indeed, it is intended to be used in that fashion), others will need some additional instruction in the classroom, and the teacher might provide a "mini-lesson" on the type of problem assigned. However, teachers should move all students in the direction of using Khan Academy content as a stand-alone learning tool.

Record Mathematics Content

In addition to using videos from Khan Academy, teachers should use some self-recorded content as the basis for a flipped mathematics lesson. Alternatively, teachers may wish to review and utilize other web-based video content. Again, both YouTube and TeacherTube are excellent options for finding specific instructional content (Edick, 2012). Generally shorter videos, rather than hour-long lectures, are recommended. These do not have to be "professionally" done, but they should present a chunk of information with adequate sound and video demonstrations if possible. Using pictures from the text, or other resources from the web can make these brief recorded pieces of information more interesting as well as more informative.

Require Note Taking

Some teachers have chosen to have students make notes on the Khan Academy content, or other video recorded content, as they practice a particular problem or watch a demo-video at home (G. Cook, 2011; Sparks, 2011; Toppo, 2011). Note taking is a skill that will well serve students throughout life, as they become life-long learners, and if students are viewing recorded content other than Khan Academy, note taking is the only means by which a teacher can check their understanding of that content. Thus, in flipped classrooms based on teacher-delivered/recording content, note taking is critical. Teachers should check those notes, since, in such a procedure, teachers get a good sense of who accomplished what the night before. Ultimately, note checking will tell who did their assigned work in studying the new content, and thus, requiring note taking is recommended both within the context of Khan Academy and for other web-based learning as well.

Try a Flipped Lesson

Once students are used to using Khan Academy content or other video demonstrations of the content in the above fashion, your class is ready to try the "flip!"

(Continued)

(Continued)

Even if some reluctant students are still having difficulty in the curriculum, teachers can assign content as a homework assignment that has not been taught at all in class, and then conduct the following class, as a project-oriented class, a drill and practice game for students, or a math-lab type of class.

Each teacher's ultimate goal should be instilling in every student the belief that they can seek out, find, and master difficult academic content on their own, with no teacher to teach them. This is truly the goal of anytime, anywhere learning, and should be a primary focus of all educational endeavors.

If differentiated instruction is best understood as students using their preferred learning styles and preferences to master difficult content, then the essence of differentiated instruction is instruction in which students independently choose how to learn, based on their personal preferences. Of course, individualized, computer-based learning facilitates such differentiated instructional choices as well as any learning approach, as students work at their own pace, take all the time they need to truly understand the content, and revisit the material as needed. During the in-class phase of flipped instruction, teachers work with students individually or in small groups as students actually do the math, rather than merely view a model problem as it is completed on the board. In these ways, the flipped class model works to effectively differentiate instruction, both in the initial instruction (homework) and in the math class.

However, unlike instructional videos from YouTube or other sources, Khan Academy has a tracking feature—the Knowledge Map for each student—that will help teachers differentiate instruction. Within the Khan Academy teachers are encouraged to set up student accounts for every student in the class. Students' work in the curriculum is saved on their individual Knowledge Map, which teachers, students, and parents can access. Teachers can then see the data on each student's progress, and this fosters increased differentiation, as teachers review what individual students have mastered, and specific topics on which they need to concentrate.

Game Changers in Education!

In conclusion, as the discussion above suggests, both the flipped classroom instructional model and Khan Academy are truly new differentiated teaching practices. These can justifiably be considered "game changers" in mathematics education! Both represent empowering students to effectively use multiple online resources for anytime, anywhere learning in mathematics that is student driven. This is learning for the future, and these tools have only become available within the last decade. With Khan Academy, students worldwide are now free to seek and master nearly any mathematics content they choose, and this can be truly empowering. Teaching students to seek information, evaluate it, and apply it will ultimately lead to highly capable life-long learners, a worthy goal indeed for all educators. This may very well be the single-most important instructional result of the 21st century technology tools now available, and I do recommend that every teacher, and in particular every teacher of mathematics, explore this powerful, free teaching option.

> *Both the flipped classroom instructional model and Khan Academy can be considered "game changers" in mathematics education!*

PROJECT-BASED LEARNING IN MATHEMATICS

What Is Project-Based Learning?

The fourth differentiated instructional model described in this book is project-based learning (PBL). Definitions of PBL are quite numerous, and various authors have presented differing perspectives (Bender, 2012b; Boss & Krauss, 2007; Bui, 2012; Larmer, Ross, & Mergendoller, 2009). Most definitions emphasize authentic, real-world projects, based on highly motivating and engaging student-generated questions. Student inquiry is emphasized, as is the fact that in PBL, the project drives the curriculum rather than serves as an "adjunct" project within various units of study. This author recently proposed the following definition.

> ***Project-based learning*** *is instruction in which student-generated questions and projects drive the curriculum and instructional time frame, and the primary focus is study of highly motivating topics, reflective of real-world problems, resulting in authentic application of the products produced. Student-generated projects must drive the time frame of study in PBL, rather than teacher-generated assignments, instructional unit structure, or even course structure. Common Core Standards must be "mapped" across projects to assure content coverage. Therefore, an excellent, teacher-generated project assignment within an instructional unit of study is not PBL. Rather PBL may be said to be taking place under three conditions, when student-driven projects (1) replace course structure; (2) replace instructional unit structure within a course, or (3) cut across multiple units of instruction, courses, or disciplines* (Bender, 2012b).

As this definition indicates, PBL involves a significant restructuring of instructional time in the mathematics class. In fact, various PBL projects are likely to replace traditional whole group instruction altogether, and each project is likely to take considerable time. Projects should be selected and developed in order to teach students mathematics content in the context of real-world problem solving, a skill strongly emphasized by the Common Core Standards in Mathematics (Bender, 2012b; Magee, 2013). Further, unlike curricula aimed at development of procedural processes in mathematics, project-based learning lends itself to development of deeper conceptual insight and applications of mathematics in applied settings. Student inquiry is heavily integrated into project-based learning, and because students typically have some choice in selecting their group's project, and the methods they would use to solve that project, they tend to be more highly motivated to work diligently toward a solution to the problem (Belland, French, & Ertmer, 2009; Boss & Krauss, 2007; Larmer et al., 2009; Mergendoller, Maxwell, & Bellisimo, 2007). This typically results in high levels of engagement with the mathematics content involved in solving the problem or completing the project, as well as higher levels of mathematics achievement overall (Larmer & Mergendoller, 2010; Mergendoller et al., 2007).

Project-based learning (PBL) may be defined as using real-world projects, based on a highly motivating and engaging student-generated question, task, or problem, to teach students academic content in the context of students working cooperatively in order to solve the problem.

PBL has been used in virtually every subject area and grade level, up through adult learning situations (Bender, 2012b; Bui, 2012; Larmer et al., 2009), though PBL has been implemented more frequently in science and mathematics in middle and high school. Because PBL increases motivation to learn, teamwork, and collaborative skills, it is now recommended as a 21st century differentiated instructional teaching approach across the grade levels in mathematics (Bender, 2012b; Bui, 2012; Schlemmer & Schlemmer, 2008). Further, with the advent of modern social networking and communications technologies, project-based learning has received increasing attention as an instructional approach that is particularly relevant for students of the digital age (Boss & Krauss, 2007).

To help teachers get a better understanding of PBL, I recommend two introductory videos. First, teachers may wish to view a five-minute video created by several Canadian teachers using PBL (http://www.youtube.com/watch?v=NPQ1gT_9rcw&feature=related). While mathematics was not emphasized in this video, note that the teachers did report on consistently high levels of student enthusiasm for PBL work. Given students' fears associated with mathematics, it is possible that PBL instruction may result not only in higher engagement with mathematics content, but also in increased positive attitudes toward mathematics in general. In fact, increased engagement with the content has been shown as one result of PBL instruction (Bender, 2012b; Boss & Krauss, 2007; Bui, 2012; Larmer et al., 2009).

The second video that I recommend is somewhat longer, but this 30-minute, student-generated video on PBL instruction helps teachers understand why all 21st century educators must consider moving into PBL instruction (http://edvisionsschools.org/custom/SplashPage.asp). It is always interesting to see how students view their academic endeavors, and clearly the students in this Minnesota high school believe that PBL is a much improved instructional model compared to traditional instruction. Indeed, these students view PBL is the best instructional method for the 21st century.

However, there is another critical aspect of PBL in this particular video that is worthy of note. Traditionally it has been the teacher's role to assure content coverage in mathematics, but in this school, the PBL instructional model makes that a student responsibility. As the students themselves stated, in this high school it is the student's responsibility to map the curricular standards across the various projects they undertake, and to assure content coverage. This fact alone can provide an important rationale to explore PBL-based instruction in mathematics. In fact, one might well argue that this is a critical skill for the 21st century workplace—that is, knowing when a task has been developed to meet the required goals. While not all PBL examples include this advantage, this high school's PBL program clearly does.

In addition to the videos above, an extensive series of additional videos on PBL are available at the Edutopia website (www.Edutopia.org/project-based-learning). I do recommend that teachers considering PBL as a differentiated instructional option in mathematics take advantage of these recommended videos, in their initial explorations.

Next, as teachers begin to implement this exciting instructional approach in mathematics, they should note that other terms have been used through the years for this general instructional procedure, including problem-based learning, inquiry learning, or authentic learning. Further, some educators prefer one term rather than another (Bender, 2012b).

Finally, proponents of PBL also disagree on the essential components of PBL, though the general list presented in Box 3.2 includes most of the general components recognized by most authors (Bender, 2012b; Boss & Krauss, 2007; Bui, 2012; Larmer & Mergendoller, 2010; Mergendoller et al., 2007). Also Box 3.2 presents several terms specific to PBL instruction.

In spite of these disagreements among some authors, the general PBL instructional approach remains the same: students identifying and solving real-world problems that they consider important, and developing various projects to address those problems (Bender, 2012b; Boss & Krauss, 2007; Bui, 2012; Larmer et al., 2009).

BOX 3.2 COMPONENTS OF MOST PBL INSTRUCTIONAL MODELS

Project Anchor

The anchor is the basis for the PBL project, and as in the example below, it sets up a narrative to set the stage and hopefully generate student interest in the project.

Driving Question

The driving question is usually part of the anchor and is intended to both engage students' attention and focus their efforts. A good driving question should, therefore, keep students focused on the task at hand and not lost in "Internet search mode!"

Artifact

In PBL projects two decades ago, student output almost always involved a written report or document. In PBL work today, an entire array of products from students may be anticipated including at a minimum, development of a website or wiki on a given topic, a slide (PowerPoint) presentation, Excel files aggregating raw data, videos demonstrating mathematical concepts, and so on. For this reason, the term "artifact" is used for any product developed in conjunction with PBL, and in most PBL projects, more than one artifact is typically required.

Collaborative Teamwork

While some PBL projects may involve individual work, most involve collaborative teamwork, and some PBL proponents believe that team-based projects are critical in developing the types of workplace skills required in the 21st century. Such teamwork also tends to make PBL projects more authentic.

Scaffolding of Tasks

In long-term PBL tasks, the work should be scaffolded; this involves providing assistance provided for mathematical procedures and operations initially (help may be provided by either the teacher or teammates working on the same project), and then systematically withdrawing that support. Later during the scaffolded project, the work emphasis typically changes to more creative, team-development tasks, intended to foster deeper understanding.

Inquiry and Innovation

Within the broader driving question, the group will need to generate additional questions focused more specifically on project tasks. Depending on how a particular project is managed, this may take place early in the project time frame, or constantly throughout that time frame.

Processes of Investigation

PBL does not involve generating a question and leaving students out in the cold! Rather, in many projects, various processes of investigation are taught. For example, in addition to finite operations, 21st century tasks such as data aggregation using spreadsheets, wiki development, Internet search procedures, and team-based brainstorming on possible problem solutions can be taught. These guidelines for various processes leading toward project completion and artifact generation can be used to frame the project. The group may also develop time lines and specific goals for completion of various aspects of the project.

Feedback and Revision

In all tasks, whether they are officially required artifacts, or merely initial tasks required to develop the final artifacts, feedback is critical. Feedback can be based on either teacher or peer input, but most PBL projects involve much more peer feedback than teacher feedback. As feedback is provided to an individual student or to part of a team, those students then revise the work, always aiming at improving the work.

Opportunities for Reflection

Creating opportunities for student reflection within various mathematics projects is stressed by all proponents of PBL. In order to aim our instructional efforts at the deeper levels of understanding envisioned within the Common Core Mathematics Standards, opportunities for individual or team-based reflection is critical.

Publicly Presented Artifacts

PBL projects are intended to be authentic examples of the types of mathematics problems students confront in the real world, and in many cases, students can make a definite contribution to their class or their school. Thus, some type of public presentation of project results is a critical emphasis within PBL.

Student Voice and Choice

Students' voice and student choices should be emphasized from the first day on any PBL project. In particular, mathematics projects should stress student choices, since this can help alleviate some the mathematics anxieties, which were described in Chapter 1. Thus, students should have the opportunity to exercise choices throughout the project.

A PBL Example in Mathematics

While every PBL project is different from the others, since students typically have a critical role in developing the project, teachers can structure general project ideas that will engage most of the students in their particular grade level, and then let students determine the project specifics. For kindergarten, primary, and/or elementary grades, various cooking projects have been undertaken, since measurement is often required in cooking, as well as addition/subtraction and perhaps estimation and so on. For older students, fractions may also be built into this type of project, and percentages. However, beyond the general project idea developed by the teacher, students at all levels should have some choice in the exact project they undertake, as this tends to increase ownership of the project, and thus, engagement with the mathematics concepts that are covered within the project.

The sample PBL project in Box 3.3 is fictional, but it does represent a sample project that might be of interest to students in middle school. Initially, a teacher might have generated the broad idea of using some of the mathematics topics to emphasize budgeting, operations, percentages, and so on in order to help students get ready for a major purchase later in life. Then, the students could have then brainstormed the general topic and come up with the idea of buying a used car. At that point, the students could consider various questions on car purchase and ownership, and they might subsequently develop specific artifacts for this project. Of course, this project could easily be adapted for elementary grades by planning to purchase a bicycle rather than a car, and adjusting the mathematics concepts a bit.

BOX 3.3 A SAMPLE PBL PROJECT—WHEN CAN I BUY A CAR?

Like most students, you will probably want to buy your first car when you are about 15 years old, because at 15.5 you can get your learner's permit and begin to learn to drive. While that may be a few years from now, you realize that it is time to plan for this car purchase now so you can save some of your money. Of course, you cannot pick out a used car today for a purchase in two years, but you can estimate how much such a car might cost. For this example, we'll say an older, small used car might be purchased for $4,000. Further, your parents have indicated that they might consider helping you with that purchase by providing 50% of those funds on your 15th birthday, if you have developed a worthwhile car-purchase plan and saved your money responsibly.

This project is intended to help you be ready to buy a car when the time comes. If the project is done well, it will also convince your parents of your maturity and personal responsibility with your own money. Further, it will show you the importance of budgeting and saving your money. Ultimately, it should help you be ready to purchase your first car, when the time comes! Up to three students may work as a group on this PBL project, or students may complete their project individually.

Required Information

In order to undertake this project, you will need records of various things. These include:

- information of what you earn (e.g., pay for doing tasks around the house such as taking out trash, mowing the lawn, raking leaves, doing loads of clothes, sweeping, washing dishes, or working part time in your family's business);
- interest your money might earn from year to year in a savings account;
- information of how much of your money you spend weekly (e.g., going to movies, buying items in stores such as make-up or tennis shoes, etc.);
- an estimation of how much you might save, based on the budget figures above;
- information on car insurance costs;
- information on car maintenance costs for an older car; and
- information on costs of operations (gas, tires, oil consumption, etc.).

Required Artifacts

In order to complete this project, you will have to convince your parents to assist you in this car purchase, and they will need to see in-depth planning on your part. These artifacts will need to be highly developed, well thought out, and must present a convincing case for help. All students will be expected to develop artifacts 1 and 2, but students (or groups working together) may choose to complete either artifact 3 or 4.

1. *Excel Budget Sheets:* You will develop a personal budget in Excel or other database. It must cover at least a two-month time frame, and must include:

   o a total of all the funds you earn in that two months;
   o a total of all of your personal funds you spend in that two months; and
   o a total of the excess funds that you can save for your car purchase in that two months.

You will need to use this budget to convince your parents to assist you in this purchase, so it must be well developed, presented in one or more Excel files, and explainable to your parents. A rubric is available to assist in development of this artifact (that rubric is described in the Differentiated Assessment Chapter, Chapter 7, of this book).

2. *Consumer Report Webquest:* You will select a car that is similar to the one you might wish to purchase in three years. You will complete a webquest that

(Continued)

(Continued)

involves seeking information on used automobiles from the Internet. In that context, each student must obtain at least two consumer's reports on the quality of that make and year of your selected automobile and summarize that information. As a culmination of the webquest, each student will prepare a written report, summarizing the quality of the auto selected and showing the operating budget for that particular car for one year. That budget must include estimated mileage for the year, and the costs of insurance, gas, oil, and so on.

3. *PowerPoint Presentation:* Students selecting this option will develop a PowerPoint presentation that summarizes all of the information you have collected. This information must be arranged in a well-sourced presentation, and based on the data in the other artifacts. Between 20 and 40 slides must be included, each slide being content rich. You will present this presentation to the class, and ultimately to your parents in order to convince them to assist you in purchasing your car.

4. *Video Presentation:* In order to convince some parents of the appropriateness of the automotive selection, a brief video may be more appropriate than a slide presentation. Instead of artifact number 3, students may choose to develop a video as their final presentation of this PBL project. Videos must be between 5 minutes and 10 minutes in length, and must present all of the information summarized for the entire project.

5. *Large Purchase Comparison* (This assignment is optional for students doing the project independently): For most people, the largest purchases they are likely to make in their lifetime are a car and a home. As time allows, students may wish to compare the purchase of a car with another type of purchase that economists consider a "large buy" purchase—the purchase of a home. To complete this assignment, students must review the Khan Academy video on purchasing a home and compare that process with the budgeting/purchasing process above. Students will then prepare either a three-page written report or a PowerPoint, comparing and contrasting these two large purchases. All students who work in small groups on this project are required to complete this artifact.

Project Time Frame

This project will consist of a minimum completion of at least three artifacts, as described above. These must be completed during the next nine-week grading period. Students will be provided some time in class to complete this work, and they will frequently share their completed work with other class members. Ultimately, each student will present their project to the class, and final grades for each student's project will be a combination of peer evaluation and teacher evaluation of the multiple artifacts above.

In this example, teachers can get a sense of the types of things a PBL project in mathematics might involve. First, part of the allure of PBL is that students are more likely to engage in study of real-world problem solving that relates to their needs and/or their desires, compared to more traditional, imaginary problems (Bender, 2012b; Boss & Krauss, 2007; Larmer et al., 2009), particularly if students are allowed some choice in the assignments required. In this example, student choices are clearly delineated, in terms of the required artifacts, as well as which specific artifact each student might complete. Also, in this example, students may also choose to work in small groups or independently.

The first two paragraphs in Box 3.3 may be considered the "anchor" or real-world scenario that relates this mathematics project directly to the desires of students in the class. Of course, the driving question here is, "When can I buy a car?" With that driving question in mind, and the option of some student choices in the project, it is quite likely that students will be motivated to work on the tasks required within the project.

> With a good driving question in mind, and the option of some student choices in the project, it is quite likely that students will be motivated to work on the tasks required within the project.

Next, most PBL projects today, as illustrated in this example, are heavily tied to 21st century technology tools for learning. In this case an Internet search, guided by a webquest, is included as one of the required artifacts, and a Khan Academy video is included in another assignment. Also, while not illustrated in this project, many PBL projects require completion of game-based mathematics activities on specific topics (gaming for mathematics instruction is discussed in later chapters). The use of these modern teaching tools helps every student to access and engage with the mathematics content, much more so than merely delivering this same content via a textbook/modeling, or lecture presentations.

Teachers should also note the detailed descriptions of the project artifacts in this example. In addition to fairly detailed descriptions such as these for each artifact, teachers should devise individual evaluation rubrics for all or some of the artifacts, to assist both teachers and students in development and evaluation of the ongoing work. Rubrics may be developed for evaluation of either single artifacts in PBL, or for entire PBL projects, and a sample rubric for one artifact in this project is presented and discussed in the differentiated assessment chapter (Chapter 7) of this book.

Also, "publication" of the project results is critical in PBL. In this case, students are required to develop projects that have intrinsic value in the real world—helping convince parents to support the purchase of a car.

Projects that do hold intrinsic value in the real world are much more likely to engage students than are the make-believe problem-solving scenarios that are typical in most traditional mathematics curricula.

PROJECT-BASED LEARNING FOR DIFFERENTIATION OF COMMON CORE MATHEMATICS

PBL was not discussed as a model for differentiated instruction until recently (Bender, 2012b; Schlemmer & Schlemmer, 2008). However, while this approach has been around for several decades, today PBL provides a 21st century instructional approach that facilitates differentiated instruction while, at the same time, fostering high levels of student engagement with the mathematics content (Bender, 2012b; Larmer & Mergendoller, 2010; Schlemmer & Schlemmer, 2008). Within the project time frame, student choice is exercised, as they select many tasks that must be accomplished, as well as aspects of various assignments that they will personally complete. That selection process typically results in students choosing learning activities that are particularly compatible with their own learning styles and preferences, and in that sense, project-based learning is an excellent example of how to differentiate instruction (Bender, 2012b; Schlemmer & Schlemmer, 2008).

As discussed previously, the Common Core State Standards in mathematics emphasize mastery learning, problem solving, in-depth conceptual understanding, 21st century communication skills, and teamwork, and each of those is, likewise, an emphasis within PBL instruction in mathematics (Bender, 2012b). PBL is an exciting, innovative, instructional format in which the teacher, working with small groups of students or with individual students independently, selects a driving question that frames their project. Then, either the teacher or the students map the Common Core Mathematics Standards onto each individual project, and subsequently to other projects throughout the year, thus assuring content coverage. The videos above provide examples of both teachers and students taking responsibility for content coverage in PBL instruction.

Finally, research has consistently shown that PBL results in higher levels of engagement with the curriculum, as well as higher levels of student achievement in mathematics when compared to more traditional instructional models (Bender, 2012b; Boss & Krauss, 2007; Bui, 2012; Larmer et al., 2009). Of course, higher levels of both engagement and academic achievement speak volumes! Because of this proven track record, PBL is the perfect vehicle for 21st century mathematics instruction in Common Core Mathematics.

Ideas and Resources for PBL Instruction

Ideas for PBL projects in math are limited only by the creativity of the teacher and the students. In particular, once specific mathematics content is identified as the basis for a project, teachers and students together can usually identify a PBL project that incorporates most of that content. Adjustment of the artifacts for a given project can also provide the teacher a method for assuring content coverage for specific content standards. Box 3.4 presents a list of examples of PBL projects in mathematics from a variety of sources.

BOX 3.4 OTHER IDEAS FOR PBL PROJECTS IN MATHEMATICS

Math Cartoon Project—In this project, elementary students must create a cartoon comic strip using six or more sequenced pictures (Wetzel, 2009) that communicates a mathematics concept or rule using humor. Since all students are not artistically inclined, students have the option of using a computer drawing program.

Creative Math Book Project—In this example, students create a book using cartoons, illustrations, and pictures to explain everyday real-world applications of math (Wetzel, 2009). This may involve cartoons created in specific instructional units throughout the year. This project supports student learning in math as they make connections with geometry, algebra, number sense, and more concepts.

Historical Mathematicians Project—Students individually, or working in small groups, research the biography of a particular mathematician (J. Cook, 2012). They might be required to develop a PowerPoint, a blog, a glog, or a scrapbook on the life of a famous mathematician, or on the contributions of women or minorities to the field of mathematics. They may also research the discovery and development of new mathematical principles and theories. They must present their projects in a way that demonstrates what they have learned and then share that new information with the class.

The Doodle Family Budget Project—This project was published previously (Bender & Crane, 2011) and deals with helping students understand the purchase of a home. It is similar to the budgeting, information gathering, and so on from the project presented in this chapter of purchasing a car.

Stock Market Project—In this project, students working individually or in small groups pick one or more stocks they want to "purchase" (Wetzel, 2009). They make a brochure for prospective investors using a publishing computer program. Students then graph the sales of the stock or stocks over a several-week period to display how well the stock fared during this time period. They make several math connections along with reading, using newspapers in the classroom, watching stock reports on television, and comparing/contrasting. Teachers may reward the individual or group that earns the most on their stock investments.

(Continued)

(Continued)

Geographic Statistics—In this project, students might research relevant population statistics about their city, state, or county, including data on minority populations, gender breakdowns, income distribution, and so on (J. Cook, 2012). They may also collect growth trends over three or more census periods, and can then present their findings in a visually descriptive way, showing trends and possibly even making predictions for the future growth of the entity under study. Alternatively, statistics-based projects might involve researching educational trends, or even the government budget.

Election Statistics—When elections come, students often get interested in the polling numbers associated with various candidates, and projects of this nature can emphasize statistical concepts such as percentages, standard errors, and sampling techniques.

Geometry Map Project—Students are required to design a map that includes lines, angles, and triangles (Wetzel, 2009). The map can be of a neighborhood town, city, or state and must include the following as a minimum:

– Two sets of streets that are parallel	– Two sets of streets that are perpendicular
– One obtuse angle street intersection	– One acute angle street intersects another
– One street that is a line segment	– One street that is a line
– One street that is a ray	– One building shaped like an equilateral triangle
– One building shaped like a scalene triangle.	

If teachers wish to extend this project, various courses can be described and distance computed by individuals or groups of students.

Math Problem-Solving Video—With Khan Academy and YouTube videos receiving so much attention, this project requires students to create an instructional video of either a specific type of mathematics problem or of everyday mathematical problems that they encounter in the real world (Wetzel, 2009). Students may work in groups to present a skit or role-playing situation as they follow the guidelines of the project.

In addition to these project ideas, there are many resources that can be found online for PBL. In particular the website for the Buck Institute for Education (www.bie.org) should be explored. That site promotes PBL as an instructional model for the future, and a series of short videos is available on a variety of projects that have been undertaken in various subject areas at different grade levels. Also, a number of other websites are available that can support PBL instruction, and several of these are presented in Box 3.5.

BOX 3.5   WEBSITES TO SUPPORT PBL PROJECTS IN MATHEMATICS

TheFuturesChannel.com—This site presents a series of short videos that link mathematics to science and/or careers. Topics include algebra, hands-on mathematics, and problem solving. Each video is accompanied by a lesson plan that further explores the mathematics concepts. Use of this site is free, and videos are added frequently. In PBL, the videos can provide content for one or more project artifacts.

Global SchoolNet—Global SchoolNet (www.globalschoolnet.org) is a nonprofit international educational clearinghouse for collaborative educational projects in a wide variety of subject areas including science and mathematics. Approximately 90,000 educators from 194 countries, and 4.5 million students, have participated in global projects through this organization, as of 2012. This site includes a projects registry of more than 2,500 annotated listings of teacher-led global projects, including several hundred projects in mathematics. It is searchable by date, age level, geographic location, collaboration type, technology tools used, or keyword. Here teachers can choose to join an existing project or announce one of their own.

Hands-On Math Projects—This is a PDF document (Carter, Cohen, Keyes, Kusimo, & Lunsford, 2002) that includes a variety of mathematics projects. For example, The Mathematics of Quilting exposes learners to plane geometry, symmetry, and tessellations. In Making Art Through Mathematics, learners explore Cartesian coordinates, 2-D and 3-D geometry, measurement, symmetry, and volume.

National Math Trail—This site (www.nationalmathtrail.org) is supported by the U.S. Department of Education's Star Schools program, through the Satellite Education Resources Consortium (SERC), and NEC Foundation. Teachers can look at this site and seek resources for primary and elementary grade level mathematics instruction.

Conclusion: PBL for 21st Century Mathematics Classes

Many educators today are encouraging all mathematics teachers, indeed all teachers, to explore the implementation of PBL instruction (Bender, 2012b; Boss & Krauss, 2007; Bui, 2012; Larmer et al., 2009). PBL fits very nicely with the emphasis of the Common Core Mathematics Standards, as discussed above, and for that reason and others, these researchers see PBL as the best 21st century instructional approach. Certainly all mathematics teachers should, at a minimum, consider developing some mathematics projects in the classroom context, and this practice with PBL may very well lead to a significant restructuring of your mathematics instruction.

WHAT'S NEXT?

At this point, four different models of differentiated instruction have been described:

1. Modification of the traditional, whole group lesson,

2. Mathematics learning centers,

3. Flipped mathematics classes, and

4. Project-based learning in mathematics.

In particular, this chapter presented two recently developed models for differentiating instruction. Both the flipped mathematics class and project-based learning are receiving increased attention in the literature on mathematics instruction, and both of these may best be understood as options for differentiated instruction in the mathematics class. Further, an increasing number of math teachers are exploring these new instructional options to better meet the needs of all students in mathematics.

However, as new instructional methods such as these are developed, teachers find that they face many of the same instructional issues as in the traditional classroom, issues such as student engagement, motivation, students' readiness to do homework, and the necessity to assess student outcomes. Finally, teachers of mathematics at all grade levels need specific instructional tactics for differentiation, regardless of the overall model of differentiated instruction they choose to use. The next three chapters will explore specific instructional techniques for differentiating instruction, and Chapter 7 focuses directly on assessment of mathematics in the differentiated math class at the primary and elementary levels.

Strategies for Differentiating Early Math Instruction

4

Early learning in mathematics may be best understood by considering two distinct phases of conceptual understanding in mathematics: the early development of number sense and the subsequent development of mathematics readiness skills. While there is clearly some overlap between these concepts—indeed some theorists may consider these synonymous—teachers should focus on these two phases of early mathematics learning as relatively distinct, in order to most easily develop and implement differentiated instructional strategies for these areas.

NUMBER SENSE IN YOUNG CHILDREN

In order to differentiate mathematics instruction in the kindergarten and primary years, teachers must understand the concept of early number sense. As defined in Chapter 1, number sense involves a student's conceptual understanding of basic number and numeration concepts such as counting, or recognizing how many objects are present in a set, and how a number may be used to represent that set of objects, as well as the understanding that sequences of numbers are often best understood as patterns (Jordan, 2007; Sousa, 2008). Research has shown that early development of number sense provides the foundation for early success in math (Jordan, 2007; Sousa, 2008).

For example, in one of the initial long-term studies, Jordan et al. (2007) showed that various measures of number sense, assessed in kindergarten, were directly correlated to mathematics achievement in both kindergarten and Grade 1.

Stages of Number Sense Development

Because the early development of number sense is so critical to success in mathematics, researchers have investigated number sense in depth, and some teaching guidelines for development of number sense are available today (Jordan, 2007; Sousa, 2008). For example, Gersten and Chard (1999) identified several levels of number sense among children with difficulty in math. These researchers likened the construct of "number sense" in mathematics to the concept of "phoneme instruction" in reading. Within the past decade, research has demonstrated conclusively that "phoneme manipulation" skills—that is, the ability to recognize and intentionally manipulate different speech sounds—represent a more fundamental and earlier prerequisite skill for reading than "phonics" (i.e., knowledge of letter shapes and the sounds those shapes represent). Of course, prior to this important research, for many previous decades, phonics had been the very first step in reading instruction; only now have teachers realized that phoneme manipulation skills is prerequisite to phonics. In short, if students cannot detect and manipulate sounds independent of letter recognition, they cannot succeed in phonics, which associates different sounds with specific letters.

> *Number sense involves a student's conceptual understanding of basic number and numeration concepts such as counting, or recognizing how many objects are present in a set, and how a number may be used to represent that set of objects.*

To pursue this comparison a bit further, the concept of number sense may be as fundamental in learning mathematics as phoneme instruction has become in learning to read (Gersten & Chard, 1999). In short, number sense seems to be a prerequisite to the many early mathematics skills that are typically referred to as math readiness skills. Thus, teachers must have strategies that facilitate the early development of number sense for students who have not yet developed a sense of numbers and what they might represent. Gersten and Chard (1999) identified several stepping stones that allow teachers to evaluate a child's understanding of number sense. These stepping stones represent increasingly complex levels of a child's understanding of numbers, as presented in Box 4.1.

BOX 4.1 STEPPING STONES FOR NUMBER SENSE DEVELOPMENT

Level 1

Children at this level have not yet developed number sense or shown any knowledge of relative quantity. A child at this level will not be able to answer questions involving "more than" or "less than." Further, children at this level would not have the basic concepts of fewer or greater.

Level 2

Children at this level are beginning to acquire number sense. A child here would be able to state and understand terms such as "lots," "five," and "ten." These children also are beginning to understand the concepts of "more than" and "less than." These children do not understand basic computation skills, but they do understand greater/lesser amounts.

Level 3

Children at this level fully understand "more than" and "less than." They also have a general understanding of computation and may use a "count up from one" strategy to solve problems. These children may use their fingers or manipulate objects to solve a problem. While these children are beginning to understand computation, there will still be many errors in counting. For children at this level, adding four and three may involve holding up four fingers on one hand and three on the other. They will start at one and count to four, and then look at the other hand, and count from one to three. Finally, they will count all of the fingers together to get an answer. Errors are seen more often when the child is calculating numbers higher than five, because these computations involve using fingers on both hands.

Level 4

Children at this level use a more sophisticated "count up" or "counting on" process, rather than the "counting all" process just described. For example, these children may hold up fingers to represent each addend, begin with the number of the first addend, and then "count on" to the second. For adding four and three, the student starts at four and adds the three, using fingers and counting out loud. "Four, five, six, seven." At this level the child can keep track of the first addend while counting to the second. Thus, these children understand the conceptual reality of numbers (i.e., they do not have to count to four to know that four exists). Children at this level may not even need to use their fingers or manipulatives to count to find a solution. Children at this level can solve any digit problem presented to them, provided they can count accurately.

(Continued)

(Continued)

Level 5

Children at this level are at the highest level of number sense. They can use a retrieval strategy. They can respond quickly and correctly, pulling from memory the answer to a problem. They have learned addition math facts to a highly automatic level and have memorized some basic subtraction facts. These children can recall $4 + 3 = 7$. They can also turn the fact around to state that $7 - 3 = 4$. With these stepping stones in mind, teachers need strategies for developing number sense in children, including older children, perhaps throughout the elementary school years. The section below describes several activities that early education teachers can use for teaching number sense. These activities will improve the number sense of students who already have the basics. Further, these tactics will help students with deficits in number sense to catch up with other students.

Mathematical Play to Develop Number Sense

With these steps in number sense as a background, prekindergarten and kindergarten teachers can proceed to number sense instruction. In fact, the Number Worlds curriculum has recently been developed to assist with instruction in number sense and early mathematics skills (Griffin, 2003a; 2004a; 2005). You may find a synopsis of this curriculum in Appendix A, or simply look at the Number Worlds website (www .sranumberworlds.com).

In addition, a number of strategies have been suggested for developing number sense, and many of these are based on informal games and mathematical play for young students (Checkley, 1999; Griffin et al., 2003; Gurganus, 2004; eSchool News, 2012a; Whitenack et al., 2002). Initially in prekindergarten, kindergarten, and the early grades, teachers should emphasize mathematical activities as "play" within the typical routines of the classroom, and a number of ideas for this informal instruction in the early grades are presented below in Teaching Tip 4.1.

Teaching Tip 4.1 Activities to Develop Number Sense in Young Children

Extend Counting to Other Number Patterns

In some of the early counting activities, students should extend their counting to other, larger numbers. Rather than counting from 1 to 10, teachers could have students count from 101 to 110 (Gurganus, 2004), and teachers should stress number patterns by pointing them out whenever possible.

Use Finger Patterns

Finger patterns are a way many young children use their fingers to represent the numbers 1 through 10 (Whitenack et al., 2002). Provide students varied exercises that allow them to represent the numbers with their fingers. Students at first only use their fingers the same way they have learned how to count. Part of number sense is recognizing that there are several different ways to represent numbers, and playing games with finger patterns allows children to think unconventionally. Students need the exercises to see that three fingers on one hand and two fingers on the other hand represent the same number as five fingers on one hand. Class discussion during the finger pattern game allows students to see the differences and the similarities between the different ways of representing numbers. Having students explain why they picked three fingers on one hand and two fingers on the other lets the students that held up five fingers on one hand see a new pattern and vice versa. This is a good type of instruction to use in a "buddy" game, where kids are paired together to generate an alternative solution.

Greater/Fewer Games

Students who need to learn the concepts of greater or fewer can generally be taught using manipulatives such as same-size blocks, papers with dots, and the like. Having the students line up and each take a different number of steps may assist students to see relationships between numbers (e.g., that a student who took four steps went farther than a student who took two steps). Teachers should use several different methods that students will be able to understand to concretely illustrate various number facts, such as the fact that seven is always greater than four. For example, teachers should use different-size blocks to illustrate the same number concept (e.g., seven is greater than four regardless of the size of the block).

As an example of a number sense activity for older children, teachers may challenge the students with questions such as the following:

I have 10 candy bars. We'll just pretend my fingers are candy bars. Here are some candy bars in this hand. (The teacher should hold up four fingers, while hiding the other hand behind his or her back.) How many am I hiding from you?

Moving on Down the Road

Using a number line on the floor, have students move "down the road" by noting the numbers as they pass. Emphasize that six steps are more than five steps, and so on. (For older students, this number line activity can be done with both positive and negative integers.)

Teaching Puppets

Teachers can teach beginning addition and help increase number sense at the same time. Using a puppet, the teacher would place a specific number of cookies in a bag

(Continued)

(Continued)

(e.g., three cookies). Next, the teacher would have a student draw a card from a pile that has "+ 2," "– 3," or "+ 4," or another such number fact on it. The teacher should ask groups of students to think through the problem and then do the problem using the puppet by calculating how many cookies are left. This can assist spatial learners as well as students with strength in interpersonal intelligence.

Pocket Games for One-to-One Correspondence

Use a hanging shoe bag with at least 10 pockets (Checkley, 1999) and put a different number on each pocket. Give students cards that have varying numbers of objects on them. Have the students match the number and the card by placing the card in the appropriately labeled pocket. Students may even make their own cards.

Snap-Together Objects

Kindergartners and first graders need to practice addition and subtraction repeatedly in various game formats. Teachers may use a group of cubes or objects that snap together to assist in this practice. First, divide the students into groups of two. Next, give each group a chain of 10 snap-together objects. Then, one student should break the chain and give the other student the portion of the chain that is left. The second student would then be required to tell how many objects are missing (Checkley, 1999). This will assist bodily/kinesthetic learners.

Using Mathematical Models

Mathematical modeling was stressed in the Common Core Standards for Mathematical Practice, and teachers should encourage students to make mathematical models for the problems they are asked to solve in the early years. For example, consider the following problem: "There are seven children; how many eyes are there?" Teachers may wish to allow the students to create their own drawing for this problem in order to help them find a solution—a technique that will be of great benefit to visual/spatial learners. Some students may just draw a circle with two dots. Other students will draw more elaborate drawings that have noses and mouths. In this approach, the students are allowed to use their creativity to solve math problems (Checkley, 1999).

Use Manipulatives and Representations

Many teachers unfortunately feel that blocks or other manipulatives are "baby toys," and some students even put them away by the first or second grade. For other students, however, manipulatives need to be used for as long as possible in the early grades. When students ask about manipulatives, point out that almost all teachers are using sections of a round pie for fractions in Grades 3 and 4, and even Grade 5. There is good evidence that using representations of numbers is an effective teaching tactic with high schoolers struggling in mathematics (Witzel, Riccomini, & Schneider, 2008). Also, teachers should not move students through the concrete, representational, abstract levels too quickly or insist on students' using pictures or "representations of manipulatives" before they are ready. Rather, use of either manipulatives or representations should be allowed for as long as students wish in the early grades (Checkley, 1999).

Make a Class Quilt

This is a creative activity that is great for spatial learners. First, each student designs his or her own "square" for the quilt. Teachers may wish to use crayon or tempera paint to color the squares of cloth. The squares are then combined and sewn together to make a quilt. This allows students an early introduction to geometry, fractions, visual-spatial reasoning, and addition, since the quilt components represent various shapes and various portions of the whole. Teachers should display or use the quilt so the students will be reminded of the concepts as well as have pride in their work (Checkley, 1999).

Pair Numbers With Objects

In the class routine, when discussing objects in the class or pictures in a storybook, pair numbers and objects. For example, there are two wheels on a bicycle, three wheels on a tricycle, and four wheels on a car. Students will thus begin to associate numbers with different values rather than merely as labels (Gurganus, 2004).

BEYOND NUMBER SENSE: MATH READINESS SKILLS

In additional to early number sense, early mathematics readiness skills should be emphasized in kindergarten and the primary grades. Studies of early math readiness have increased recently, as the importance of both number sense and early mathematics skill development has become clearer (N. C. Jordan, 2007; N. C. Jordan et al., 2007; National Mathematics Advisory Panel; 2008; Sousa, 2008). This body of research on early math has paralleled the research in early reading and literacy skills, though research on early math is not nearly as developed as research on literacy. Still, research in early mathematics has documented a set of skills that students generally master either prior to school or in kindergarten and Grade 1 that are predictive of math skills through the primary grades (L. S. Fuchs, Fuchs, Compton, et al., 2007; N. C. Jordan et al., 2007). While not all studies of early math involved all of these indicators, the list of early math readiness skills includes the ability to:

Compare sets of objects to determine which is greater (2 objects or 3 objects)

Count to 10 (or 20, or perhaps 25)

Recognize written digits (1 through 10, or greater)

Recognize patterns in numbers and predict the missing digit to complete the pattern (an example might be 1, 2, 3, 4, _, 6, or perhaps 2, 4, 6, _, 10)

Verbally repeat a sequence of numbers (either in the original order or in reverse order)

Write digits 1–10 in correct order

Complete basic number combinations (e.g., simple addition of two digits involving one-step strategies such as counting on)

Of course, the overlap between number sense and early math readiness skills is fairly obvious in this list, as items one, two, and perhaps five above could be considered number sense, whereas the last item represents number manipulation. Further, while both number sense and these early math readiness skills are important, this body of research has not yet answered certain questions. For example, in the literature on early phoneme and reading skill, a set of early literacy skills has been identified (e.g., the student's ability to recognize the initial sound in a word based on a picture representing that word, and then find another picture that has the same initial sound). Further, the reading research has shown that those skills may be used as both benchmarks of early literacy and as the basis for the early literacy curriculum. In mathematics, comparable research is not yet available. For example, while the list of skills above do predict mathematics achievement in the early grades (N. C. Jordan et al., 2007), it is not clear if these represent the best predictors of early math achievement, or if other skills yet to be identified might be better predictors. Further, it is not known if specific instruction during kindergarten or the first grade on these math readiness skills, as listed above, will help struggling learners overcome their difficulties in early math. While some research has suggested that such early instruction may foster more successful mathematics achievement in later years (Griffin, 2004a; 2004b; 2005; N. C. Jordan et al., 2007), more research needs to be done in this area.

Steps in Developing Early Math Skills

With those limitations on math readiness research noted, there are some conclusions that may be reached on current research. First, a number of researchers have considered how students master early math skills, and the common element, appearing repeatedly in the teaching guidelines, is the "concreteness" necessary for successful early math instruction (Allsopp et al., 2008; Fahsl, 2007; Fuson & Wearne, 1997; Griffin, 2003a; 2005; Gurganus, 2004; Witzel et al., 2008). In short, the mastery of early math skills beyond the number sense level also involves use of concrete objects or representational instruction in which pictures of objects are used as teaching tools, or both. Of course, for students throughout the elementary grades who may be struggling and thus several years behind in mathematics achievement, concreteness is no less important than in kindergarten and the early grades.

The UDSSI Model of Early Math Skills

In addition to the need for concrete instruction, teachers must understand the various levels of skill development in early math. Fuson and Wearne (1997) developed a sequence of early math skills that many teachers find helpful in considering how young brains learn math beyond the number sense level. These researchers postulated that children learn their numbers in a pattern—consistent with the emerging brain research suggesting that all brains search for patterns. Again, this is the reason that the Common Core Mathematics Standards have emphasized patterns in mathematics so heavily. Specifically, this research has become the basis for the emphasis on pattern seeking, as embedded within the Standards for Mathematical Practice within the Common Core State Standards in Mathematics (see item 7 in Box 1.1 in chapter 1).

> *Children learn their numbers in a pattern—consistent with the emerging brain research suggesting that all brains search for patterns.*

Fuson and Wearne (1997) attempted to identify the patterns in early math, and subsequently identified five different stages of early learning. The stages are referred to as the UDSSI model, as presented in Box 4.2. Each letter represents a stage of learning, and Fuson and Wearne (1997) suggest that children must learn each step in sequence in order to understand multi-digit numbers and higher math problems.

BOX 4.2 STAGES IN THE UDSSI MODEL OF EARLY MATHEMATICS SKILLS

The Unitary Stage—This represents the early understanding of numerals and the numbers they represent. Children initially learn that 10 means "10 objects." Knowing the order of the numbers one through nine allows young children to understand numbers, and their early understanding of the concept of place value allows students to understand numbers up to the early teens. Thus, children in the unitary stage comprehend the numbers one through 19 fairly well.

(Continued)

(Continued)

The Decade Stage—This stage involves children's understanding the concept of counting by tens, as well as numbers higher than 19. Many children comprehend the order of sequences such as 21, 22, 23, or 35, 36, and 37, but they do not know the order of the numbers in the tens place for subsequent groups of ten (e.g., is 32 higher than 51?). These children may count up through the 20s and then go to the 50s. Children who understand the decades know the order of the numbers in the tens place (i.e., the decades). Children who understand the decades can count from 1 through 99.

The Sequence Stage—This involves children beginning to understand the sequence of tens and ones. Children learn that 53 means five tens and three ones. They realize that when a person states a number, the first part is written first and the last part is written second (i.e., 53 is written by writing a 5 and then a 3, in that order). These children are then able to write the numbers in order. Prior to this understanding, children may write 53 as 50 and 3 and then combine these as 503.

The Separate Stage—This involves children realizing that the numbers mean something even though such meaning is not stated. Children at this stage understand that even though "ten" is not stated in the number 55, the first digit really means five tens and the second digit means five ones. Children who comprehend this step can separate the tens and ones.

The Integrated Stage—This stage begins when children begin to combine the sequence and separate stages. Students who understand numbers at this stage have flexibility in approaching and solving problems using two-digit numbers because they can rapidly shift attributes of the "10s" in the tens place to either the background or foreground in their thinking. They also understand that the order of one through nine is repeated throughout the hundreds, thousands, and so forth.

With this model in mind, we can understand how students learn early operations in addition and subtraction. According to this model, children learn addition and subtraction of single-digit numbers in three levels, as shown below (Fuson & Wearne, 1997).

Level 1: *Children at this level use objects as a model for addition or subtraction. Children move the objects to solve the problems, and thus are using a very concrete learning method. The objects may either be part of the total or part of the addend, but the objects are essential at this level.*

Level 2: *Children at this level use the "count on" method by counting onto the addend, and in using this method do not need the concrete objects in order to solve the problem. This is based, in part, on growing memory skills, since children at this level are capable of keeping track of the amount represented by the first addend as well as the second addend.*

Level 3:   *Children at this level can "chunk" the information together to get a total. These children can look at the problem and chunk (i.e., mentally regroup the numbers), which allows fairly easy calculation of the answer. This is the highest level of early addition skill. These students no longer need models or the "counting on" method to reach the solution, but are able to get to the total by grouping and chunking known facts.*

Fuson and Wearne (1997) also suggested that these levels may apply in understanding mathematics at higher levels also. For example, children solving two-digit addition and subtraction problems go through basically the same steps as above. Children at Level 1 use a model by placing the first number of objects and either adding or subtracting the next number and then counting the total to reach the solution. Children at Level 2 tend to use mental markers to get the total. These children remember where they start and either "count up" or "take away" to get the answers. Children at Level 3 can chunk information to get the total.

Using this model can benefit teachers in almost all elementary grades with students who are challenged by early operations; they can better understand exactly where a child's mathematical strengths are. Further, this construct provides a solid theoretical basis for the use of manipulatives or concrete examples across the elementary grades for students struggling in math, and much of the research on instruction in mathematics emphasizes concrete instruction.

THE CRA DIFFERENTIATION TACTIC

Students master early math beyond the number sense and math readiness levels most effectively when mathematics content is presented in concrete, representational (or pictorial), and abstract ways. This type of three-level presentation is referred to as CRA instruction, and is currently recommended by most researchers focused on mathematics instruction (Allsopp, 1999; Allsopp et al., 2008; Fahsl, 2007; L. Jordan, Miller, & Mercer, 1998; Mancl, Miller, & Kennedy, 2012). This approach is also occasionally referred to as CSA, and in that instance, the letters represent concrete, semi-concrete, and abstract. This instructional method has been shown to be highly effective, but, unfortunately, it is still not in widespread use in many mathematics classrooms beyond the first few grades.

However, both the brain research and the Common Core Standards emphasize conceptual depth in mathematics instruction, and mathematics concepts that are presented in a variety of different ways are much more

> *CRA is now recommended for use in general education classrooms throughout the elementary and middle grades to help all students successfully learn difficult math concepts.*

likely to be conceptually understood, as well as retained over a longer period of time (Sousa, 2008). Thus, CRA is now recommended for use in general education classrooms throughout the elementary and middle grades to help all students successfully learn difficult math concepts (Harris, Miller, & Mercer, 1995; Marsh & Cooke, 1996). Further, research has shown that this approach should be used more frequently even in high school for students who are struggling in mathematics.

What Is CRA?

Almost all educators would agree that abstract learning is the most efficient means of problem solving in math at any grade level, because concrete or representational examples can get quite cumbersome for higher-level mathematics. However, for many students across the elementary years, concrete or representational learning may be necessary during the initial instruction in a particular math concept. In the differentiated classroom, providing tear-out group work using concrete or representational examples is one way to offer varied instruction and meet the needs of all students. Further, with the emphasis on inclusion of students with special needs in the general education math classes, teachers will out of necessity begin to use CRA methods to teach math skills simply because many students with disabilities will require this type of instruction.

Shaw-Jing, Stigler, and Woodward (2000) refer to CRA as the "mental tool" view of math instruction, which suggests that mental images of mathematical equations or problems may best be formed using physical materials or concrete objects. You will recall from Chapter 1 that visual processing is highly correlated with mathematical thinking (Sousa, 2008), suggesting that students need to "visualize" math problems in order to understand them. Clearly, concrete objects, or pictorial representations of them, can greatly assist in this visualization process. These mental tools are then used to guide the students in their problem solving. The mental tool view uses highly organized and structured representations of the numbers. This view suggests that if the representation is highly structured, it will provide the student with a tool that can assist in visualization of the math problem.

While the use of CRA has received a boost from recent brain research and the current emphasis on differentiation of math activities,

Shaw-Jing and colleagues (2000) point out that this instructional paradigm is not new. Many years ago, Stern (1949) developed a pattern that used a wooden stick with grooves to slide into wooden blocks. Ten sticks would go in each wooden block, and students would use these counters to assist in problem solving. Others subsequently developed a variety of grids or counting devices to reflect the base-ten number system. Thus, concrete and semi-concrete models have been employed in math for a long time, and there are many variations on this older instructional approach.

However, because of brain-compatible research as well as the necessity to differentiate instruction in the general education class, the CRA approach has been revitalized. Further, the current recommendations from the research suggest that application of this approach for higher-level learners will be quite useful (Witzel et al., 2008). To get both younger and older students who may be having difficulty in math used to using concrete or semi-concrete mathematical representations, Shaw-Jing et al. (2000) developed a set of game-like activities, as presented in Teaching Tip 4.2. To make many of these games a "peer buddy" activity, pairs of students can merely use a spinner, rather than have the teacher call out numbers or patterns, as in the description below.

Teaching Tip 4.2   Games for Teaching Representational Math

Pattern Number Bingo

This uses a standard Bingo-style board with pictures in patterned sets on it. These may be tally marks in groups of five; thus "7" would be represented as ///// //. The board should include patterns representing numbers 1 through 10. Teachers hold up a pattern card, and students place a marker on their Bingo card if that pattern is present. This game is meant to help students learn to enumerate and associate numerals with patterns.

Memory Cards

This game uses two different colored decks of cards. One deck of cards has the numerals 0 through 10 on them. The other deck of cards has groups of objects representing 0 through 10 on them. The students turn one card from each colored deck over. If the cards represent the same number, the student collects the cards and goes again. This game is intended to motivate students to memorize the representational patterns for the numerals.

(Continued)

(Continued)

Flash Pattern Cards

This game assists students in quickly recognizing patterns for numerals. Children have to quickly find a correct numeral card for a pattern card flashed by the teacher for three to five seconds. The students will enjoy seeing how fast they can find the card matching the number pattern presented by the teacher.

The Relay Race

This game is similar to hopscotch. Students line up in front of a number grid that is pre-drawn on the floor. Students draw pattern cards from a bag, decipher the pattern, and stand on the correlating number on the grid. The students can use this idea to work on numeration and number sets. This activity makes mathematics fun and incorporates movement into learning, as recommended by the brain-compatible research discussed previously.

How Many Do You See?

In this game, students are shown a numeral on a big picture card. The students then create a pattern to correspond to the numeral, using pictures of any object they wish. The group may then be asked questions about the pattern made. For example, a student who used pictures of human "stick men" to represent the numeral five might be asked how many legs the stick figures had altogether. This game assists in relating mathematics to the real world.

Addition Quizmo

This game has several steps. First, the teacher calls out a number between 0 and 5. The students place that many markers (use any type of concrete counters here) on a Bingo card. Then the teacher calls out another number, and the students next place that many additional markers on the card. The students then look on their Bingo cards for the total number represented by the markers, and place a marker over that number on the Bingo card if they find a match. Teachers may have the students explain their answers.

The Difference War

This game is the same as Addition Quizmo, but the students practice subtraction (referred to as "take away"). The Bingo cards and the markers are used for subtraction in the same fashion as in Addition Quizmo above.

Start From Five

This game is a combination of Addition Quizmo and The Difference War. The teacher always starts with a 5, and presents addition or subtraction problems (e.g.,

5 + 4 = _____, or 5 − 2 = _____). If the student's Bingo card has a match to the sum or the difference required, the student places a marker on the Bingo card.

Make Ten

This game uses a deck of cards for each student and a target card deck used by the teacher. A target card is flipped over. The students then turn over a card from their deck. If the sum of the two cards adds up to 10 (i.e., Make Ten), then the student moves the card off to the side. If the turned card does not make 10, then the card is placed back into the deck. The student who gets rid of his or her deck of cards first wins.

Using CRA in the Classroom

CRA focuses instructional planning on explicit instruction using three cognitive levels for instruction in math skills (Allsopp, 1999; Allsopp et al., 2008; Mancl et al., 2012). The first level, representing the lowest level of comprehension, is the concrete level. This involves the use of manipulative objects during instruction and the manipulative may be almost anything, including paper clips, circles divided into fractional parts, or even edibles such as an orange divided into its sections (Fahsl, 2007). The second level is the representational (or the semi-concrete) level, which uses representations of concrete objects in instruction, such as drawings of objects. The abstract instructional level uses no hand-on support materials.

In the concrete phase, teachers use manipulatives that can readily be configured to portray the concept being taught. These can be purchased (e.g., counters) or may be inexpensive, teacher-made materials. In this stage, the teacher would instruct students in how to manipulate the objects to simulate the math problem. Also, teachers should include worksheets of computer work in order to help students record the results of their problem solving. Most students in schools today are exposed to foam rubber sections of a "pie" and can recall examples of concrete instruction of this nature, particularly in the lower grades.

In the representational phase, teachers use visual representations of items rather than manipulatives. Students may be exposed to graphic representations on paper, as well as spaces to draw their own representations as needed. Mathematics teachers, over the years, have been highly creative in devising ways to represent mathematics problems, often pairing representations of problems with concrete manipulatives. Teaching Tip 4.3 presents an array of ideas from teachers focused on concrete and representational mathematics examples.

Teaching Tip 4.3   CRA Teaching Tips From Teachers

Counting Money: Coins With Stickers

One CRA technique that has been around for many years is the use of coins to teach counting change. Here are a couple of new and interesting variations on that theme. In counting change, students must be proficient at counting by fives, and many students are not. Thus, teachers may place stickers on the coins themselves to represent their value. Place a white sticker with a "1" written on it on the nickels, a sticker with a "2" on the dimes, and a sticker with a "5" on the quarters. Next, you should model for the students how to count change using this system. When presented with a pile of coins, students should separate them and begin counting with the large coins first (the coins with the highest number on the sticker—not the physically largest of the coins). Students are told to count by fives as many times as the coins' stickers indicate (e.g., for a quarter they would count by fives, five times, saying, "5, 10, 15, 20, 25"). Next, the students should be told to remember that amount, and then move to the next largest of the coins, and "count on," beginning with the first amount. Again they count by fives for as many times as that coin says. When they are finished with the quarter, dimes, and nickels, all they have to do is count by ones for the pennies. Often, students who seem unable to learn to count change in any other fashion can suddenly count by fives to reach correct sum. After the students are proficient in the strategy, the teacher should slowly phase out the use of stickers.

Hairy Coins

As another interesting variation on this theme, teachers can use "hairy money." Rather than stickers with numbers written on them, teachers may tape short hairs (perhaps using yarn if hair is not available) to large pictures of the coins on the dry erase board. The picture of a quarter would have five hairs on it, a dime two hairs, and a nickel one hair. Pennies have no hairs and are counted by counting ones.

Traditionally, both concrete manipulatives and pictorial representations have been frequently used in mathematics curricula in the primary grades and up through about Grade 3. As one example, both manipulatives and representations are used in most curricula to teach fractions in Grade 3. However, representational instruction is not often used in the general education mathematics classes beyond the lower grades for teaching more complex math skills. In one widely used math curriculum for elementary grades, this author recently found the semi-concrete representations of operations to be quite common in the Grade 1 teacher's manual. These representations were still present in the Grade 3 teacher's manual. However, by Grade 5, such pictorial representations had disappeared from the teacher's manual altogether.

This represents a significant problem in most modern math curricula, because the representational, or semi-concrete, phase can be critical for many students in the higher elementary and middle school grades who are experiencing difficulty in math. In the differentiated math class, teachers must make certain that they do not skip this stage simply because the curriculum materials do so. Rather, teachers should develop and provide examples of all types of math problems in a representational fashion. Further, each time a concrete or representational demonstration is given, the teacher (or another student) should verbally describe the representation, stressing the relationship to the math concept under discussion. Thus, in presenting either concrete or representational instruction, the teacher will likewise be presenting abstract instruction.

Today, there are a number of online resources that teachers can access for ideas on representational mathematics. For further assistance in mathematics readiness, early math skills, and CRA instruction, teachers should investigate the mathematics instructional tools at several websites. These are presented in Box 4.3.

BOX 4.3 ONLINE TEACHER ASSISTANCE TOOLS FOR EARLY MATH AND CRA

Math Fact Café—This website provides teachers with a tool to set up a math facts activity and other activities on the computer (mathfactcafe.com). This can be a quick, free way to generate computer-assisted activities that are specific to individual sets of math facts (e.g., three's times tables, or math fact division by six), and/or word problems at specific grade levels. The math fact problems typically involve presentation of 20 math facts, one at a time, with the opportunity for the student to type in his or her answer and check the accuracy of that answer. The software keeps a running tally of the percentage of corrects and errors, and after 20 problems are completed, the screen shows each problem with the incorrect problems corrected and highlighted. Graphics are not included, and the reward for a correct answer is presentation of a term such as *Awesome;* problems answered incorrectly result in presentation of terms such as *Bummer.* In general, for today's software this provides minimal stimulation for either corrects or errors, and this presentation may result in students being less than motivated to do this activity after the first few times. Still, this is one option for quick presentation of

(Continued)

(Continued)

computerized math facts. In addition, this presentation can provide teachers with data on daily problem completion in a variety of math tasks (math facts, word problems, etc.), and those data may then be used as daily performance-monitoring data in the response to intervention process.

Intervention Central—This website includes a free tool for generation of worksheets in early mathematics, among many other math intervention and assessment resources that teachers will find useful (www.interventioncentral.com). Also a wide variety of intervention strategies are presented such as incremental rehearsal of math facts, self-monitoring of mathematics performance, and math self-correction worksheets. Curriculum-based measurements in mathematics can also be generated at this website for targeted, highly specific mathematics skills in all of the whole number operations, and combination worksheets.

SuperKids.com—This website has a worksheet-generation tool for much more complex mathematics work in fractions, prime numbers, percentages, order of operations, exponents, rounding, and factorials. In the lower grades teachers can generate worksheets on telling time, greater than/less than, and odd or even numbers.

MathVids—This website is intended for teachers working with students who struggle in mathematics (www.coedu.usf.edu/main/departments/sped/mathvids/index.html). This site provides video models of teachers using research-supported instructional techniques in real-world math classes, working with struggling learners. Teaching plans and various instructional modifications are also presented, along with a special section devoted to cognitive learning strategies in mathematics.

National Library of Virtual Manipulatives—The National Library of Virtual Manipulatives presents many manipulative objects that you may purchase, all of which are sorted by grade level (nlvm.usu.edu/en/nav/siteinfo.html). These are categorized for various math topics, based on the National Council of Teachers of Mathematics content standards. You can find an online abacus, online fraction parts, a grapher for exploring functions, and many other tools that range across the grade levels and facilitate CRA instruction.

Research on CRA

Research has strongly supported the use of CRA for students across the elementary and middle grades (Allsopp, 1997; Allsopp et al., 2008: Fahsl, 2007; Harris et al., 1995; L. Jordan et al., 1998; Mancl et al., 2012). One study by L. Jordan and colleagues (1998) used the CRA method to teach three groups of students in a fourth-grade inclusive general education class. The study included 125 students, some with learning disabilities, some average students, and some gifted students, who were taught a lesson on fractions. The results demonstrated that CRA produced significantly better learning and maintenance for *all students* than the traditional textbook-based instructional method. This study found that the CRA method was effective in teaching students fraction identification, comparison, equivalence, and computation using fractions, and teachers should note that this very content has been strongly emphasized by the Common Core State Standards in Mathematics. Further, the students also maintained these new skills in posttests one and two weeks after the end of instruction. These results suggest that CRA can be used successfully in the general education classroom to help all students, including students with mathematics learning problems, to master difficult math concepts.

The study described above is critical because of its demonstration of the efficacy of CRA for students with learning disabilities. Students with learning disabilities, the single largest group of students with disabilities, are also the students with disabilities who are most likely to be included in the general education math curriculum. Thus, in the differentiated math class, teachers must find ways to include these students in the activities. Yet these students often struggle with mathematics, and many display certain learning characteristics that amplify difficulties in various areas of math. For example, many students with learning disabilities exhibit visual and auditory perception problems that negatively affect mastery of math. In general, students with learning disabilities will also have trouble reading the math problems or using highly specialized mathematics language such as the language of fractions (i.e., with terms such as *numerator, denominator, mixed numbers,* and *tenths*). The use of CRA can foster efficient learning of math concepts and provide these learners with strategies to solve problems in every math area (L. Jordan et al., 1998; Mancl et al., 2012).

> *Research has strongly supported the use of CRA for students across the elementary and middle grades.*

CRA in the Higher Grades

Researchers now urge teachers to employ CRA in higher grades (Allsopp et al., 2008; Witzel et al., 2008). Typically, in the abstract phase of instruction, mathematics problems without any representations are used, but such worksheets also can be constructed to include space on the sheet for students to develop their own representation of the problem. Further, teachers should encourage students to do so, if such visualization and drawing helps students better understand the math problem.

Again, all math curricula include abstract problems as the final assessment of skill mastery, and such abstract thinking should be the teacher's overall goal. However, many students need representational instruction in higher grade levels. Box 4.4 presents several examples.

BOX 4.4 USING CRA IN THE HIGHER GRADES

Sample Semi-Concrete Math Problems for Elementary Grades

1. Jennie had $82 but she owed $31 to Jonathan. After paying that debt, how much did Jennie have left?

Jennie's Money	Money She Gave to Jonathan
$$$$$ $$$$$ $$$$$ $$$$$	$$$$$ $$$$$ $$$$$ $$$$$
$$$$$ $$$$$ $$$$$ $$$$$	$$$$$ $$$$$ $
$$$$$ $$$$$ $$$$$ $$$$$	
$$$$$ $$$$$ $$$$$ $$$$$	
$$	

$82   Minus $31 equals _____

To solve this problem, the students should draw a circle around the dollar signs in Jennie's money that are equivalent to the money she gave to Jonathan. They will then count the remaining funds, using the groups of fives.

2. Here is a sample of a regrouping problem for three-digit subtraction: $324 - 245 =$ _____?

First, 3 100s, 2 tens, and 4 ones can be shown like this:

////////// ////////// ////////// ////////// ////////// ////////// ////////// ////////// ////
////////// ////////// ////////// ////////// ////////// //////////
////////// ////////// ////////// ////////// ////////// //////////
////////// ////////// ////////// ////////// ////////// //////////
////////// ////////// ////////// ////////// ////////// //////////

Next, we need to picture 2 100s, 4 tens, and 5 ones:

////////// //////////   ////////// //////////   ////////// //////////
////////// //////////   ////////// //////////   ////////// ////////// ////
////////// //////////   ////////// //////////
////////// //////////   ////////// //////////

Beginning with the digit on the left, the student must regroup the top number and group marks in the problem in the tens and ones places as follows:

3 100s and 2 tens and 4 ones =
2 100s and 11 tens and 14 ones

/////////// /////////// /////////// /////////// /////////// /////////// /////////// /////////// ////

/////////// /////////// /////////// /////////// /////////// ///////////

/////////// /////////// /////////// /////////// /////////// ///////////

/////////// /////////// /////////// /////////// /////////// ///////////

/////////// /////////// /////////// /////////// /////////// ///////////

Next, the student will cross out the number of tally marks equal to the subtrahend and then calculate the remaining tally marks.

Using CRA

Multiplication Tables and Popsicle Sticks!

One teacher developed a great way to represent multiplication using Popsicle sticks to represent the lower times tables. For example, in teaching the three's times tables, students may use three sticks to make a triangle on their desk. Then they count the sides (which equal three). They should then say, "One triangle with three sides equals three Popsicle sticks," and then shorten that to "One times three equals three."

Next, they add another triangle and count all of the sides (which equal six). They would say, "Two triangles with three sides each equal six sticks," or "Two times three equals six." They continue this process until they have ten triangles on their desks, representing the entire math fact family.

The same activity can be repeated using squares to represent multiples of four and stars to represent fives and sixes. This activity involves many brain processes in the sense that students are manipulating objects, repeating verbal equations, and visually seeing the demonstration of the times tables. Thus, this activity would involve a variety of multiple intelligences (bodily/kinesthetic, spatial, linguistic, logical/mathematical).

Math Facts on the Floor!

One fun movement game involves use of a large piece of construction plastic (a shower curtain will do nicely). You should cut a piece of plastic in a square approximately six feet on a side. Across the top and down the side, write the numbers 0 through 9, thus forming a number grid. You may wish to station a student at each corner of the grid to keep it from moving. Next, you call out a math fact problem, and pairs of students (or individuals) have to move to the appropriate square and

(Continued)

(Continued)

call out the answer. For example, if a teacher calls out "5 × 6 = ?" the student will hop first on "5" then move down to the intersection with the sixes, while saying "5 × 6 = 30!" Having students work in pairs offers students the opportunity to discuss their answer before shouting it out. This is a great tear out activity, and can be played by as few as four students or as many as an entire class.

Teaching Percentages

Students are often most motivated when they see that their educational activities can help them in real-world situations, such as shopping. In most shopping experiences, students confront percentages, and teachers can use shopping experiences as a teaching tool. To set up a lesson on percentages, teachers may bring in some old clothes on hangers and create a "Boutique." With only twelve to twenty items in the store, students can be challenged to learn percentages. First, place a price on each item and then place a percentage discount tag on each item. The discount tags could read "10% off," "25% off," and so forth. Each student will be responsible for recording a description of all pieces, the original price, and the final price after the discount.

For a tiered version of this activity, have students in one tear-out group compute the final price, as described above, but add the percentage associated with the local tax on the item. Another idea would be to compute prices for a grocery list, complete with multiple items and percentage of tax for each.

Further, although many students do not do well in math across the grade levels, curriculum materials companies have continued to present abstract problems in the upper grades without appropriate representational examples. Thus, many teachers may be reluctant to include the representations of math problems described here beyond a certain grade level. Again, while CRA problems have always provided the basis for most mathematics instruction in kindergarten and the lower grades, teachers today are urged to employ representational instruction in higher grade levels throughout the public school years. Modern theorists have provided examples of representational instruction for introductory algebra (Allsopp, 1999; Witzel et al., 2008). An algebraic example of CRA instruction is presented in Box 4.5.

BOX 4.5   TEACHING ALGEBRA WITH CRA

A CRA Example in Algebra

Imagine solving for "a" when teaching the algebraic equation $2a + 3a + 5 = 25$ (Allsopp, 1999). This can be represented by physical objects as follows. A saucer or paper plate can represent "a"; thus, two paper plates would represent "2a." Put two paper plates together on a desk. Cut a piece of tag board into strips that are one inch wide and three inches long. Use two of these to make a cross to represent the addition sign. Then place three plates in a group to represent "3a."

Next you will need some smaller counters (perhaps plastic counters) to illustrate the "+ 5" in the equation. Place two more strips to represent the second addition sign, and then place five counters to represent the "5." Finally, place two strips of tag board parallel to represent an equal sign. Your example would then look like this:

Next, you will need to introduce the concept of a balance beam to "balance" the equation in the middle. The equal sign represents the fulcrum, and your balance beam will look like this:

$$\frac{2a+3a+5 \qquad\qquad = \qquad\qquad 25}{\triangle}$$

When we take away five counters from one side, the beam is unbalanced, and will look like this:

We'll correct that by taking away five counters from the right side also, and then the beam will look like this:

$$\frac{2a+3a \qquad\qquad = \qquad\qquad 20}{\triangle}$$

Next we'll add the 2a and the 3a to make 5a, but since we took nothing away, the beam is still balanced:

$$\frac{5a \qquad\qquad = \qquad\qquad 20}{\triangle}$$

Finally, we'll divide both sides by five to find the value of "a." Thus, the value of "a" is 4.

The CRA Differentiation Tactic

In differentiated classrooms, teachers need access to a wide variety of math strategies, and the use of concrete or representational instruction can assist many students who are currently struggling in math. Moreover, CRA can provide a variety of tear-out activities across the elementary and middle school grade levels. In planning the mathematics lesson, teachers may provide exclusively abstract examples to some students, such as modeling a math problem on the interactive whiteboard, or referring students to a video for that type of math problem, whereas for other students teachers might provide both the model problem, coupled with a graphic or representational example of the problem. Such differentiation of instruction will, effectively, assist many struggling students in the mathematics class, while allowing the average and advanced students to move forward at their own pace. As is apparent from the examples above, the representational stage of learning is now being employed in much higher grades, and the research on the use of this tactic is strongly supportive (Allsopp, 1999; Fahsl, 2007; Harris et al., 1995; L. Jordan et al., 1998; Marsh & Cooke, 1996; Shaw-Jing et al., 2000; Witzel et al., 2008). Clearly, teachers who wish to move into differentiated instruction should implement instruction using this CRA tactic, tailoring the instruction to each specific student's level of understanding. This is differentiated instruction at its best!

TECHNOLOGY OPTIONS FOR DIFFERENTIATED MATHEMATICS INSTRUCTION

In the 21st century mathematics class, various technology options exist for mathematics instruction that were not available only a few years ago, and many of these are becoming critically important differentiated instructional tools (Bender & Waller, 2013; eSchool News, 2012a). In fact, within the Common Core, the Standards for Mathematical Practice specifically emphasize the use of technological tools in mathematics classes (see Standard 5 in Box 1.1, in Chapter 1 of this book), and these tools continue to evolve almost daily. Of course, many schools are still struggling to provide Wi-Fi availability in each classroom, and/or with computer/instructional tablet availability for most students. However, almost all schools are gearing up for widespread Wi-Fi, and many schools are using BYOD (bring your own device) initiatives to get tablets or laptops into the hands of the students. Thus, technology is likely to play a key role in teachers' efforts to differentiate instruction in mathematics for the next several decades of the 21st century.

> *Technology is likely to play a key role in teachers' efforts to differentiate instruction in mathematics for the next several decades of the 21st century.*

Of course, the amazing array of newly developed software programs, apps, and other instructional tools is much too extensive to describe in this book, and the reader might wish to consult Bender and Waller (2013) for more information on recommended technology applications for the 21st century mathematics class. However, in this context, it is important to note several instructional, tech-based tools that are particularly useful in mathematics, and this chapter, along with subsequent chapters, will describe technology applications and tools that can greatly assist in differentiating the math class.

As noted in Chapter 1, many students have significant mathematics anxieties, and such fears are likely to hamper those students in their mathematics classes, even in the earliest grade levels. This is another reason many mathematics teachers, in particular, are employing various 21st century teaching tools; these technologies often help to alleviate students' fears of mathematics. Below I describe the use of avatars for mathematical explorations in the digital environment, as well as educational games for mathematics instruction. These modern instructional tools provide a much less threatening way to teach mathematics for young students, and they typically result in higher levels of engagement with the mathematics curriculum (Baird, 2012; International Society for Technology in Education [ISTE], 2010; Maton, 2011; Stansbury, 2012a; 2012b). Of course, this ultimately leads to higher achievement in mathematics.

> *Many mathematics teachers are employing various 21st century technology-based teaching tools in order to alleviate students' fears of mathematics.*

Avatars for Differentiating Math Instruction

Nothing can be less threatening for many young children than a friendly cartoon character, so it seems quite reasonable to use self-generated, animated characters for teaching mathematics. An avatar is a character that represents oneself or someone else in a digital environment, and self-created avatars can be used to teach mathematics (or other subjects) within the digital world. Today, many teachers find that their students love using avatars while they study math and other subjects (Stansbury, 2012b). The creation of an avatar involves having a student create a cartoon or digital image of himself or herself, and then using that image to individually explore mathematics concepts. Of course, this can be a highly engaging way to explore those concepts, since visual representations of mathematics concepts certainly grab students' attention, and avatar-based activities often seem more like "play" for many students. Of the wide array of new tech-tools for teaching, use of avatars in primary and elementary math is

> *An avatar is a character that represents oneself or someone else in a digital environment, and it can be used to do activities in mathematics within the digital world.*

the one tool I recommend most often, simply because kids learn to love mathematics when taught in this manner.

Avatars and CRA Instruction

Use of avatars for mathematics instruction compliments, quite nicely, the representational or CRA emphasis in mathematics instruction that was discussed previously. In a digital environment, students cannot only construct representations of mathematics problems, they can use their personal avatar to manipulate those representations! While representational examples of mathematics are certainly encouraged, as discussed above, avatars coupled with representational math have an even stronger effect, since the representational image actually includes the students themselves! Early anecdotal reports from teachers indicate that these animation activities are quite powerful. In fact, animation might well be considered a universal language that has the ability to reach virtually all students, including students with varying ability levels in mathematics (eSchool News, 2011; Stansbury, 2012b).

Further, allowing students to learn through animation of their own characters lowers the intimidation of the mathematics curriculum and provides an avenue for learning in a nonthreatening environment. As discussed in Chapter 1, getting through math anxiety is critical for many young learners, and avatars can provide another tool to accomplish that. Finally, many teachers have reported that students are much more engaged and retain more content material when they are able to creatively express themselves through animation of their own avatars in the classroom, in the context of their academic work (eSchool News, 2011).

Voki in the Math Class

While some teachers may feel somewhat intimidated with the idea of having students create virtual selves in the classroom, there are various computer programs available to facilitate that, and these will help make animation a reality in the mathematics classroom. Voki is an online animation tool that allows students to create an avatar for themselves and use that in ongoing class instruction (www.voki.com). Voki is one of the easiest animation programs to use, and teachers can experiment with it free. Like most animation programs, Voki allows students to create their own avatar and then write dialogue for their avatar to speak. To get a sense of how avatars (avatars are called *vokis* in this

> *Allowing students to learn through animation of their own characters lowers the intimidation of the mathematics curriculum and provides an avenue for learning in a nonthreatening environment.*

software) can fit within the curriculum, I recommend that teachers view an introductory video on the Voki Classroom, available on YouTube (www.youtube.com/embed/ao9KQltMkP0).

Although the most basic Voki service is free, this basic level of service is funded by ads, which pop up on the side of the computer screen. The next level of service, Voki Classroom (see Figure 4.1), is a subscription service available for educators. For around $2.50 a month, a teacher is given access to all standard Voki features as well as a system to manage vokis created by each student in the mathematics class. Once a teacher has purchased this level of service, he or she can create student accounts, manage mathematics assignments, and receive unlimited tech support through the website, while having each student in the class create his or her own voki. In this level of service, there are no ads displayed.

The possible uses of Voki-based avatars in the mathematics class are virtually unlimited. For example, in one mathematics lesson plan for sixth graders available on the Voki website, teachers are encouraged to have their students use their avatars to create a description and example of a mathematics term from the lesson. Students can use their avatar to explain concepts in mathematics to each other, or to the entire class, and having students (via their avatars) actually teach about a term represents a higher level of understanding that construct. In fact, communication about mathematics is a strong emphasis within the Common Core, and vokis can facilitate such communication.

Figure 4.1 Voki Classroom

Source: © 2012 Oddcast Inc.

Avatars can be used to practice automaticity in math facts in the primary and elementary grades. Working together, older students can create scripts to explain entire mathematics problems, and all of these avatar-based explanations can then be uploaded to a class website, blog, or wiki, thus creating a catalogue of review problems for the class.

> *Voki is an excellent animation-based teaching tool and will serve virtually all teachers in mathematics at every level.*

As part of the Voki Classroom, teachers can outline a mathematics assignment on the website for students to complete. Once students have completed their assignment with their avatar, the teacher can go online, access each student's avatar, and evaluate the work. Teachers will be able to manage several different classrooms on the account, as well as different lessons and assignments for the same class. In short, Voki is an excellent animation-based teaching tool and will serve virtually all teachers in mathematics at every level.

Differentiated Instruction Using Vokis

As the explanation above suggests, Voki creates many avenues for differentiating mathematics instruction. One fairly obvious option is differentiated requirements for student presentations. For students who are intimidated by presenting mathematics content in front of the class—a fear often resulting from fear of negative feedback or a general lack of self-confidence in mathematics—presentations for the class can be done through their avatar. Avatars, such as those created within Voki, take the pressure off of the speaking portion of the mathematics explanation, since the student will have developed and recorded that presentation in advance. Thus, this teaching idea will allow all students to focus more directly on the math concepts under study.

Teachers can also vary the Voki creation assignments in mathematics to accommodate various learning styles and student strengths. Students struggling in math material may have modified creation requirements; those students may merely be required to create a relatively simple, 30-second avatar presentation on a mathematics term, while other students might be required to create longer, more in-depth content.

Peer tutoring avatars can be created and used in math classes as well, by having higher-level students create "peer tutor" explanations of math constructs for other students. This is an excellent differentiation tactic for both the advanced students and the students with more learning challenges, since the skills associated with synthesizing mathematics content and explaining that material gives the tutors more time to analyze the math constructs or problems under study. Once the avatar explanations are uploaded to class blogs or wikis, the students who need that explanation of content may access the avatars and get clarification on concepts exactly when such clarification is needed. Again, they are able to access these avatars and hear the review material and never have to fear asking questions in the math class itself.

Student avatars can even assist in formative assessment in mathematics. Students needing extra assistance might be required to create avatars to help them review the material and think through the mathematics problems that are causing confusion. In that context, they would create the dialogue for their avatar to use in explaining the concept. Once that avatar-based content is uploaded, the teacher can access that information, listen to the student's explanation, and find the areas where the student needs extra help. This process, again, allows the student to receive individualized help in a nonthreatening environment.

Finally, using avatars as part of the teacher presentation also helps differentiate for various learning styles. Students who are more visually oriented will benefit from being able to see the avatar versus simply listening to a teacher discuss the math problem, and in many cases, students pay more attention to a teacher's avatar than they do to the teacher during such explanations. Like the student-created avatars, the teacher-created avatars can also be loaded onto blogs or wikis so that students can access them at a later date, both in class and at home, for review.

Games for Differentiating Math Instruction

In addition to personal avatars for math instruction, computer-based games provide many additional, technology-based differentiation opportunities for the mathematics class. Instructional gaming was by 2013 coming into its own as a viable instructional method, and mathematics teachers were quickly boarding the educational gaming bandwagon (Baird, 2012; Hudson, 2012; A. Miller, 2011a; Sheehy, 2011; Takahashi, 2012). Of course, teachers have used various game formats, including both game boards and technology-based games, for decades. However, as the commercial video gaming market has reached new highs in sales, sales that are well into the billions of dollars, educators have begun to use tech-based games to teach important content such as mathematics (Baird, 2012; A. Miller, 2011b, 2012). Many websites present educational games in a wide variety of mathematics areas, and some of the most frequently used sites for mathematics games are described in Box 4.6.

BOX 4.6   WEBSITES AND APPS FEATURING EDUCATIONAL GAMES FOR MATHEMATICS

Math Playground—This website provides free mathematics games for learning subject content across the grade levels (www.mathplayground.com/games.html). Students need to sign in and create a profile. The one or more players (up to four) can play the specific math game selected. A number of videos on specific mathematical topics for the elementary grades, similar to Khan Academy (as described in Chapter 3), are also provided, making this website useful in flipping one's instruction.

BrainPOP—Another website that is used increasingly in lower grades is BrainPOP (www.brainpop.com). BrainPOP is a fee-based site and uses animated characters to teach curriculum-based content in a variety of areas, including math, science, social studies, English, engineering and technology, arts and music, and health. The site includes a free short tutorial video, as well as extensive movies, quizzes, experiments, timelines, and activities. The content is aligned to, and searchable by, state standards but not by Common Core standards (as of February 2012). These instructional activities are appropriate and recommended for all grades, and in particular, the site features 45 games (click on the BrainPOP Jr. icon) for kindergarten through Grade 3.

SoftSchools.com—This is another website that provides free online math games for primary and elementary students (www.softschools.com), including operations, estimation, fractions, decimals, and number sense. While many activities are free, other services are provided via this website on a subscription basis. At this site, teachers can also generate free math worksheets for a variety of topics including place value, statistics, decimals, conversions, and other topics, up through and including algebra.

JumpStart World of Learning—This is an integrated alternative reality world in which students (kindergarten through Grade 2) interact with their environment, and in that process learn reading, math, and critical-thinking skills (www.jumpstart.com/school). The game environment encourages interactive play while building important educational skills. It is designed for use by teachers and/or home-schooling parents. Teachers can access and review each child's (or the entire class's) progress through a classroom management system. Each child's alternative world is completely personalized with individual photos, artwork, achievement badges, and gems. The characters and environments change repeatedly throughout the game experience, reacting to a child's progress through the world.

Pop Math Lite—This is an award-winning app that can turn any smartphone into a mathematics game focused on basic operations (https://itunes.apple.com/app/pop-math-lite/id303258911?mt=8). Many parents have their children use this app, so teachers can expect students to show up in their primary class with experience using this program.

Many refer to the increasing use of educational games in the classroom as the "gamification" of the school curriculum (Baird, 2012). While mathematics games of the 1980s tended to emphasize procedural processes in mathematics, many of today's gaming options represent deeper understanding of mathematical processes, as well as applications of those processes, two skill sets that are emphasized within the Common Core (Magee, 2013). The term gamification has been used to stress that all of these levels of mathematics—procedural, deep conceptual, and application—are now expected within any modern curriculum. One high-profile proponent of educational games for instruction is Bill Gates, who views gaming as the basis for most educational endeavors within the next decade. In fact, the early research data do suggest that gaming and/or simulation scenarios are highly effective instructional tools for mathematics content (Baird, 2012; ISTE, 2010; Maton, 2011), though, like most early math games, that research tended to focus on procedural understanding rather than mathematics applications. Still, every mathematics teacher today simply must consider gaming options as one of the emerging 21st century teaching techniques.

Today, many games have been developed specifically for teaching mathematics in the primary and elementary grades, as well as the later grade levels, and some of these games are available free of charge. For example, PEMDAS Blaster (teaching the order of mathematical operations), and Algebra Meltdown are designed to teach a wide range of mathematics skills, and like many recently published games, these games are aligned with the Common Core State Standards in mathematics (see www.mangahigh.com). The games at this site are targeted for students ages 7 to 16.

> *"Gamification" is the trend toward teaching virtually all curricular content in the context of technology-based, educational games.*

These educational games all stipulate a goal for students to achieve by repeatedly practicing the core mathematics concept, and teachers can track the progress of their students using their own login and passwords. Teachers reported anecdotally that these exciting mathematics games resulted in some students playing math games long after school was over, and sometimes well into the night (see the website above for several teacher reviews). Certainly, any mathematics teacher should take advantage of games for instruction, such as those on this website, and access some educational games that will motivate students to learn mathematics.

While educators have recently used either laptops or tablets as the platform for tech-based gaming, many games exist for alternative Internet platforms. For example, Math Mate is a free game for rehearsal of mathematics skills that works on any Android smartphone (see www.android 4schools.com/2012/04/03/math-mate-practice-math-skills-on-your

-android-phone/). Two modes of play are available, practice and challenge, and the challenge mode times a student's performance and ranks that against other players. Within each of those modes, there are three levels of play, with skills ranging from addition/subtraction up through more complicated multiplication and division problems. Teachers can certainly use free games such as these if smartphones, or any similar tech platform, are available. Further, math teachers should share info on these games with parents, and request that parents encourage their children to play such games on the smartphone from time to time. Personally, I've seen many young children playing such games on smartphones while their parents shopped or merely waited for a doctor's appointment.

Alternative Reality Gaming for Differentiation

The newest innovation in educational games involves the creation of individual student interactions in a digital world, or "alternative reality." This is referred to as alternative reality gaming, or ARGs (Maton, 2011). Thus, ARGs are games played in the real world as well as in the digital world. In ARGs, students select an avatar, and that character serves as an action figure that represents them throughout the online, digital game environment (or in the "alternative world"). In addition, the students themselves often go on "quests," completing mathematics assignments in the real world.

> *Teachers reported anecdotally that these exciting mathematics games resulted in some students playing math games long after school was over.*

Of course, a number of ARGs have been developed recently for educational use in various settings, ranging from public education to the United States military (Maton, 2011). In fact, both industry and the United States armed services use ARGs for teaching everything from individual combat tactics in confined spaces (e.g., city terrain) to tank warfare, to airborne fighter combat. While ARGs in industry and the military are still being explored, this ARG trend may represent nothing less than a fundamental paradigm shift in the future of education generally, and mathematics and science education in particular.

As one example, the ARG Math Trek involves students using photographs and mathematics as virtual parts of the game, and their hometown or community as the physical basis for the game (http://naturalmath.wikispaces.com/Math+Trek). This ARG involves sending students on quests that require them to notice patterns, mathematical relationships, and abstract concepts embedded within their town or community. You may recall that students' ability to demonstrate understanding of mathematical patterns was emphasized in the Standards of Mathematical Practice (see

Standard 7, Box 1.1, in Chapter 1). This game is applicable for all ages. In November 2012, mathematicians in the North Carolina Natural Math Club were making the game up week by week, and inviting mathematics teachers worldwide to participate. Teachers are invited to start such a group for the game, and add a link to this webpage for the game.

To sense the potential of ARGs, teachers might imagine the entire mathematics curriculum, at some point in the near future, taught via educational games and ARGs! While curricula in most areas have not developed to that point as of 2013, teachers should, nevertheless, explore gaming and ARGs that might be appropriate for their mathematics content, in order to remain current with 21st century classroom instructional methods. Games and ARGs are quite likely to dominate instruction in the

> *ARGs involve the creation of an alternative reality in which avatars play a role, while also learning from the physical world, in order to learn mathematics content during the game.*

mathematics classes in the near future, and teachers today should certainly begin to use mathematics instructional games and/or ARGs as they become available.

Advantages of Mathematics Games and ARGs

There are several advantages to teaching mathematics with games and ARGs. Perhaps the most important single advantage is that today's students are highly motivated to complete schoolwork when the mathematics content is presented in game formats (Hudson, 2012; ISTE, 2010; A. Miller, 2011a, 2011b; Takahashi, 2012). As all teachers recognize, many students prefer gaming as a preferred after-school activity as well as an in-class expec-

> *Imagine a future curriculum in which all subject areas are taught via educational games and ARGs!*

tation. For this reason, the early data on gaming or ARGs in the classroom, though mostly anecdotal, does suggest that games and ARGs are effective instructional tools in a variety of subject areas including mathematics (Ash, 2011; eSchool News, 2012b; ISTE, 2010; Maton, 2011).

Next, gaming as a tool in the mathematics class provides an opportunity to alleviate many of the fears and anxiety associated with math for some students. In general, instruction delivered via educational games is viewed as fun by most students, as reported by many teachers using games in the classroom (Baird, 2012). Compared to traditional instruction, games seem much less threatening, and this will alleviate many of the math anxieties that have been described over the years.

> *The early data, though mostly anecdotal, suggest that games and educational simulations are effective instructional tools in mathematics.*

Additionally, many educational games and ARGs are interactive, and interaction can greatly enrich the learning experience in mathematics. In fact, interactive games allow many students to play the game together, and thus master the content collectively, adding a social element to their learning. Further, depending on the game, that type of instructional competition can involve students in different locations worldwide. Imagine the impact of having American students, Canadian students, students from London, and students in France compete in a simulation game focused on import/export economics between North America and Europe! Interaction such as this, including the option of worldwide instructional interactions on mathematics topics, increases student engagement and can be quite motivating for students. While such options can be somewhat difficult to arrange and manage, the payoff, in terms of students' interest in and excitement for mathematics, is high. Further, instructional gaming provides the promise of more easily arranged options such as this in the near future.

Another advantage of modern games is the richness of the video content, and the similarity between video-rich educational games and other noneducational gaming content. As almost any parent realizes, kids love video games in which the quality of the video content is enhanced, and the video presentations become more real with each passing month. Most modern games come complete with highly complex video presentations, and such visualization options can boost mathematics learning. Further, the complexity of this video content makes these games seem similar to activities that many students today choose to do, via their home gaming consoles. Gaming is quite enjoyable for many students and that seems to be the main reason that games increase student engagement with the mathematics content, which, in turn, increases achievement (eSchool News, 2012b; Sheehy, 2011).

However, the debate on the effects of instructional gaming is still ongoing, and one caution on the use of gaming in the classroom is related to these high levels of student engagement (eSchool News, 2012b; Shah, 2012). Engagement resulting from computer games is often so high that it may, at some point, become a negative effect of gaming. This has been noted in several Asian cultures, where noneducational games have become much more entrenched, and in some countries, some psychologists view gaming as "addictive" to young minds (*Frontline*, 2010). Of course, it is critical to note that this concern is related to noneducational, commercial games that are played strictly for personal enjoyment, rather than educational gaming. To date, over-engagement with game content, to the exclusion of everything else in life, has not become a major concern relative to educational games used in the classroom, and with this caution noted, instructional gaming in mathematics does hold many advantages for students, as noted previously.

Teachers need to be aware of the concern noted above, as parents might share that concern with the impact of gaming. Still, in spite of this caution related to noneducational gaming, teachers should certainly explore use of educational gaming in the classroom as one differentiated instructional technique.

> *The debate on the effects of gaming is still ongoing, and there may be negative effects of gaming, including over-engagement with the game to the exclusion of everything else.*

Teaching Tip 4.4 presents several suggestions for teachers who may be just beginning to use educational games for teaching mathematics.

Teaching Tip 4.4   Guidelines for Using Games and ARGs in the Mathematics Classroom

Carefully Select Several Games or Virtual World Websites

Many websites offer educational games for content at various grade levels; some are free and others require a nominal monthly fee. The websites below will provide you with some gaming resources for your class, and for more selections, we suggest that you do a Google or Bing search for indicators such as "educational games primary elementary mathematics."

www.funbrain.com	primarygames.com	funschool.kaboose.com
www.knowledgeadventure.com	pbskids.org	arcademics.com
www.kidsplaygames.com	http://www.sheppardsoftware.com	
www.edutopia.org		

1. Match Games/ARGs to Your Mathematics Content!

Of course, finding educational games is merely the beginning. Teachers should carefully select games that match the content under study, as well as the Common Core State Standards and/or state standards that may apply. While gaming is a great activity that students are supposed to enjoy, teachers must select games to maximize student learning, and some games have much richer content than others. Also, teachers must consider their use of the game. Is the game to be used for initial instruction or practice of previously learned content? Different uses can inform which games or ARGs teachers might use in the classroom.

While we presented several examples above of teachers creating educational games, we generally do not recommend that, unless a teacher is highly fluent with

(Continued)

(Continued)

technology. Further, we do not recommend that most teachers attempt to "import" content into games, as that can be quite complex, and teachers typically need highly developed technology skills to do so. Rather, we recommend that teachers attempt to draw the natural lessons from the game content itself (Sheehy, 2011), and then relate those to the Common Core or state standards that might apply in a given instructional unit.

2. Preview the Game

Of course, teachers must preview any game or ARG selected for classroom use; in many cases teachers simply play the game they have selected one time. This preview will allow the teacher to determine possible uses of the game and, in many cases, set up different levels of the game for students at various academic levels. While a preview is essential initially, once a teacher begins to know and trust the games available at a given website, he or she might be able to merely implement those games and activities without a preview, or use other resources from that same location with increased confidence.

3. Explore Fee-Based Games/Sites

While many math games are free (see www.mathfactcafe.com for examples), I also recommend teachers explore various fee-based websites (e.g., www.brainpop.com or www.softschools.com). Fee-based sites for mathematics games that involve a set monthly access fee, or a per student fee that is set for the year, are the best locations for teachers to use, as those costs can be predicted in advance. School administrators may be able to find some funds to cover these costs, but many teachers likewise have found games so useful that they occasionally pay these fees themselves. In most cases, one-class subscription fees are nominal.

4. Relate Game Themes to Nongame Content

Games and ARGs are most effective as educational tools in mathematics when the relationship between game activities and the math content under study in the instructional unit is highlighted. While some games present these relationships well, others do not, and it is ultimately the teacher's role to demonstrate for the students the relationship between the game and the content under study. Thus, for many games, some type of post-game activity that reinforces the mathematics concepts is appropriate.

5. Teach Cyber Safety!

Instructional games and ARGs provide a wonderful opportunity to teach students about cyber safety and appropriate uses of the Internet. Interactive gaming is likely to become a large segment of education in the future—but student safety should always be paramount—and various guidelines have been presented for educators. Teachers may wish to see the "Appropriate Internet Use" policy described by this author (see Bender & Waller, 2013).

Differentiated Instruction With Educational Games

Educational games and ARGs offer many options for differentiating instruction. First, in instructional gaming, students are required to act more independently than in traditional activities in the mathematics classroom, so students become much more active in the learning process. Given the student selection options built into most educational games, students tend to differentiate themselves within these gaming scenarios by their selections and choices within the game, particularly in ARGs that mix online and real-world activities. Linguistically talented students, for example, are likely to select game activities that focus on language-based learning options for mathematics, whereas students with a visual learning strength will select more visually based mathematics activities.

Next, in setting up the parameters of the mathematics games, teachers can create many differentiation options for their students. Depending on the game, many factors can be preset such as the activities within the game, the level of play selected for and by various students, or the pace of the math activities. In making those choices with individual students in mind, teachers can differentiate the mathematics content and the processes within the game. Thus, differentiating the instruction during mathematical gaming is not difficult, and students are almost always highly motivated to participate in these types of highly differentiated mathematics activities.

> *In gaming environments, students are forced to act more independently than in a traditional mathematics classroom environment, and thus, they are typically much more active in the learning process.*

ERRORLESS LEARNING FOR DIFFERENTIATING MATHEMATICS INSTRUCTION

The research on learning and the human brain—specifically the "emotional brain" basis of learning as described in Chapter 1—has emphasized that children require high levels of success in order to be motivated to continue their work in any subject area. Of course, there is no area of the curriculum in which this is truer than in mathematics, because of the negative emotional baggage associated with math as discussed previously. Psychologists generally indicate that students need to succeed at least 85% of the time in order for learning to take place. Given that emphasis on high levels of success, some theorists several decades ago began to experiment with instructional techniques that resulted in high levels of success and few errors on the part of the students (Schuster, Stevens, & Doak, 1990; Wolery, Bailey, & Sugai, 1988; Wolery, Cybriwsky, Gast, &

Boyle-Gast, 1991). Those theorists postulated that learning would be less painful and more fun if it could be constructed to result in almost no errors. The resulting instructional procedures became known as errorless learning procedures (Wolery et al., 1988; Wolery et al., 1991).

> *Learning would be less painful and more fun if it could be constructed to result in almost no errors.*

Like all behavioral instructional procedures, errorless learning is dependent upon accurate daily recording of the number of corrects and the number of errors a student achieves during the mathematics lesson. That record of success is necessary in order to assure that the student is learning the material in an errorless or nearly errorless fashion.

Wolery et al., (1988) presented a number of reasons for using errorless learning procedures. First, errorless learning is very efficient in that time is saved. This procedure usually results in mastery of material in fewer instructional sessions than are required when other instructional procedures are used. Also, for general education math classes, the errorless procedures may be used in a peer buddy fashion, making this a great tear-out or differentiated math activity, as well as a mainline instructional activity for everyone in the class.

Researchers suggest that errorless learning promotes positive social interaction between students. Using these procedures, very few errors are made, and much less social stigma is associated with any errors that do occur (Wolery et al., 1988). This makes the errorless learning procedure very effective as an interpersonal learning format in a differentiated math class. Also, errorless procedures should certainly be considered an option of choice for special education students working in inclusive mathematics classrooms. For these reasons, teachers should consider using errorless learning for many types of instruction in early math.

The Prompting Tactic

A prompt is defined as teacher or peer tutor assistance before a student responds to a question. Prompts may be either verbal or gestural, and are used to increase the likelihood of correct response (Wolery et al., 1988). Further, if enough appropriate prompts are used to effectively eliminate most errors and correct responses are sufficiently rewarded, prompting becomes an errorless learning technique. Thus, the student will master new mathematics content with very few errors.

An illustration may be helpful. If a student struggling in math has some difficulty with place value decisions (i.e., regrouping) in the addition of whole numbers, the teacher may present a series of double-digit addition problems written vertically like those below.

25	44	62	47
+37	+19	+34	+39

The child would have to discriminate between the problems that required regrouping and those that did not, as well as to solve the problems that required regrouping. In assisting the child to complete the problems, if the child summed the digits in the ones column and began to write a two-digit answer under that column rather than placing one digit at the top of the next column (a common error among young children), the peer tutor or teacher may prompt the child by merely tapping the paper at the top of the next column to remind the student to write the "tens place" number down at the top of the next column of numbers. This prompting procedure would tend to eliminate most errors (presuming that the child had previously acquired the prerequisite skills in math facts), and errorless learning would result. While teachers could do such prompting, this tactic is very effective for differentiated classes that utilize a peer tutor or peer buddy instructional approach.

The Time Delay Tactic

Time delay is another errorless learning procedure (Schuster et al., 1990). The time delay procedure is implemented by presenting a problem to a student, waiting a given time, and then verbally providing the answer to the problem. Over time, the teacher or peer tutor should increase the amount of time between the problem and the answer on successive trials (Schuster et al., 1990; Wolery et al., 1991). For example, this procedure has been used for teaching multiplication facts to students with learning disabilities (Koscinski & Gast, 1993), and a time delay procedure could easily be applied to teach virtually any other math facts across the primary and elementary grades.

Implementation of Time Delay

Here is an example of how multiplication math facts may be taught using a time delay procedure coupled with peer buddy teaching in Mr. Varella's third-grade mathematics class. Mr. Varella should preselect peer buddies based on common skills in multiplication math facts (or any other type of math problem). Students who need help with the five and six times tables should work together while students who haven't mastered the eight and nine times tables should be partnered together. These peer buddies would work together for 20 minutes each day for a period of days on their math facts.

Mr. Varella would first need to teach the time delay procedure by modeling it for the class. He would select a student and work with that student doing a time delay instructional procedure with the class watching. Mr. Varella would present math facts to that student using flash cards that showed the math fact on the front (e.g., $4 \times 8 =$ ___), and the math fact with the answer on the back ($4 \times 8 = 32$). During the first instructional session a zero-second time delay would be used. This means there would be zero seconds between when Mr. Varella presents the problem and when he verbally reads the problem and the answer. Specifically, Mr. Varella would hold up a flash card with the math fact on it (so that the student could view the side without the answer), and immediately Mr. Varella would read the equation and the answer; thus, there are zero seconds between the math fact being presented visually to the student and the student's receiving the verbal prompt. Mr. Varella shows the card and says

---

BOX 4.7   TIME DELAY SCORE SHEET FOR EIGHT TIMES TABLES

Student's Name _____ Date _____ Time Delay _____

Math Fact	Corrects		Errors		
	Anticipations	Waits	Anticipations	Waits	Nonresponses
$8 \times 1 = 8$					
$8 \times 2 = 16$					
$8 \times 3 = 24$					
$8 \times 4 = 32$					
$8 \times 5 = 40$					
$8 \times 6 = 48$					
$8 \times 7 = 56$					
$8 \times 8 = 64$					
$8 \times 9 = 72$					
$8 \times 10 = 80$					

"4 × 8 is 32." The student would then repeat that equation; "4 × 8 is 32." Mr. Varella would then show the reverse side of the card to the student, as feedback on the student's correctness. Mr. Varella would also place a slash mark by the "4 × 8 = _____" equation under the "correct wait" column on the daily score sheet such as the one presented in Box 4.7. This mark indicates that the student waited to hear the answer and then correctly restated the problem and answer. Mr. Varella would present all 10 facts twice using the zero-second time delay in order to assist the student in learning the facts. Thus, there would be 20 marks on the score sheet at this point.

In the next step of the time delay procedure, Mr. Varella would present the facts with a three-second delay between presentation of the flash card and the correct completion of the equation. This time, the student should be encouraged to read the equation and give the answer before the teacher does if he or she knows the answer. If the student correctly answered the math fact, Mr. Varella would mark this response down as a "correct anticipation." Otherwise, the student should be instructed to wait until the verbal prompt, in order to get the answer right. If the student does not know the answer, and waits for the teacher's verbal prompt and subsequently repeats the equation correctly, the student should be rewarded with a mark in the "correct wait" column.

Each "correct anticipation" would be noted with a check mark by Mr. Varella. Each correct wait would be noted with a slash mark. Other responses would be noted with an "x." Mr. Varella would again present all of the facts twice, using the three-second delay, and thus 40 slash marks would be present on the child's score sheet at the end of the instructional session. The student's "correct waits" and "correct anticipations" should be charted daily, since increasing the "correct anticipations" is the overall goal of the procedure. Also, charting both correct waits and correct anticipations emphasizes for the student that both of these are correct—hence the term *errorless learning.*

On the next day, Mr. Varella should consider using a zero-second time delay for only one presentation of the 10 math facts in the eight times tables, and to use a three-second delay for the presentation of those math facts three times. The student's progress, or lack thereof, will assist in making that determination. Finally on the third day, pending appropriate student progress, only the three-second time delay is used. The 10 facts are, again, presented four times each, and the student's score is again tallied and charted.

The data chart presented in Box 4.7 presents a relatively standard recording format for time delay instruction. Note that each type of student response is listed in the five columns so that the teacher can note the specific type of response made. "Waits" indicate that the child waited to hear the prompt from the teacher before responding; "anticipations" indicate that the child did not wait for the verbal prompt from the teacher. For both the anticipations and the waits, the child could possibly answer either correctly or incorrectly. Alternatively, the child might not verbally respond at all. Thus, there are five possible answers: the terms used for these five possibilities are *correct anticipations, correct waits, anticipation error, wait error,* and *nonresponse.* Obviously, the goal of the teacher is to increase correct anticipations and decrease all other responses until the child performs with 100% accuracy and all of the corrects are anticipations rather than waits. It is important to note that the child "feels" rewarded for correct waits also, thus assuring an experience of success for the student. The emotional impact of such errorless learning in math cannot be overstated; students simply must experience high levels of success in mathematics in order to continue to be motivated to do increasingly difficult mathematics problems.

Time delay works particularly well in the differentiated math class when the teacher couples this tactic with a peer tutoring strategy, such as the classwide peer tutoring strategy described later in this chapter. Once Mr. Varella has demonstrated this with himself as the tutor, he should also demonstrate how the roles of tutor and tutee may be reversed. In other words, the student who was formerly the tutee now presents the math facts flash cards to Mr. Varella, and the student is taught to mark a daily score sheet for Mr. Varella's success. From that point on, it is fairly easy, even in the lower grades, to teach students to tutor each other. Ideally, once the students in the class learn this procedure, they can serve equally well as tutors or tutees, and they will typically serve in each role each day. Students should be tutored on math facts for approximately 10 minutes and then should serve as tutees for their peer buddies for an additional 10 minutes. Using this tactic in the differentiated class will not only strengthen interpersonal intelligence, it will also involve all students in meaningful tutoring roles and will make mathematics much less emotionally threatening for many struggling learners.

Uses of Time Delay Across Grade Levels

Research results indicate that students in elementary general education classes quickly mastered almost any factual material presented to them using this errorless learning procedure (Schuster et al., 1990; Wolery et al., 1991). Also, maintenance probes indicated that the students' mastery of factual material has been maintained for more than three months as a result of time delay instruction. Again, for almost any type of elementary math problem, consistent use of the time delay procedure would result in building automaticity and consistently high performance in a nonthreatening way.

Time delay works particularly well in the differentiated math class when the teacher couples this tactic with a peer tutoring strategy.

Furthermore, time delay may be used in higher grade levels as well. For example, recent research has indicated that factual material from various curriculum areas in higher grades can be mastered by the use of time delay. For example, Wolery, Cybriwsky, and their coworkers (1991) used time delay to assist adolescents with learning disabilities to master factual material from their secondary content curriculum areas. In that particular study, the content included the functions of federal offices, the services provided by local offices and agencies, over-the-counter medications, and the effects of specific vitamins and minerals on the body. As these diverse topics indicate, any mathematics content that can be specified as isolated factual material (for example, the meaning of PEMDAS, or mathematics problem-solving techniques), can be structured as curricula for a time delay procedure.

Any mathematics content that can be specified as isolated factual material can be structured as curricula for a time delay procedure.

A Copy, Cover, Compare Tactic

Another errorless learning procedure that assists in differentiating instruction and likewise results in a high level of success in math is the copy, cover, compare tactic. Stading, Williams, and McLaughlin (1996) used this errorless learning technique to teach multiplication math facts to a third-grade student with a learning disability. In this procedure, the student is presented with a set of math fact equations to be mastered— perhaps the seven's multiplication and division facts. These equations should be written on flash cards that contain a math fact equation and the answer. The student then performs each task: copy, cover, compare.

When presented with one of the flash cards, the student first copies the equation and the answer while reading it aloud. Next, the student covers the problem by turning the flash card face down and covering his or her written equation with a cover sheet and then writes the equation from memory. Finally, the student compares the two written equations. This is a fairly simple errorless learning procedure that students can accomplish by themselves. Also, working with the flash cards makes this a bit more "manipulative" than merely presenting the same math facts on a worksheet.

Differentiation With Errorless Learning

As these several errorless learning procedures demonstrate, students can master the basic math facts, as well as even more complicated math problems, in an errorless or nearly errorless fashion. Because errorless learning is an individualized instructional procedure, the instruction is highly differentiated, based on students' exact learning needs. In fact, this procedure has repeatedly been shown to be successful in both special and general education math classes (Stading et al., 1996; Wolery et al., 1988).

However, there is one critically important additional advantage to using errorless learning procedures in math. As described previously, the emerging brain research has demonstrated convincingly that when students fear a particular subject, they are much less likely to be actively engaged in that subject or to master the content (Sousa, 2008). Given the fear many students experience in math class, teachers of mathematics have a unique responsibility to address this emotional baggage, and errorless learning can be a critically important instructional approach in the differentiated classroom for that reason. One may imagine the joy of teaching in a public school math class, if every single student was initially taught in an errorless learning—and thus a much less threatening—fashion. Perhaps students would then experience the joy and beauty of mathematical problem solving, and this is the dream of almost all teachers of mathematics.

CLASSWIDE PEER TUTORING FOR DIFFERENTIATING MATH INSTRUCTION

You may not have realized it, but in the discussion of errorless learning above each reader received a highly practical instructional strategy idea that will make differentiated learning activities not only possible in the average-sized general education class, but also quite fun. Embedded within the discussion of time delay above, was an applied description of an instructional approach for differentiating the general education math classroom that is referred to as classwide peer tutoring. In this system, all students in the class learn to tutor each other in mathematics work that is individually selected for each student. This provides a wonderful opportunity for both mainline instruction and tear-out group work in the differentiated math class (Allsopp, 1997; Greenwood, Delquadri, & Hall, 1989).

For the past three decades, a number of researchers, principally led by Dr. Charles Greenwood at the University of Kansas in Kansas City, have developed a system of peer buddy tutoring that can easily be employed in elementary classes of almost any size (Allsopp, 1997; Greenwood et al., 1989; Mortweet et al., 1999). This procedure and other peer tutoring instructional tactics have received considerable research

> *In classwide peer tutoring, all students in the class learn to tutor each other in mathematics work that is individually selected for each student.*

support (Baker, Gersten, & Lee, 2002; Foegen, 2008; Kroeger & Kouche, 2006; Kunsch, Jitendra, & Wood, 2007; National Mathematics Advisory Panel, 2008). For that reason, the classwide peer tutoring tactic served as the basis for the discussion of the time delay strategy above. In that procedure, students who are paired together serve the role of both tutor and tutee in the class.

Although classwide peer tutoring should not be used for initial instruction in any type of math problem, this type of instruction is very useful during the guided practice and independent practice phases of instruction in math. In fact, this instructional model may be more helpful than traditional instruction for monitoring student progress since a record is kept of all errors each student makes. The teacher can review this record outside of daily class time and make determinations about an individual student's level of understanding of the math problems. Should a student be struggling, that will quickly become apparent in his or her daily worksheet scores.

Essentially, in classwide peer tutoring, time—perhaps 20 minutes—is set aside each day in the mathematics class for the tutoring experience. The students are paired together (teachers should vary these pairs daily) and provided with the appropriate materials for the tutoring session— typically either flash cards or a worksheet that involves only one specific type of problem (e.g., two-digit addition with regrouping). During a tutoring session, one student will first serve as the "tutor" and will record the corrects and errors of the "tutee." The tutor will present math facts, equations, or problems on flash cards to the other student and record the responses. When the problems are presented on a worksheet, the tutor is still responsible for marking the daily record of errors. When a worksheet is used, each student should be provided a copy—the tutee completes the problems while the tutor marks correct or incorrect on his or her worksheet.

The tutee is awarded two points for correct answers. Should an error be made, the tutor can assist the student in figuring out the problem, and upon correction of the problem the tutee is awarded one point. Zero points are awarded for nonresponses. Should the tutor and tutee both need assistance, they are instructed to raise their hands to request help. After 10 minutes, the roles will be switched for each pair of students (i.e., the tutor becomes the tutee), and the new tutor begins to record the progress of the tutee. Of course, each student's progress is charted each day, and students are typically highly motivated to improve their scores over previous performances. During the 20-minute tutoring time, the teacher should move throughout the class and assist students as necessary. The teacher thus becomes a facilitator of learning, which frees the teacher for more in-depth, one-on-one instruction for students who need extra help. Moreover, teachers are responsible for setting up the classwide peer tutoring setting. This is accomplished by consideration of three things.

1. Close examination and/or specific assessment that will depict the exact skill level of every child in the class so that specific types of math problems may be identified and either flash cards or worksheets can be developed for those problems. These flash cards or worksheets should include only those specific types of problems on which the student has received initial instruction but has not mastered.

2. The development of daily recording sheets that allow the tutor to record the correct and error responses on the specific math problems for the student he or she is tutoring. For worksheet-based activities, the teacher can review the copy of each student's worksheet after class and analyze any errors that were made.

3. A training period in which the teacher demonstrates how the tutoring should be done. This should emphasize the reciprocal nature of the tutoring—that is, that each student serves as both tutor and tutee each and every day.

At this point, you may wish to reread the discussion of the time delay tactic above, and consider how classwide peer tutoring was embedded within that discussion. In that section, you can see the relatively easy application of this research-proven instructional method for the differentiated class.

Most of the research on classwide peer tutoring has been undertaken in elementary general education classes and concentrated on reading and language arts subject areas. Nevertheless, this teaching procedure has been shown to be effective in elementary math (Mortweet et al., 1999), as well as in middle school or secondary algebra (Allsopp, 1997, 1999; Foegen, 2008; Kroeger & Kouche, 2006). Further, peer tutoring procedures have now been endorsed by the National Mathematics Advisory Panel (2008). Application of this tactic for almost any type of math problem during the elementary and middle school grades would be quite easy, and thus, almost every teacher in the early and middle school grades should learn to apply this tactic.

DIFFERENTIATED INSTRUCTION PLAN: PRIMARY GRADES

Many professional development books, such as this one, can be justifiably criticized for offering an array of instructional ideas, but rarely do such books actually put the pieces together in a meaningful differentiated instructional plan. I will seek to alleviate that concern by recommending specific tactics for teachers in various grade levels. Of course, every class is different and teachers have varying comfort levels with the different instructional ideas. However, these are my suggestions as to how I would teach a general education math class, using brain-compatible, differentiated tactics and 21st century teaching skills, in conjunction with the Common Core Mathematics Standards. The plan for kindergarten through Grade 3 is presented in Teaching Tip 4.5.

Teaching Tip 4.5   Differentiated Instructional Plan: Kindergarten Through Grade 3

These guidelines are based on the assumption that teachers in the early grades will spend about 60 minutes daily in mathematics instruction. This is not intended as a daily math lesson schedule, but I do include recommended times for certain activities as general guidelines for teachers to consider.

Khan Academy—I recommended that teachers set up every member of their class within Khan Acad emy, and allocate 15 minutes daily work for this, for all students in kindergarten through Grade 3. This assures students receive exactly the level of work they need, while helping them meet with success in mathematics. Teachers should praise students for earning badges.

Begin Instructional Gaming in Mathematics—In addition to the gaming nature of Khan Academy, I suggest all teachers, kindergarten through Grade 3, select a website for other educational games (www.brainpop.com or www.soft-schools.com), and use those games several times each week. Again, this will help students experience the joy of mathematics in a nonthreatening way, early in their school years.

Mathematics Learning Centers—Learning centers should be established—a minimum of two centers—in every primary grade. Various activities can be structured for

(Continued)

(Continued)

the centers for some students while the teacher works more directly with other students. Learning centers focused on whole number operations and/or measurement are good topics for the early math curriculum. Teachers should use the learning centers daily for at least some students.

Use Student Avatars—I recommend that all primary teachers in Grades 1 through 3 should have students create avatars for themselves and use those once or twice weekly. Voki is one option for this. As discussed in text, avatars help students enjoy mathematics more and will alleviate much of the stress associated with math.

Classwide Peer Tutoring—Beginning in Grade 2, teachers should establish a routine of classwide peer tutoring. The reciprocal nature of this tutoring assures that students receive the differentiated instruction they need and provides a social nature to mathematics instruction. I would suggest 20 minutes of peer tutoring daily.

Stress CRA—For initial instruction, I urge all kindergarten through Grade 3 teachers to stress CRA instruction. I'd recommend a maximum of 15 minutes of initial instruction daily in these grade levels, and most math texts do include CRA examples in the primary grades, though teachers in Grade 3 may need to supplement the CRA examples, using several of the websites provided in the chapter.

Use Time Delay as a Tier 2 Intervention—As mentioned in the introductory chapter, differentiated instruction is now considered the epitome of Tier 1 instruction in the response to intervention effort. For students who continue to struggle in mathematics, I suggest a time delay procedure that targets their specific weaknesses. Thus, teachers will use time delay with some students while most other students are working in learning centers, doing Khan Academy, or doing the 20 minutes of classwide peer tutoring on a daily basis.

By using this differentiated instructional plan, all students will receive exactly the instruction they need, at their level, and the fears and anxieties associated with mathematics will be alleviated, based on the fun associated with math games and successful experiences.

WHAT'S NEXT?

This chapter has presented a variety of differentiation strategies for young children in mathematics. Initially, both number sense and mathematics readiness/early math skills were discussed, and strategies were provided for teachers working with very young children in math. Next, the CRA tactic, a strategy that must be heavily emphasized in mathematics instruction across the grade levels today, was described. Technology options for differentiated instruction that will help alleviate fears of mathematics were discussed, as were errorless learning and classwide peer tutoring. All of these tactics are excellent differentiated instruction tactics and will help teachers alleviate the math anxieties of so many young children. Also, a differentiated instructional plan was presented, with specific recommendations about structuring the differentiated mathematics class in the primary grade levels.

In the next chapter, the focus is on the mid-elementary grades. Additional technology options will be presented, as will a discussion of scaffolded instruction, to help students build their deep understanding of the conceptual issue in mathematics that are emphasized within the Common Core Standards in Mathematics.

Strategies for Differentiating Instruction in Grades 3 Through 6

5

CHANGING MATHEMATICS INSTRUCTION FOR THE MID-ELEMENTARY GRADES

As students move into Grades 3 through 6, both the students and the mathematics curricular content change. Of course, students mature throughout school, and it is generally the case that maturity engenders deeper levels of number awareness, number sense, and mathematical skill. Number sense was discussed in the last chapter, and as noted, activities that continue to strengthen number sense are recommended across the elementary and middle school grade levels. The strategies presented in Teaching Tip 5.1 should assist students with number sense in Grades 3 through 6.

Teaching Tip 5.1   Developing Higher-Level Number Sense

Plan Estimation Experiences

Estimation is a critical skill for success in higher mathematics, and teachers should teach estimation both directly and indirectly by discussing topics such as "less than" and "more than" with students. Some students are uncomfortable with estimation since students typically strive for the "right" answer. Encourage students to provide estimates within a certain range (e.g., "How many shoes are in class today? Give me a number between 40 and 70," or "How many students are sitting in a single group in the media center?").

Counting Off in Line

Students in lower grades frequently line up to go to the lunchroom or elsewhere. Every time students line up, teachers could encourage them to count off, and thus stress number sense (Griffin et al., 2003). As an interesting variation in the upper grades, have students count off when in line using a "quiet voice" but have each person who is a multiple of a certain number (say a multiple of five) say his or her number louder. This makes learning multiplication more interesting since multiples will be frequently used in the classroom.

Stress Numbers in Other Subjects

When encountering a number in a reading story, take a few moments to explore the number. When a group of characters in a story does something together, stop for a moment and say, "I want to get a sense of how many are doing that in this story. Let's have students in the first row stand up to represent that number."

Emphasize Measurement

From the early days of kindergarten, teachers should take measurements of objects and discuss them with the class. Teachers may use a short tape measure to measure the length of the teacher's desk or a student's desktop. When measuring distances on the floor, teachers may add the element of counting steps (e.g., "How many steps are there in the 10 feet between the front row of student desks and the teacher's desk?" Have a student walk that distance and count his or her steps. Next, the teacher would measure another floor space of 10 feet in a different area of the classroom, and ask the class how many steps the same student would use to cover that distance.

Chart Making Money

Using charted data in higher grades (which takes only one or two minutes at the beginning of the class period) can encourage students to investigate the use of numbers in a real-world environment. In an economics course, as one example, a teacher might start each student with $1,000 in make-believe money in the stock market, and have each student pick stocks to buy and to chart stock price changes for. This can be a fun learning activity with real-world significance.

Model Enjoyment of Numbers

Perhaps the most important legacy a teacher can leave with a student is enjoyment of number play. Gurganus (2004) emphasizes the importance of the teacher modeling the enjoyment of numbers and establishing a climate for curiosity in mathematics.

(Continued)

(Continued)

Musical Fraction Squares

The report of the National Mathematics Advisory Panel (2008) strongly empha-sized the need for increased instruction on fractions. In this "musical squares" game, the parts of a fraction can be demonstrated. Begin with four students and four chairs and write "4/4" on the dry erase board. Discuss the fact that the chairs represent the numerator and the students represent the denominator. Thus, if the teacher removes one chair while the music plays, there will be ¾ or 3 chairs and 4 students. The teacher can then discuss various fractions with the students and talk about, "What is left when the music ends?" or "What has been taken away?"

Of course, teachers should note that many strategies introduced for primary grades are equally applicable in the higher elementary grades, just as some strategies introduced below will be applicable in the middle schools mathematics classes, as discussed in the following chapter. Veteran teachers are, in reality, masters at adapting strategies, or instruc-tional ideas, to fit their grade level and curriculum, as students' maturity increases across the grade levels.

In addition to increased student maturity in Grades 3 through 6, instruction in mathematics is also impacted by at least two changes in the mathematics curriculum. After Grade 3 or 4, mathematics becomes both more abstract and more complex. For this reason, some students who suc-ceeded in mathematics in the primary grades may begin to experience difficulties when com-plex concepts such as fractions, decimals, or two-step word problems are introduced. Further the demands of the mathematics cur-riculum change somewhat around Grade 3. As

> As students move into Grades 4 through 6, both the students and the mathematics curricular content change.

noted previously, most instructor's manuals in mathematics do not pro-vide many representational examples of math problems in Grades 4 through 6, and as the grade levels increase, there is an increased emphasis on problem solving.

The Standards for Mathematics Practice associated with the Common Core (see Chapter 1) suggest that students at every level should be provided many opportunities to develop skills in mathemati-cal modeling, and while it is relatively easy to make that statement, such mandates become more of a challenge when a fourth-grade math teacher is confronted with a number of students in the class who have not quite mastered basic operations, or fractions, or one-step word problems. Many students in the middle elementary grades demonstrate increasing difficulties in mathematics, on work involving simple or complex operations such as multiplication, division, or fractions, and thus, teachers across the mid-elementary grade levels can benefit from tactics for teaching such basic math skills as the times tables, or operations with fractions, and so on.

For that reason, the use of teaching aids such as addition, multiplication, or division math fact charts should be encouraged not only in the primary grades when the times tables are introduced, but in the later and elementary grades as well (Foegen, 2008). Of course, teachers should also make every effort to assist students in reaching automaticity, since automaticity is required in order to succeed in later mathematics courses (National Mathematics Advisory Panel, 2008).

In addition to use of fact charts, there are a number of relatively simple, yet innovative instructional modification options that should be used in the elementary math class (Foegen, 2008; Jitendra, 2002; Joseph & Hunter, 2001). I recommend that teachers implement most of these modifications, presented in Box 5.1, as ideas that will assist struggling students in becoming more comfortable with mathematics.

BOX 5.1 Modifications for the Differentiated Math Class

- Structure new instruction for mathematics concepts as games between teams or as peer buddy activities, using either traditional game boards or computer-based gaming technology. This helps involve students with interpersonal learning styles in the activity.
- Stress "think alouds" to demonstrate how to think through a problem. This provides opportunities for students to communicate on mathematics with each other, as stressed in the Common Core Standards for Practice, (Box 1.1, Standard 3). Teachers should always follow up both correct answers and incorrect answers from students with a question about how the student arrived at that answer. As a modification of this idea, have students consult with a group of "peer colleagues" prior to answering the question, and have other students suggest alternate ways to get the answer.
- Use cue cards for students involved in various types of math problems. The cue cards should present practical steps in problem implementation, and students should be taught how to discriminate when to use which set of cues. Post these around the room for immediate access.
- Use graph paper to assist in lining up numbers and visualizing concepts.
- Always have many counters or pictorial representations available in the classroom, and challenge students who get the correct answer to represent that problem solution for others in the class using these materials.

With these simple teaching modifications as a backdrop in the general education math class, this chapter presents an array of additional strategies for differentiating mathematics instruction in the middle elementary grades, with an emphasis on constructivist instruction to facilitate deeper understandings of mathematical concepts, as envisioned within the Common Core. Also, several more technology-based instructional techniques will be described, in order to foster collaborative work in mathematics, as well as the development of 21st century communication skills among all students as they, working together, discuss mathematical concepts. Finally, a variety of scaffolded instructional strategies are presented later in the chapter, since scaffolded instruction is a very effective platform for differentiating instruction for all students in the math classes.

Of course, readers should note that there is much overlap in instructional techniques across the primary, elementary, and middle grades, so many of the instructional techniques previously discussed (e.g., CRA instruction, technology-based teaching ideas) should be used in these mid-elementary grades as well. However, at least as early as the mid-elementary grades, instruction should focus more on problem solving, in an effort to develop deep, broad knowledge and understanding of mathematics.

CONSTRUCTIVIST THEORY AND CONCEPTUAL MATHEMATICS

Embedded within the Common Core Mathematics Standards, as well as preceding iterations of standards for mathematics, is a strong emphasis on developing deep understanding of mathematics concepts and problem-solving skills (Garelick, 2012; National Mathematics Advisory Panel, 2008). Many instructional experts have suggested that "constructivist theory" might be the most appropriate perspective from which to develop deep conceptual understanding in math across the grade levels (Grobecker, 1999; E. D. Jones, Wilson, & Bhojwani, 1997; Woodward & Montague, 2002). Constructivist theory calls for students to be perceived as learners who may be immature in their mathematical understandings, but who can develop deeper knowledge in math as long as they

> Have mastered the prerequisite skills for a particular problem, and are supported by the teacher and curriculum as they "construct" meaning or further understandings of the mathematics problems under study.

In the constructivist view, teachers are not information providers (demonstrating problems on the board), but rather are facilitators who provide opportunities to learn along with appropriate supports to assist students in developing their growing understanding of various mathematical skills. In that sense, mathematics teachers should function more as "coaches" rather than "modelers" of problem-solving techniques. Further, as students mature in their cognitive understandings of mathematics concepts, the teacher should withdraw the supports and allow students to work more independently.

According to this perspective, in order to accomplish effective instruction teachers need to develop an array of instructional skills. First, teachers must understand what supports a student may need based on the student's current mathematics skills and their understanding of the problem. Next, for a given student, the teacher must apply the specific type and level of support needed, and at a later point withdraw it, as student comprehension increases. Closely aligned with this perspective is the notion of "guiding" the cognitive understandings of students as they develop in their mathematical experiences (Alsup, 2003). I should note that I have chosen to present this constructivist concept in the discussion of mathematics instruction for Grades 3 through 6, but this construct is every bit as relevant for lower grades, as well as middle school grades.

Teachers do this "guiding" by listening to a student's solution to a problem and then asking pointed topical questions that are designed to guide students cognitively through the problem-solution process. Thus, students are responsible for using the information they have learned to solve the problem, and the students are exposed to the mystery and the fun of problem solving in math. Students may use manipulatives or models as described in previous chapters in order to solve the problem, but the emphasis will be on moving students past the necessity for concrete or representational models and into a deeper level of conceptual understanding. In that sense, the constructivist perspective fits very nicely with the main emphasis of the Common Core Math Standards on development of deep conceptual understand of mathematics processes.

> *In the constructivist view, teachers are not information providers, but rather are facilitators who provide appropriate supports to assist students in developing their growing understanding of various mathematical skills.*

Scaffolded Instruction

Arising from this constructivist perspective, teachers began to use the term "scaffolded instruction." Scaffolding is an instructional technique used in many different subjects, including mathematics, and originally represented a procedure whereby teachers strategically guide students in the learning process by questioning students in order to assist in building their understanding of a mathematics problem (Woodward & Montague, 2002), and then withdrawing that guidance as the student's skills increased. However, it was soon realized that many instructional procedures other than individual teacher tutoring can support student learning by assisting the student to understand content (e.g., graphic organizers, pictures). Thus, scaffolded instruction may best be understood as a sequence of prompted content, materials, and teacher or peer support to facilitate learning (Grobecker, 1999; Karp & Voltz, 2000). In scaffolded instruction, the emphasis is placed on a teacher's assisting the student in the learning process with individual prompting and guidance that is tailored to the specific needs of the individual student and offers just enough support (i.e., a scaffold) for the student in a new task (Karp & Voltz, 2000). Further, that support should gradually be withdrawn, allowing the student to eventually "own" the task performance. The student, then, is initially considered an apprentice, and soon to be an expert, in the learning effort.

Constructivist Perspectives and 21st Century Technology

In the collaborative instructional world of the 21st century classroom, the constructivist perspective is perhaps even more relevant than in more traditional classes. As students use various apps in mathematics, different math websites, and various Web 2.0 tools (e.g., blogs, wikis, Google docs, and collaborative, cloud-based assignments, etc.), they will be using technology as scaffolds to support their understanding. Further, these 21st century tools allow students to collaborate in completing mathematics problems in ways that could not be envisioned even 20 years ago. In this collaborative context, students often assist other students in their efforts to "construct" understanding of various math examples, many times using these 21st century tech tools. From the constructivist perspective, these student peer-buddies are using technology to do the instructional "guiding," and for many students who might fear mathematics somewhat, this can be much less threatening than traditional instruction from the teacher, even if that instruction is delivered in a one-on-one teacher tutoring session.

In that sense, as this book is written in 2013, constructivist theory is becoming even more influential in education, because it does stress deeper conceptual understanding and applications of math, and cross-pollinates nicely with the ongoing development of tech-based teaching strategies. Math teachers should certainly avail themselves of these powerful, new constructivist, tech-based teaching tools.

TECH-BASED TOOLS FOR DIFFERENTIATING ELEMENTARY MATHEMATICS

> *In the collaborative instructional world of the 21st century classroom, the constructivist perspective is perhaps even more relevant than in more traditional classes.*

The last chapter presented two tech-based instructional strategies—computer-based gaming and use of avatars to personalize mathematics—to make this curricular area less threatening and more engaging. However, 21st century teaching tools can go much further than this, and can actually make mathematics a collaborative, creative activity for individual students or for groups of students. Using recently developed tech-based teaching tools that are generally referred to as Web 2.0 tools, students can grapple with mathematics content collaboratively, in a highly engaging, social manner, and assignments based on these tools tend to transform the mathematics class into a much more exciting learning experience. In today's classroom, students are not merely consumers of information, but actually create content that can then be shared worldwide, and studied by others, using technology. Thus, mathematics is transformed from "learn these procedures and formulas" to "creatively engage with your peers in the class and online, to devise a workable mathematics solution for this problem."

Both class blogs and wikis are presented in this chapter, as the initial tools teachers might use in fostering such collaboration. Even for teachers with little background using instructional technologies, these tools can be easily mastered. These are 21st century teaching tools that can enhance differentiated instruction, and generally enrich the mathematics experience for all students.

Blogs for Mathematics Instruction

Students in the mid-elementary grades typically begin to socialize much more with their peers than in earlier years, and many technology tools can use this growing desire for socialization and harness that desire as an instructional tool. For example, many teachers today—math teachers among them—are using blogs to help students collaborate in mastering curricular content. Specifically, this tech tool helps mathematics teachers address Common Core Mathematical Practice Standard Number 3, which emphasizes the construction and communication of viable mathematics solutions.

A blog is a collaboratively developed, online journal in which posted information from both teachers and students is arranged and archived in reverse chronological order (W. M. Ferriter & Garry, 2010). Using a blog, teachers and students can work individually or together to create a solution to a mathematics problem or recommend information to their peers relative to that problem, by creating online links to other material such as videos or model problems. All blog entries are listed, in order, so teachers can follow which students added specific comments. Students can collaboratively work on a math problem, with each student in the group completing steps in the problem in turn. Blogs provide the opportunity for connectivity in that the students can leave comments on the work from other students. Finally, when teachers create classroom blogs, students are able to interact with the mathematics content long after the school day has ended.

I recommend that 21st century mathematics teachers use blogs professionally, in at least two distinct ways: as a professional learning tool and as a class instructional tool to foster student excitement about mathematics. First, blogging has become an excellent way to share information and teaching ideas professionally, and many blogs for math teachers are available. Teachers may wish to check some of the most popular general topic blogs for teachers (edudemic.com/2011/12/teacher-blogs/). However, several mathematics-related blogs are also good starting points for teachers interested in mathematics instructional ideas, as presented in Box 5.2. From blogs such as these, teachers can pick up an amazing array of teaching ideas, with relatively little reading time.

> *A blog is an online journal where posted information from both teachers and students is arranged and archived in reverse chronological order.*

BOX 5.2 BLOGS FOR TEACHING IDEAS IN MATHEMATICS

The Number Warrior—This blog, written by an Arizona high school math teacher, offers a mix of riddles, observations, and videos on higher-level topics in mathematics (numberwarrior.wordpress.com). Various games and cooperative learning ideas are included here as well, and all mathematics teachers are invited to join the discussions.

Math for Primates—This blog includes a series of podcasts on math that present various mathematics topics in an entertaining fashion (www.mathforprimates .com/). This site can be used to glean teaching ideas, as well as by more advanced math students. Recent posts explore the idea of infinity, as one example.

Continuous Everywhere but Differentiable Nowhere—This blog is written by a math teacher in New York, and describes various questions faced by mathematics teachers (samjshah.com/). I found several discussions of how this teacher might manage his class (e.g., do one problem initially, then assign peer buddies to complete a problem), and it can be informative for math teachers to see another math teacher "think through" how to structure the math class.

Let's Play Math—This blog presents a great deal of content on teaching mathematics, including various games and teaching suggestions (letsplaymath.net/).

I Speak Math—This blog is written by a middle school math teacher in North Carolina and presents many creative teaching ideas such as creation of a video on operations with fractions, or hold a free-throw competition on decimals (ispeakmath.wordpress.com).

Keeping Math Simple—This blog focuses on math pedagogy, and provides many instructional ideas (math4teaching.com/). The blog author/creator, Erlina Ronda, seeks to narrow the gap between theory and practice.

Math Teacher Wiki—This is an open wiki that teachers can share ideas on for math instruction (msmathwiki.pbworks.com/w/page/27071816/Math-Teacher-Wiki).

When considering a blog for student use, teachers should realize the value of social learning in the 21st century classroom. The extreme popularity of the many social networking sites available today demonstrates students' desire to be socially connected, and math teachers should certainly tap into that desire for social interaction. A blog is the simplest way to do that.

Utilizing class blogs fills that desire for socially mediated learning by offering high levels of student-to-student interaction focused on the mathematics content (Richtel, 2012). Students are more likely to enjoy mathematics taught in this fashion (Richtel, 2012), and they are much more motivated to complete mathematics homework when it involves collaborative blog postings on the problem or problems under study.

To use a blog as a classroom teaching tool, teachers simply write a note (called a "post") about a particular topic to begin the blog, and then encourage students to respond to that post, with a post of their own. The teacher's initial post might be a general question on a mathematics concept, or an actual math problem for students to discuss. Here is a sample blog post teachers may use when teaching rounding from the Common Core Math Standards in Grade 3:

> *Students are much more motivated to complete mathematics homework when it involves collaborative blog postings on the problem or problems under study.*

Use place value understanding to round the whole numbers to the nearest 10 or 100. (3.NBT.1)

Teacher: *Who has an idea about how to round off the number 76? Can anyone explain how we do that?*

Student posts might include a variety of ideas such as:

Laquisha: *I think that the six in the one's place is higher than five so we need to round up. That means the answer is 80.*

Billy: *It would be 70. Right?*

Students can then post their responses to the teacher, or respond to other students' comments. Here are several examples.

Stacy: *Laquisha has it right. I think we need to go up to 80, because you go up if the number in the one's place is five or higher.*

Adam: *Laquisha and Stacy are correct. The answer is 80.*

As this simple example indicates, even a general blog discussion tends to be quite collaborative in nature. Further, students, with just a bit of coaching, can be taught to focus on the correct ideas, and ignore the incorrect ones, such as Billy's idea above. Alternatively, students may be taught to gently coach other students on the blog when an error is made. In these ways, blogs can be nonthreatening, and yet highly interactive. Further, blogs are highly accessible as students can log onto blogs via their personal computers, mobile devices, or any other technology tool that has Internet capabilities, either at school or at home. On some blog platforms, students even have the option to "follow" blogs, so that the students would be notified via e-mail whenever there is a change on the blog itself.

Blogs have been used by various educators for many years now, and do tend to increase student engagement and collaborative learning. However, other teachers have not employed this tool. In some cases, the school was not Wi-Fi equipped, or few computers were available for students. Still, this is a tech tool that mathematics teachers should begin to utilize in the class, since it is a 21st century communication skill, and provides many collaboration options. Finally, blogs are fairly easy to set up, even for the uninitiated teacher who has not used this tech tool before. The steps in Teaching Tip 5.2 should help in that regard.

Teaching Tip 5.2   Setting Up a Math Instructional Blog

Select a Blog Hosting Site

First, teachers must select a blogging host website for their blog. Some sites are available at no cost, but these tend to be funded by advertising, while others are ad-free. Teachers should also consider the levels of privacy (who can participate in or view the blog—students only or students and parents?), as well as student security. A number of hosting sites are available including:

www.classblogmeister.com—This is a free website designed specifically for teachers and classroom use. All articles and comments are sent to the teacher for approval prior to being published, which helps the teacher ensure acceptable behavior on the blog. Teachers can also ensure that the site is password protected.

www.21classes.com/—This is a blog host with several options for teachers. A single teacher blog is free for teachers and provides the teacher with a central dashboard for controlling accounts and comments. This free option allows for uploads of videos and images. The blog can be made public or private for the classroom. Regardless of the setting, the teacher has control over which posts are approved and even if certain posts are only approved for certain groups. 21 Classes also offers fee-based programs where students have their own personal blogs monitored by the teacher.

edublogs.org/—Edublog is another host created entirely for educational use. It allows teachers to make their blogs private or public. Edublogs boasts an adult-content-free site, making it safe for students to browse through the site. There are several options for teachers when using Edublogs. The free version allows students to create their own blog without having an e-mail address. The site recommends that a single teacher use the Pro version, which is $3.33 a month for 50 student blogs as well. This Pro version has more options for teacher monitoring.

education.weebly.com/—Weebly is a free service for teachers. Due to the emphasis on education, no advertising appears on the blogs. The service is completely free for up to 40 student accounts. The host supports picture, video, document, and photo gallery uploads. All websites (either teacher or student created) have the option to be password protected, offering higher levels of security for parents and teachers. Weebly boasts an easy drag-and-drop editor, making the creation of any site easy.

Consider the Blog Audience

Generally, students are more motivated to actively participate in mathematics activities on the blog if the blog audience is larger; a bigger audience fosters excitement about the blog (Richtel, 2012). Blogs that require a student login and password can be secure while allowing a wide audience. Making blogs available to the school and parent community encourages students to think about their audience and how to engage them, and fosters student excitement about using the blog. Ultimately, this will increase students' motivation and commitment to the mathematics discussion.

Follow Blog Host Instructions

Finally, teachers should follow the hosting and set-up instructions for their particular blog. Again, anyone who currently uses e-mail can set up a blog, but instructions are different on the various hosting sites. I generally recommend that teachers look at one or two of the blog hosts, and watch the tutorial videos

(Continued)

(Continued)

on that website, in order to learn the tips and tricks of that particular blogging host.

Create the Initial Post

The initial blog post should be something that will engage students' curiosity and motivate them to want to participate. Teachers might initially ask a general question, and, somewhat later, post a specific mathematics problem for students to consider. Links to outside documents, model problems, video demonstrations, pictures, or audio clips can also be included in the blog.

Blogs provide many differentiated instructional options in the elementary mathematics class. For example, blogs allow teachers to make meaningful, content-rich assignments for some students, while still allowing them to provide direct instruction. As one example, imagine a fourth-grade mathematics teacher, Ms. Chang, who is teaching measurement and focusing on the Common Core Measurement and Data Standard (4.MD.3);

> *Apply the area and perimeter formulas for rectangles in real-world and mathematical problems. For example, find the width of a rectangular room given the area of the flooring and the length, by viewing the area formula as a multiplication equation with an unknown factor.*

In most fourth-grade classes, both the academic skill level and the learning preferences vary considerably. Thus, Ms. Chang would probably have several students in her class that require extra instruction from her on that standard, while others may have mastered that work and need more challenging work. In order to differentiate instruction, Ms. Chang could use her class blog to make a collaborative, creative assignment. She could require the advanced students to work on the blog, reviewing a link to a video about areas of multishaped buildings (e.g., instances in which students must calculate areas for two or more building sections, and then add those areas together for the total floor area). Those students would view that video, and then post questions and comments on the blog about that type of calculation. Those students might then be required to make up several such area calculation problems, based on rooms within the school. At the same time, Ms. Chang could provide direct instruction for the other group of students. In this manner, Ms. Chang would be able to differentiate the content through the use of the interactive class blog without embarrassing any students in a class setting.

Blogs can also help differentiate in other ways. Because teachers and students can link any digital document, audio, and video clips to a class blog, many learning options are offered for students with different learning styles that may not be offered in the tradi-

> *Blogs make differentiating instruction easier by providing ways to differentiate the class activities.*

tional classroom setting. Material presented in class can be differentiated on the blog by including various presentations of the same math content. For students who may need a more visual representation of the math example, such an example could be posted by the teacher. In contrast, students needing auditory explanations may be referred to a podcast on the content, with a link to that podcast posted within the class blog. In fact, with multiple materials linked to the class blog, students can search for the media selections that best help them understand the math content in a clear manner.

In this sense, class blogs can be used as a time saver. Teachers often note that their actual instructional time in the class is quite limited, and as the example above demonstrates, well-developed class blog assignments can provide teachers with an assignment option for one or more groups of students while leaving the teacher free to work with others.

Blogs can also provide limited options for student creativity. For example, when studying various shapes in mathematics, teachers may have students use their mobile phones to take a picture and upload examples of the shapes they see in the community or in their home. Further, students may be required to post some brief comments on the blog about their shape and why they found it interesting.

Wikis in the Mathematics Class

While blogs do facilitate class interaction, as noted previously, a more effective tech tool for increasing collaboration and joint problem solving in mathematics is the wiki (Watters, 2011b; Wetzel, 2012). A class wiki is similar to a blog in that all students can post contributions to the wiki, and this results in more options for true collaboration on mathematics projects. However, wikis involve much more functionality, and more instructional options than merely class blogs. In fact, a wiki is, essentially, an editable website for the class, and may include class blogs, as well as many other 21st century instructional tools. Wikis can be used as instructional tools in the mathematics class, or they may be set

> *A wiki is an editable website, usually with limited access, that allows students to collaboratively create content and post their work in the form of digital files.*

up as communication tools, to let parents, other teachers, administrators, or anyone else review the work done in their class. Wikis usually involve limited access, in order to protect student identities, but they do allow students to collaboratively create and post written work, or share digital files, such as digital photos or even digital video projects (Watters, 2011b; Wetzel, 2012).

Wikis, like blogs, have been used in some classrooms since the late 1990s (Richardson, 2010; Watters, 2011b). Some teachers use the class wiki as a combination of a unit syllabus and instructional activities assignments page for math students. Today, teachers can do virtually all of their instruction based within a class wiki, because wikis are so very versatile and can include any type of assignment a teacher might imagine. Box 5.3 presents a number of ideas for using wikis in the mathematics class.

BOX 5.3   INSTRUCTIONAL IDEAS FOR WIKIS IN THE MATHEMATICS CLASS

All of the following teaching ideas for wikis could also be represented by pages within a class wiki. Teachers would set up the parameters for these teaching ideas on a locked wiki page, and then provide unlocked wiki pages for students to work with.

Problem of the Day—Wikis can present a teacher-developed problem of the day or a problem of the week, and students can work, individually or in teams, on that problem with reinforcement offered for the first team to solve it.

Create an Example—Wikis can provide a location for students to upload interesting images representing mathematics concepts that they take with a digital camera (typically a parent's smartphone) in the local community. Students should be required to write a brief paragraph about the image, and its importance in the mathematics unit under study.

You Write a Problem—Working in teams, students can be required to create a sample mathematics problem based on the topic under study, and upload that to the wiki. Others would then critique that problem and perhaps solve it.

My Math Problems Today—Students might individually present a mathematics problems that they encountered in their daily lives. Unlike the "You Write a Problem," this assignment involves a mathematics problem of any type and is not related to the unit under study.

My Math Vocabulary—On this page, the teacher should input all math terms for that specific unit of instruction, and perhaps any review terms from the previous unit. Students would then be expected to define and provide examples for those terms.

Around the World Collaboration—Using a wiki, teachers can help students work with other students anywhere in the world on mathematics problems. For example, students in Utah might share pictures of a mountain valley and a calculation of the rough area of that valley, while students along coastal North Carolina might provide a picture of a sound or river basin, and likewise present an example of the area of that geographic feature. The website iEARN (www.iearn.org) is dedicated to helping teachers around the world connect their classes for this type of collaboration.

As described earlier, blogs preserve students' and teachers' posted comments separately, in chronological order, and while the blog can facilitate some collaboration, students generally cannot work directly on the same mathematics problem at the same time. However, by using a wiki, teachers can encourage a much richer student collaboration, since in the wiki students can actually edit the work of others, rather than merely comment on it. Thus, students can collaboratively solve problems while working within the same digital file in the wiki. The most recognized example of a worldwide wiki is, of course, Wikipedia, a free, online encyclopedia that anyone can contribute to or edit (www .wikipedia.org).

These collaborative and creative options make a wiki a true Web 2.0 tool, since creative collaborative options can be explored in wikis that have not been possible previously. Thus, when a group is working as a small group on a specific mathematics problem, students can and will correct each other's mistakes. This functionality makes wikis an excellent tech tool for increasing the types of collaboration and social learning that students today enjoy. Also, like blogs, most wikis allows teachers to track every posted entry to see who is making entries and who in the class is not, and even in collaborative work, that feature is quite useful for following individual student contributions.

Wikis can also be used to encourage students to publish their own work contributions in a mathematics problem-solving scenario (Wetzel, 2012). Students will quickly get used to editing everyone else's content, and over time, this leads to an online, collaborative community of math learners who serve as a resource for each other. In that sense, wikis will move your students toward increased participation and increased enjoyment of math. Again, students

With a wiki, teachers can encourage a much richer student collaboration, since in the wiki students can actually edit the work of others collaboratively, while working within the same digital file.

are demonstrating by their out-of-school actions that they love social networking, and by using that motivation for increased social exchange in the context of mathematics instruction, teachers can use a class wiki to encourage students to participate more fully in the classroom and while completing math homework.

Further, the skills developed within the wiki truly represent 21st century skills. In developing written or video content for the mathematics wiki, students learn how to work together, sort through information, evaluate information using various sources, create newly synthesized information, and make contributions to the content already on the wiki (Bender & Waller, 2013; Richardson, 2010). These are the skills that will be demanded by the 21st century workplace, and merely using a wiki teaches these skills.

Wikis serve one instructional function better than any other teaching tool: Wikis are excellent for teaching mathematics vocabulary! From the mid-elementary grades and up, mathematics curricula involve developing vocabulary, and many teachers spend some time on math vocabulary in each unit of instruction. In contrast, using a class wiki in math can save that time!

Within the wiki, teachers can merely list the vocabulary terms for the instructional unit and have students define the terms and provide examples in the wiki. Students can pick up the definitions for each term as they work through the wiki, while checking the work of their peers. Teachers should merely list vocabulary terms on an "unlocked" (i.e., editable) wiki page, and have the students define those terms. By requiring that such work be completed on the class wiki, the teacher saves valuable class time. Students still get the content, however, in a manner similar to their use of Wikipedia. Most students enjoy this type of activity and will learn vocabulary terms based on this activity, without the teacher having to take additional class time to teach the vocabulary for mathematics.

> Wikis serve one function for teachers, perhaps better than any other teaching tool: Wikis are excellent for teaching mathematics vocabulary.

As schools today are striving to make Wi-Fi and computers or tablets (e.g., iPads) available, many teachers are considering how to use this Internet connectivity in the math class. A wiki is one of the best ways to do so. In fact, teachers who have never used a wiki previously can set up a wiki for their class in approximately 30 to 45 minutes. Further, the Internet provides many sites that will assist teachers in developing and using wikis. I typically suggest that teachers use the Wikispaces website (www.wikispaces.com) for setting up a class wiki, since that service is free for teachers (see Figure 5.1).

Figure 5.1 Wikispaces Website

Source: Wikispaces © 2012 Tangient LLC

Today seven million teachers and students are already using Wikispaces for their class wiki. In order to help you learn how to use this wiki, we recommend that you review brief videos from the Wikispaces homepage (www.wikispaces.com/content/wiki-tour). While the actual steps in setting up a wiki for a math class vary depending on the website you choose, the general steps in Teaching Tip 5.3 should help you get started on your class wiki.

Teaching Tip 5.3   Creating a Math Wiki for Your Class

Select a Wiki Name and Password

Begin by going to the Wikispaces website (www.wikispaces.com/site/for/teachers). There you may select the option to set up a free wiki (toward the lower right of the homepage). Next you will be asked to select a username, password, and a Wikispace name.

Select Your Security Level

Student security is critical as students begin to use the Internet, so I suggest that teachers create a private wiki, which only class members and school administrators can view or edit. Later you may wish to make the wiki available to parents for viewing only (not editing). The private wiki option is free for educators.

(Continued)

(Continued)

Create a Wiki Homepage

As the first page within the wiki, you should create a homepage that includes a brief introduction to the class and other basic information. Teachers first create a title for the wiki at the top of the homepage, using the "Heading" function at the top of the page (select "Level One Heading)." That will bold the heading and increase its size.

Next, I suggest that a title page should have an opening or introductory paragraph. This should be a paragraph-long description of the content and purpose of the wiki. You should phrase this paragraph as an "interest grabbing" paragraph, and using questions is very appropriate.

Add Videos or Digital Photos

The goal of the wiki homepage is to excite the interest of the students, so teachers should add a set of interesting photos or videos on mathematics related to the topics that will be studied. You may also add another heading such as "Recommended Videos," or "Problems you will soon learn about!" Below that heading you will put links to videos you select that can grab students' attention, or examples of problems to be studied. You can find interesting math videos on many of the websites previously mentioned or on YouTube, TeacherTube, PBS.org, or the Discovery Channel. Generally you should select shorter rather than longer video segments (3- to 10-minute video examples).

Add a Navigation Option

Next, you should select a navigation option, since you will add many more pages to your wiki. The navigation option lets students know how to get from one page to the next. In the edit bar at the top of the page is a button called "wedgets." Click that, and a list of options to add to your wiki will open, one of which is "add the navigation tool." When you click that, a navigation tool will be added at the bottom of the page you are on that will allow you or your students to navigate to other wiki pages.

Create Locked and Unlocked Wiki Pages

Now you are nearly finished with the homepage, and you now need to lock up the content that you don't want students to edit. In most cases, teachers don't want the students (or anyone else) to edit the content on the homepage, so that page of content needs to be locked down. While many wiki pages are available for students to edit, the homepage generally should not be.

To lock a page in a wiki, move the cursor to the top right of the edit bar, over the series of dots, and click there. Then you are presented with options, one of which is "Lock" this page. Click that once you are completely done with your homepage. You will need to repeat that "lock" for each page you want locked down. As creator of the class wiki, you will always have the option of unlocking any page for your own edits. However, you will need to lock it down again at the end of that process.

Create Other Wiki Pages

Next, you will need to create additional wiki pages on the math content that students can edit. These "unlocked" pages allow students to make creative contributions to the wiki. One of these should be a vocabulary page, discussed previously in text, and Box 5.3 presents a series of instructional ideas, each of which could be a separate page in your class wiki.

Adjust the Look of Your Wiki

There are a variety of options to change the color of items or the background color of your class wiki, and you should play with those options over time. Teachers can use the "edit this page" tab in the tool bar at the top of the page to manipulate text, change fonts, and adjust spacing for each page. While this is not really essential, a nicer looking wiki can be more engaging for students.

Invite Students and Parents to Join Your Class Wiki

Once your wiki is ready, teachers must invite students to join the wiki using the "User Creator feature." In some cases, teachers can sign their students up directly, and that is preferable to the invitation process. After using two or three wikis for the initial instructional units in your math class, you can consider inviting the parents to join the wiki as observers. This can foster a great deal of good will for you, and it is almost guaranteed to improve the parents' perception of your instructional skills.

I always recommend, as a student safety option, that at least one other educator be included on a class wiki. This might include administrators, department chairpersons, or other school leaders, who would not really follow the wiki, but might access it from time to time. This can serve as a useful oversight function if anyone ever raises a question about any of the content on the wiki.

Differentiating instruction using a class wiki is relatively easy, because any differentiation option you can use in the general education classroom is likewise an option for the wiki. However, since wikis allow students to participate in their learning through actual creation of content for the wiki, students will tend to segregate themselves somewhat, based on their learning styles, preferences, and strengths, as they complete activities collaboratively within the wiki framework. In that sense, differentiated instruction begins to take place almost without teacher input, when instruction is based in a class wiki.

For example, interpersonal learners may be more inclined to work together on an online of a geometry problem, whereas students who are more

Since wikis allow students to participate in their learning through actual creation of content for the wiki, students will tend to segregate themselves somewhat, based on their learning styles, preferences, and strengths.

inclined to movement-based learning may wish to work together and develop a "walk-through map" of the geometric problem. Either of those could be used to generate a digital video-tape that could then be uploaded to the class wiki. As this example illustrates, students will have many options to exercise their learning strengths when wikis are used within the math class.

Calculators in Mathematics: A Running Debate

For years, teachers of mathematics have debated and even decried the use of calculators in mathematics (Fahsl, 2007; National Mathematics Advisory Panel, 2008). Some teachers in elementary, middle, and high school allow or encourage the use of calculators, whereas others discourage such use, based on concerns that calculators may ultimately impair a student's instant recall of math facts. Some teachers suspect that use of calculators may even impair the student's deeper understanding of mathematics.

Clearly, as students progress into higher mathematics including problem solving, their knowledge of math facts becomes critically important, and most students do ultimately reach some level of automaticity (instant memory) for math facts. In later mathematics, when the emphasis in the mathematics lessons may have shifted away from calculation and math facts into more complex problem solving, such automaticity greatly facilitates success in math. However, many students with learning disabilities and others who are struggling in math may not have achieved automaticity in basic math facts (Foegen, 2008; L. S. Fuchs, Fuchs, Powell et al., 2008), and the use of a calculator for certain functions in mathematics may be desirable for struggling students.

The Common Core Mathematics Standards, and in particular the Standards for Mathematical Practice, allow for the use of calculators (see Standard 5, in Box 1.1 of this book). However, this should not be taken to mean that students should not learn their basic math facts. The National Mathematics Advisory Panel (2008) reviewed research on the use of calculators and found little support either for or against the use of calculators in the math curriculum, though the report did note that use of calculators in lower grades was a serious concern among algebra teachers. The report further cautioned that to the degree that use of calculators impedes development of automaticity with math facts, the student's fluency in computation would be adversely affected.

With these concerns noted, caution is advised concerning the use of calculators in mathematics, and teachers who allow the use of calculators should judicially consider appropriate use of these technology supports. Fahsl (2007) suggested that students be allowed to use calculators on only certain types of tasks (e.g., on checking work that has already been completed or solving complex problems). However, if the aim of a particular mathematics lesson involves automaticity in math facts, the use of calculators should not be allowed.

DIFFERENTIATED INSTRUCTION FOR DEEP CONCEPTUAL UNDERSTANDING

As noted previously, the cognitivist perspective suggests that students construct their understanding of new math concepts based on previous knowledge and various supports provided by the teacher relative to new content material. In addition to the tech-based strategies above, a number of other strategies are used as scaffolds within this cognitivist perspective to help students construct mathematical understandings in the mid-elementary grades. The strategies presented below exemplify the types of instructional practices recommended today, ranging from graphic instruction for math facts, to various strategies for problem solving in the mid-elementary grades.

Graphic Instruction for Times Tables

Instead of rote memory for learning the times tables, representational examples or even concrete examples can also help. Woodward (2006) described a graphic example for teaching times tables, based on conceptual and representational manipulation of previously derived facts. Specifically, in teaching the higher times table facts, students might be taught to utilize what they already know and from that derive the correct answer. When a student is confronted with the fact $7 \times 8 = ?$, and he or she already knows that $7 \times 7 = 49$, the student can derive the necessary math fact by thinking the problem through based on what is already known. The problem of $7 \times 8 = ?$ may be conceptualized on a number line as demonstrated in Figure 5.2.

Pattern Times Tables Instruction

The Common Core Math Standards clearly emphasize patterns in mathematics (see Math Practices Number 7 in Box 1.1, Chapter 1), and times tables are an excellent vehicle for pattern-based teaching. In fact, teachers have discovered that for many children it is critical to start with

Figure 5.2 Number Line

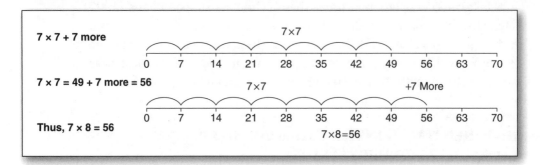

easy patterns prior to moving into more difficult patterns (Lock, 1996). As an example of a skill progressing from easy to more difficult, consider instructions in times tables (multiplication math facts). Rather than teaching the times tables in order (1 x table; 2 x table; 3 x table; 4 x table, etc.), as is typically done, teachers can teach the multiplication patterns fact from easy to more difficult by teaching the 1 x table and the 2 x table, followed by the 5 x table and the 10 x table. This is easy because students can be taught (or may already know) the one and two levels, and may even be able to count by five or by 10. Thus, the first tables taught tend to be confidence building and easy to memorize.

Next, one might teach the "squares" pattern (i.e., 3×3; 4×4; 5×5; 6×6, etc.). Then, the teacher might emphasize the commutative property in reversed problems ($3 \times 4 = 4 \times 3$). Next, the teacher might produce a multiplication chart of math facts of all the multiplication tables from one through 10, and use that to illustrate how many facts in the new times tables the student already knows from the lower times tables. Thus, the times tables can be made easier by teaching from easy to more difficult patterns.

Process Mnemonics for Computation

Another tactic that facilitates differentiated instruction in computation is based on process mnemonics (Higbee, 1987; Manolo, 1991; Manolo, Bunnell, & Stillman, 2000). Mnemonics are acronyms or sentences that may be used for assisting with memory tasks, and this tactic has been used for many decades in reading instruction. For example, simple process mnemonics have been used as reminders of processes in a variety of language arts tasks over the years (e.g., "'i' before 'e' except after 'c' and when sounding like an 'a' as in neighbor and weigh"). However, little use has been made of process mnemonics in math instruction, until the last several decades (Manolo et al., 2000).

Mnemonics are used in Japan to summarize the organization and the process of problem solving (Manolo, 1991; Manolo et al., 2000). Manolo and his coworkers (2000) hypothesized that since process mnemonics had been shown to be an effective teaching tool for students with normal abilities, it could hold promise for use with students who are struggling in math.

Process mnemonics utilizes representations of constructs in math that assist students with memory. In one research study, Manolo and others (2000) found they could engage students more actively in the mathematics process by presenting numbers as "warriors" and mathematical operations as situational military stories to teach the rules and procedures necessary for numerical addition, subtraction, multiplication, and division of whole numbers and decimals. Several example adaptations of this tactic are presented in Box 5.4.

BOX 5.4   Process Mnemonics Examples

Process Mnemonics for Teaching Decimals

Subtraction: The process mnemonic for subtraction of whole numbers and decimal fractions tells students to imagine that the two numbers are different sets of warriors doing battle. The digit on each warrior denotes his strength. Warriors to the left of the decimal point are ranked, and those to the right of the decimal point are not ranked. To fight, the warriors must be lined up ranked against ranked and unranked against unranked in battle—this reminds the students to line up the decimal places prior to subtracting. The top group of warriors in the subtraction problem is designated the defenders and the bottom group is the attackers. The attackers can be recognized because they have their swords drawn (i.e., the minus sign in the problem).

$$24.6 \qquad \text{defender}$$
$$-12.7 \qquad \text{attacker}$$

When subtracting, if the defender's strength in any column (i.e., the number in the top row) is less than the attacker's strength (the number in the same column on the bottom row), the defender has to be increased by ten in order to do battle. The consequence of this is that the next defender has his strength reduced by one. For example,

$$24.6 \qquad \text{changes into} \qquad 23.6 + 10$$
$$-12.7 \qquad\qquad\qquad\qquad -12.7$$

Students then solve for the answer: $\qquad\qquad$ 11.9

Addition: Addition problems are presented as the warriors getting into a boat (Manolo, 1991; Manolo et al., 2000). The addition sign is the mast and the line

(Continued)

(Continued)

below is the boat itself. Students should be taught that the warriors (numbers) to the left of the decimal point are ranked and those to the right are unranked, just as in the subtraction example above. They must always line up the lines of warriors ranked with ranked and unranked with unranked. If there is an unranked warrior lined up in the same column with a blank on the right of the decimal point, then the student should put a zero in that blank space, since a warrior with a rank of zero really doesn't matter and doesn't affect the outcome at all. In that type of situation, the problem changes as follows:

$$
\begin{array}{r} 39.4 \\ + 12.45 \\ \hline \end{array}
\qquad \text{becomes} \qquad
\begin{array}{r} 39.40 \\ + 12.45 \\ \hline \end{array}
$$

If the numbers have no dots, then students could put dots to the right of the warrior farthest to the right, and then line up the warriors by using the dots. Finally, they would solve the problem.

$$
\begin{array}{r} 47 \\ + 9 \\ \hline \end{array}
\qquad \text{becomes} \qquad
\begin{array}{r} 47. \\ + 9. \\ \hline \end{array}
$$

Multiplication: Multiplication problems are presented as warriors at a meeting to exchange battle strategies (Manolo, 1991; Manolo et al., 2000). The warriors in the bottom set are the "experts," and are found next to the X or "times" sign. Each of these "X-perts" must meet each of the members of the group of warriors on the top row to teach them their "special battle techniques." For example, in the problem below, the "×-pert" 4 must meet with the 7, 5, 6, 8, and 3 of the top group. Students should be reminded to place ranked above ranked and unranked above unranked when they first copy down the problem. Multiplying the respective numbers and then writing the answers below the line produces the products of their planning meetings. The skills of the warriors become more specialized the farther left they are. Placing zeros whenever the student moves on to a more specialized warrior marks these specialized results.

$$
\begin{array}{r}
386.57 \\
\times 23.4 \\
\hline
154628 \\
1159710 \\
7721400 \\
\hline
9035738 \\
\end{array}
$$

Students should be shown how to count all the unranked warriors and then count that many places from the right to the left of the final answer to place the decimal point in the answer correctly. See the example below.

$$386.57 \text{ (In this problem, the student would count 3 unranked warriors)}$$
$$\times\, 23.4$$
$$\overline{}$$
$$154628$$
$$1159710$$
$$\underline{7721400}$$

9035.738 (Thus, the 3 unranked warriors mean that the student should place the decimal between the 5 and 7 in the answer.)

Division: In division, the students are told to imagine the warriors standing in front of a rack of various pieces of armor (Manolo, 1991; Manolo et al., 2000). Each warrior is trying on a set of armor inside the cupboard, and the cupboard is represented by the long division symbol itself or $\sqrt{}$. However, only ranked warriors may try on armor, so if the divisor has a dot (or a decimal), the dot must be moved all the way to the right. Also, the dot in the cupboard must be shifted the same number of places to the right. Thus, division problems are changed as indicated below.

$.08\sqrt{34.26}$ becomes $08\sqrt{3426}$ with all the decimals shifted two spots to the right.

Additional pieces of armor can be added to the rack if there is not enough armor already in the cupboard to shift the decimal the number of spaces needed. Students should be told that a decimal above the cupboard separates "expensive" armor from "inexpensive" armor. The warrior tries on the first piece of armor (in this problem, the size of that piece of armor is 3) and finds that it is too small to fit a big warrior (who in this problem is size 8). Therefore the warrior gets the next piece also, and the size now becomes 34. To tell how well the armor fits, the students should use a multiplication chart to look under the warrior's size (8) and go down that row in the table to find the size of armor closest to size 34 but not more than 34. Students should write the "measure of fit" below the armor piece in the question, then go across the table to find the number of times the warrior fitted the armor (in this example, it is 4).

Students should be told to write that number above the armor size in the cupboard, above the second digit in 34. At that point the student will have written:
$$\begin{array}{r} 4 \\ 08\sqrt{3486} \\ \underline{32} \end{array}$$

To find out how much of the armor was not used, students should subtract the "measure of fit" from the pieces of armor being tried on. This leftover number (in this case, 2) should be checked to make sure it is not larger than the size of the warrior. The next piece of armor is then brought down from the cupboard and the warrior tries it on, looking for the "measure of fit" once again. This process is repeated until the warrior has tried on each piece of armor.

Source: Adapted from Manolo, 1991; Manolo et al., 2000.

Various research over the last two decades has shown that process mnemonics such as this is very effective for students with difficulties in math (Higbee, 1987; Manolo, 1991; Manolo et al., 2000). This tactic increases students' motivation in that the use of "warriors" makes math operations seem similar to many of the movies and video games that are so popular today. The metaphors involving warriors and their battles facilitate better retrieval of correct procedures.

Another reason why process mnemonics is so effective is that this tactic actively engages numerous fundamental mental principles of learning and memory, including organization of the constructs, association with well-understood concepts (e.g., warriors have enemies and battles), attention, and visualization. Higbee (1987) also suggests that process mnemonics provides structure that makes better sense to students. It uses concrete associations to like abstract symbols into a cohesive combination of relevance. For these reasons, teachers moving into differentiated math classes should consider using this innovative tactic for either tear-out or mainline instructional groups.

Visualization

As noted previously, there does seem to be a relationship between visual processing skills in the brain and number sense and early mathematics readiness skills. For that reason, various researchers have explored the use of visualization in mathematics instruction (Foegen, 2008; Sousa, 2008). Visualization has been used to problem solve from the mid-elementary grades and up (Foegen, 2008), and the visualization tactic allows a teacher to cognitively guide the student during the math problem, and thus help the student to bridge the gap between concrete or representational understandings, and more abstract problem solving. In fact, teaching children how to visualize the problem graphically when problem solving can help them to make sense of the problem and develop increased abstract thinking ability. Thus, the intentional construction of an "image" of the problem will typically enhance a student's conceptual understanding of the problem.

Several researchers have suggested a cognitive guided inquiry method to assist students in visualizing problems (Behrend, 2003; Foegen, 2008). All children, including children who may struggle in math, have some natural problem-solving abilities, and Behrend (2003) suggested that teachers begin with the problem-solving strategies that students generate naturally. From that basis, teachers will use a series of focused questions to help students visualize the problem more completely. In this technique, the teacher asks focused questions that draw the students' attention to various aspects of the math problem. As an example, a series of such focused questions is presented in the teacher-student dialogue in Box 5.5.

BOX 5.5   Cognitive Guided Visualization Example

Problem:

Maria has 4 bags of cookies. There are 3 cookies in each bag. How many cookies in all?

Dialogue:

Teacher:	Jay, tell me about how you got your answer of 7.
Jay:	I didn't really know how to do it so I said 4 and 3 makes 7, so 7 is my answer.
Teacher:	Does that tell you how many cookies there are? Would you like me to read the problem again?
Jay:	OK.
Teacher:	Think about it. There are 4 bags of cookies. Got that in your head?
Jay:	Yeah. (He might grab for counters.)
Teacher:	And there are 3 cookies in each bag.
Jay:	Three in each bag?
Teacher:	Yes, 3 cookies in each bag.
Jay:	OK, so I need some more of these [counters]. (Jay puts 3 "cookies" in each of 4 "bags" represented by circles on a piece of paper.)
Teacher:	So, how many cookies are there? (Jay counts the "cookies" and finds that . . .)
Jay:	There are 12 cookies!
Teacher:	That's right! There are 12 cookies in all.

As shown in this dialogue, the visualization begins with students' natural attempts to problem solve. Next, teachers should ask focused questions to assist students in understanding the problem more thoroughly in order to help them visualize it. Over time, being reminded of the conditions in a particular type of problem coupled with visualization of the problem will strengthen a student's problem-solving ability. The use of visualization also helps students generalize these newly awakened problem-solving strategies. Further, focusing on problem visualization even allows students to solve multiple-step problems that include extraneous information, because the visualization assists students to attend to only relevant information (Behrend, 2003; Carpenter, Fennema, & Franke, 1996).

Thus, instead of automatically assuming that their own answer is wrong—as many struggling students do—students can become more confident in justifying how they arrived at their own answer. When students explain their own answers to others, they and others can often spot errors that have been made and correct them. The group work basis of this tactic makes it very effective in a differentiated math class, as either a tear-out tactic or as a tactic for use with the mainline instructional group.

The implementation of cognitively guided visualization is simple, but it will be different for every student or group of students. First, working in a small tear-out group, the teacher would provide a problem for the students to consider. Next, the teacher should allow students to solve the problem in their own way. Then, the teacher will have the students share the strategies they used. Finally, using focused questions with students who got an incorrect answer, the teacher should guide them through the visualization process to arrive at the correct answer. In fact, after students have participated in this method, it should be possible for the teacher to use students for the final step above—having students ask the "guiding" questions. Initially, this should be done under the supervision of the teacher, but as students become fluent in this technique, it is possible to use this in a tear-out group, with an experienced student doing the guiding.

Behrend (2003) used this strategy to assess whether visualization would foster more accurate problem solving in two elementary-age students who were having difficulty in math. The two students explored a problem similar to the one in the dialogue above, and each devised a strategy to answer the problem. Each answer was incorrect. By encouraging one student's desire to explore mathematics and teaching the other student to "think more and guess less," Behrend demonstrated that those students with math deficits could be taught to use visualization to make sense of the word problems. They learned how to model the problem situation using manipulatives to aid their own visualization, and were thus more actively engaged in the problem than they would have been had the problem been presented merely as a paper-and-pencil task. Further, when errors were made, they were able to realize where and why their own problem solving broke down and to see how to solve future problems correctly.

As this example illustrates, cognitive guided visualization is a technique that can assist students in moving from concrete or representational mathematics toward deeper, more abstract thinking (Foegen, 2008). Also, research has shown that these techniques result in greater conceptual understanding of math than merely rote memory or static, "practice sheet" types of instruction. Clearly, this is the direction emphasized by the Common Core, as discussed in Chapter 1.

Teaching Cue Words

In helping students understand word problems, many teachers begin by teaching certain cue words that represent operations. Words such as "more than," "less than," "extra," "gave away," and "add" often represent specific operations, and learning these can be a first step in problem solving. In fact, in almost all word problems, certain terms are used that are suggestive of various operations, and word problems generally involve translation of these cue words into mathematical operations. Many teachers find that students are more motivated when they are taught that solving word problems really involves a "secret code" or set of cue words that the teacher can teach them. Because these words do not always have the same meaning in all word problems, teachers should caution students to verify their interpretation of cue words by other information within the problem. At the very least, the teacher can assure students that the cue words "often indicate" a particular operation.

> *Cognitive guided visualization is a technique that can assist students in moving from concrete or representational mathematics toward deeper, more abstract thinking.*

Initially, during instruction involving cue words, the teacher should select only problems in which the cue words mean the obvious operations. The student in Grades 3 through 5 should be trained to use the cue words and write a "number sentence" to represent a single operation problem. Then multiple operation problems that require multiple number sentences are introduced. When grading this work, teachers may wish to assign a certain number of points to correctly identifying this number sentence independent of points awarded for problem solution.

> *Many teachers find that students are more motivated when they are taught that solving word problems really involves a "secret code" or set of cue words that the teacher can teach them.*

Teachers using the cue word strategy may wish to prepare a poster of these cue words and place it in front of the class, and refer to it often when discussing word problems. When a word problem is initially read in class, the teacher should challenge the students to find the cue words in the problem. Each of those should then be investigated to determine its meaning in that particular problem.

Finally, teachers should require that students complete some problems in which the cue words represent different operations from those they typically represent, and offer instruction on how the meaning was changed based on sentence construction in the problem. Initially, however, the teacher should present a simple word problem. Here is an example:

Both Alonzo and his sister, Mia, had an opportunity from the teacher at school to take home some extra crackers. Now, Alonzo knew that his mom loved him and worked hard to feed the family each day, so he decided he'd bring her 10 crackers to show his love in return. From his teacher, he took 14 crackers, and Mia picked up 6 more. When Alonzo told Mia about his plans to give some crackers to Mom, he and Mia agreed to add their crackers together, take 10 crackers home for their mom, and split the rest. With that in mind, how many crackers could each one eat before getting home?

Next, the teacher should ask the students what words in the problem might be cues on how to solve the problem. The students and teacher should note the terms (i.e., more, how many, add). The teacher may wish to discuss that the term "more" may often mean addition, as it does here, whereas phrases like "how many crackers could each one eat" might suggest subtraction.

Differentiation using the cue word strategy is not difficult. After the introduction of the sample problem described above and before the teacher-led instruction, the teacher should use the Guess, Assess, and Tear Out tactic described in Chapter 2 to identify a group of students for a differentiated activity. While the teacher conducts the lesson for the remaining students in the mainline group, the tear-out group could do a related activity. These activities may include the following:

One subgroup "analyzes" a different problem by noting the cue words in the problem. Depending on the level of the group overall, the teacher may provide a tiered version of this activity by either providing the list of cue words to the students in this group or not doing so. Later in the lesson, that problem could be used as a class illustration.

Another tear-out group may be instructed to make up two new word problems, using a minimum of two of the cue words in each problem from the list of cue words presented above. Next, that group should solve the problems before presenting them to the class.

A Word Problem Map

Another example of a scaffold that can assist students in understanding word problems is the word problem map. As noted throughout this text, many students with learning difficulties in math have problems organizing their thoughts during any learning task; this can be devastating to students' efforts to comprehend math word problems. These students may not understand that in most word problems there is an underlying structure that can be identified, and that identification of this structure can assist in problem solution. A number of researchers have encouraged specific instruction in identification of the overall structure of the math problem for students who are struggling in math (Gagnon & Maccini, 2001), and this has become known as the word problem map. A sample word problem map is presented in Box 5.6.

BOX 5.6   A Word Problem Map

A Word Problem Map

Name:_____Date:_____Problem Number:_____

What type of problem is this?
_____
_____

The problem asked for what information?
_____
_____

What cue words were used?
_____
_____

These cue words suggest what operations?
_____
_____

Is there a particular order in which I must perform these operations?
_____
_____

(At this point, the student should attempt the problem.)

Did I get an answer that seems correct?
_____
_____

Have I rechecked the problem to make certain I understand it, and is there anything I missed?
_____
_____
_____

Source: Bender (2012a).

As indicated within this word problem map, the concept of cue words is stressed once again (Gagnon & Maccini, 2001). However, this tactic goes beyond merely using cue words and actually helps students structure their cognitive understanding of the word problem. The word problem map is intended to assist the student with a learning problem in math to organize his or her thoughts concerning the structure of the word problem. Thus, when a student reads a math problem in the general education classroom, he or she should be required to simultaneously complete the word problem map as a scaffold on which to build understanding of that problem.

This word problem map activity is also very effective when completed as a buddy activity; two or three students may partner together to complete the map. Furthermore, these word problem maps should be reviewed in class as a post-problem activity to check for accuracy and for comprehension of the problem.

The word problem map may be adapted as necessary across the grade levels, and teachers should feel free to implement this in any fashion they desire that works for their students. Finally, the word problem map can be used as a study guide for any future tests on that content. In fact, a wide variety of instructional activities can be built around the word problem map concept.

DIFFERENTIATED INSTRUCTIONAL PLAN: GRADES 3 THROUGH 6

As mentioned in the previous chapter, I intend to make some general recommendations as to how teachers may wish to use these strategies to differentiate math classes at the various grade levels. Once again, every class is different and teachers have varying comfort levels with the different instructional ideas, so these suggestions should be used merely as guidelines. In some of the cases below, I recommend that teachers merely continue with the recommendations made for earlier grades. A differentiated instruction plan for math classes in Grades 3 through 6 is presented in Teaching Tip 5.4.

Teaching Tip 5.4   Differentiated Instructional Plan: Grades 3 Through 6

These guidelines are based on the assumption that teachers have explored many of the differentiated instructional options presented in Box 4.5 in the previous chapter.

Continue Khan Academy

I recommended that teachers throughout the grade levels set up every member of their class within Khan Academy, and allocate 15 minutes daily work for this.

Continue Instructional Gaming in Math

Teachers should find a gaming website that meets their needs, and have students practice mathematics using educational games, using those several times each week. This will facilitate positive experiences in mathematics.

Flip the Math Class

Beginning as early as Grade 3, but certainly by Grade 4, teachers should experiment with flipping the mathematics class, as described in Chapter 3. I recommend that teachers begin a new content or conceptual area by having students view a video demonstration as homework, and use the next math class period as a peer-buddy practice time on that type of problem. I'd recommend such peer-buddy activity for 20 minutes daily.

Ideally, all initial instruction in mathematics could be completed in a "flipped" fashion by Grade 5, saving teachers a great deal of instructional time in the math class.

Set Up a Blog

Beginning in Grade 3, if not before, teachers should have students working within a class blog. This will facilitate much student-to-student coaching on mathematics problems, and should foster increased engagement. Teachers may require students to make a blog posting a minimum of twice a week, as an out-of-class assignment.

Teach With a Mathematics Wiki

At least by Grade 4, teachers should migrate from the class blog to a wiki format to increase students' social interaction and communication on mathematics. Students should interact with each other via the class wiki on a daily basis for 10 to 15 minutes.

Continue Using Student Avatars

Many students enjoy using avatars, and if students are used to this, I suggest that avatars be used throughout the elementary math years.

Devise a Range of Tier 2 and Tier 3 Intervention Options

Any of the scaffolded interventions described in this chapter could become excellent interventions, since scaffolded instruction often means individual instruction anyway. Using word problem maps, process mnemonics, or graphic illustrations can greatly assist students struggling in math, and thus these make effective interventions at the Tier 2 and 3 levels.

By using this differentiated instructional plan, all students will receive exactly the instruction they need, at their level, and the fears and anxieties associated with mathematics will be alleviated, based on the fun associated with math games and successful experiences.

WHAT'S NEXT?

This chapter has presented a variety of differentiation strategies for the mid-elementary grades, including more advanced strategies for increasing number sense in 8- to 11-year-old students. Within the context of constructivist theory, a variety of additional tech-based teaching strategies were discussed including blogs and wikis for the math class. Also, several scaffolded instruction tactics were presented, including graphic representations for math facts, process mnemonics, cue words, and word problem maps. As in the previous chapter, a differentiated instructional plan was presented with specific recommendations about structuring the differentiated mathematics class in the primary grade levels.

In the next chapter, the focus is on the higher elementary and middle school grades. Social networking options will be described, as many teachers in middle school are using social networking as a teaching tool, and cognitive instructional strategies for the early teen years will be presented, that will assist in developing conceptual understanding in mathematics.

Strategies for Differentiating Instruction in Grades 6 Through 8

6

DIFFERENTIATED INSTRUCTION FOR THE MIDDLE SCHOOL GRADES

Moving Into Middle School Mathematics

As students progress in mathematics into the middle school grades, the demands within the mathematics curriculum, once again, increase. For example, within the Common Core Math Standards there is increasing emphasis on conceptual understanding, math modeling, problem solving, and on operations with fractions of all types in the higher grade levels (Garelick, 2012). With this recent emphasis on increasing conceptual understanding, students are increasingly exposed to problems embedded in real-world scenarios. Further, within the Common Core, middle school mathematics requirements are likely to change significantly (Magee, 2013). There will be two different pathways in mathematics at the middle school level: one that allows students to take algebra, and a second that provides general mathematics classes to prepare students for ninth-grade algebra. In states that had previously required algebra as an eighth-grade mathematics class, this represents a significant curricular change.

> Within the Common Core Math Standards there is increasing emphasis on conceptual understanding, math modeling, problem solving, and on operations with fractions of all types in the higher grade levels.

189

Emphasis on Mathematical Reasoning

Within the Common Core Mathematics Standards, mathematical reasoning is stressed for all grades, but in particular it is stressed for the middle grades (see Standard 2 of the Standards for Mathematical Practice, in Box 1.1, Chapter 1). As students mature, their ability to practice inductive and deductive reasoning in applied situations increases. Inductive reasoning involves generating understandings from specific cases, while looking for patterns in the information, and then making generalizations. Thus, students are using inductive reasoning when they make and justify a conjecture based on what they have observed. For example, students exploring the angles of a triangle might investigate several angles in several different triangles and determine that the sum of the angles for those triangles was, consistently, 180 degrees (Annenberg Learner, 2013). The students' conjecture is based on what they have observed from testing many triangles, so they are using inductive reasoning.

In contrast, deductive reasoning involves using general rules to prove a hypothesis about a particular case. In other words, deductive reasoning uses statements that we already know are true to prove other statements. In the example above, once students make the observation on the sum of the triangles in an angle, they would move toward a generalized rule that the sum of angles in any triangle is 180 degrees. Middle grades students usually justify their reasoning through the use of inductive reasoning, initially (Annenberg Learner, 2013). However, the goal of the mathematics teacher is helping students move toward more formal justifications or proofs using deductive reasoning.

Within the Common Core, reasoning and proof are not isolated topics, but rather should be integrated into all aspects of middle school mathematics. In that sense, students should be highly engaged in rich mathematical content that develops a mathematical concept and encourages students to extend their findings into other situations through development and testing of hypotheses. It is critical that students have the opportunity to share and justify their reasoning with others, as emphasized in Standards 3 and 4 of the Standards for Mathematical Practice (see Box 1.1, Chapter 1). Effective questioning by the teacher (or by other students) is critical for fostering inductive and deductive reasoning skills. Asking questions (e.g., "How did you come to that conclusion?"), or simply saying, "Justify your answer, please," are teaching habits that all mathematics teachers should develop. Teachers might have students work in teams in developing such justifications, and then have various other teams explore the accuracy of those justifications or proofs. There should always be many opportunities for students to share different strategies through these classroom interactions, as they reason mathematically, justify their ideas, and evaluate their own and others' thinking (Annenberg Learner, 2013).

New Strategies for Differentiating Math Classes

Even with these changes, many of the strategies and tactics presented previously continue to be quite effective in the middle school grades and upper elementary grades. However, there are several additional tactics that should enhance the learning for all students in these differentiated middle school and perhaps even secondary mathematics classes (Bottge, Rueda, LaRoque, Serlin, & Kwon, 2007; Shaftel, Pass, & Schnabel, 2005). This chapter presents a series of strategies that can be used to differentiate the mathematics classes from Grades 5 through middle school. First, several cutting-edge, tech-based teaching ideas are presented that can facilitate differentiated instruction, including the use of social networking for teaching. Specifically Facebook, Twitter, and Ning will all be discussed as social networking options for teachers to consider. Next, various tech-based collaborative or instructional support suggestions are presented. Then, a series of cognitive strategies, representative of the ongoing research in the cognitive sciences, is presented.

SOCIAL NETWORKING AND PERSONAL LEARNING NETWORKS

Facebook: A Powerful Teaching Tool for Mathematics

Facebook has become the premier social networking site, worldwide. It is not an overstatement to say that Facebook has become something of a cult phenomenon over the last decade, and it is difficult to find any middle grade or high school student who does not have a Facebook account. There is a lower age requirement for setting up a Facebook page (participants must be 13, and have an e-mail account), so this social networking option is not appropriate in primary or mid-elementary grades. However, many upper-grade teachers are using a Facebook page that is established strictly for use in their mathematics class, in order to engage students in math using a tech tool that students are very comfortable with. Facebook is, currently, the most popular social networking site used by students and adults worldwide to present information on themselves to the world, and by May 2013 over 1.1 billion individuals worldwide had chosen this social networking medium.

Facebook is the most popular social networking site used by over 1.1 billion students and adults worldwide to present information on themselves to the world.

On a typical Facebook page, an individual might post some information about himself or herself, including sets of pictures of themselves or their activities. They might list their hobbies and interests, or simply post a written entry one or more times each week (some do this many times a day) about their activities. Anyone else on Facebook can read those entries, if they search for and find the original person who posted the information. However, there are some controls that individuals can exercise to limit the information available about them. In most cases, students and teachers select a group of friends to share information with (leading to the new verb, "friend me"). Thus, over time, Facebook participants develop a network of "followers" who access the information and can post back to each other's Facebook page.

Because of the high popularity of this social medium, many teachers in the middle grade levels or high school have begun to set up Facebook pages dealing exclusively with problems, assignments, or other topics in their mathematics class (B. Ferriter, 2011; W. M. Ferriter & Garry, 2010; Watters, 2011c). These educationally based Facebook pages are not intended for social networking interactions; rather, these pages typically present information about the topic under study, including the teacher's notes, reminders, multi-post collaborative discussions, or student-created posts on the topic of study (Kessler, 2011; Phillips, 2011).

To illustrate the power of the Facebook instructional phenomenon, allow me to share a personal example of a teacher in an Atlanta-area high school. That teacher had previously encouraged students to use her cell phone number, on a very limited basis; they were to call her directly only on the evening before a unit test, if they needed help. She told the students she would specifically address any content questions they had only on that single evening. She reported that she had received no calls at all before the first three unit assessments, and after the third unit test, she asked why the students had not reached out to her with their questions as they studied prior to the tests. Their reply was enlightening!

We are all on Facebook anyway. Can't you just set up a Facebook page and let us contact you there?

This example, which is similar to the experiences of many other teachers today, demands that teachers consider reaching out to students in the medium that the students are comfortable using. When our students specifically request help via a specific communications option, shouldn't we, as mathematics teachers, set up that communication tool?

Of course, the impressive power of using technology to create learning opportunities for our students is only now being explored, but the advantages of networking via Facebook on various mathematics topics cannot be overlooked. For example, one recently developed

> *When our students specifically request help, via a specific communications option, shouldn't we, as mathematics teachers, set up that communication tool?*

educational app has been devised for Facebook, called Hoot.me (http://hoot.me/about/). This tool connects students from the same school or even the same math class that happen to be studying the same mathematics content on a given evening (Watters, 2011c).

Imagine this scenario. When a student gets online via Facebook, rather than ask the usual Facebook question, "What's on your mind?" the Hoot.me app prompts the student with the question, "What are you working on?" When students answer that question, with something like, "I'm doing homework on addition of fractions with unlike denominators," they might be presented with the option to join a study session with other students from their own math class related to that topic, who happen to be studying and on Facebook at that same time! Teachers can even encourage this by, on the evening before a unit test on that skill, reminding students to get on Facebook when they begin their homework studies that evening. In short, this application will seek out other students with a Facebook account, from the same school or class, who are likewise working on that topic (Watters, 2011c) and then suggests that those students chat with each other about that math content. Thus, this app is effectively pairing students together for joint study opportunities!

There are also many other uses for a math class Facebook page. For example, teachers can post reminders for students concerning what they should study, or add video links that explain specific math problems from YouTube, Khan Academy, or other such sources. Students can post questions they have on a math problem, and get multiple answers from other students within a matter of minutes on the class Facebook page. The ideas for using a powerful networking tool like Facebook are limited only by the teacher and students' imagination.

While many teachers have begun to explore Facebook as a teaching tool, there are some problems that teachers and schools must consider. For example, many schools that specifically block this content via a schoolwide "firewall." Other districts prohibit teachers and students from any social network contact. When schools consider these issues, it is obvious that prohibiting use of an effective 21st century communication tool is not advisable, and it is relatively easy for the instructional technology person at the school district to turn off a firewall.

Further, the concern of social networking between students and teachers can be effectively managed in many ways. One simple option, used at many schools, involves including a school administrator or lead teacher on each class Facebook page. This is typically enough to discourage inappropriate teacher/student social networking contacts.

Clearly, it is inappropriate for teachers to "socialize" with students on Facebook or in any other fashion beyond certain, very limited boundaries. However, in the 21st century world, one must consider a critical counterpoint. While social networking between teachers and students is not appropriate, it is also inappropriate for schools to *not* introduce students to the concept of using social networks as learning networks, focused on specific topics of study. Further, schools should model the idea of using the most advanced 21st century learning tools for every learning endeavor.

Given the importance of social networks in today's world, some schools have found other, more protected options for creating such networks. Box 6.1 presents several suggestions for helping teachers and students set up networks for instruction in the math class, independent of a Facebook page.

BOX 6.1 PROTECTED SOCIAL NETWORK OPTIONS FOR THE CLASSROOM

Edmodo

Edmodo is a free social networking option at which teachers and students can share information on the topic under study in a Facebook-type fashion (www .edmodo.com). Teachers can store links to relevant websites, digital files, assignments, and class calendars, and teachers and students alike can create and respond to information posted by others. After teachers create their free account, they invite their students to join. Students then sign up using a teacher-generated code that specifically assigns them to that teacher's class. Teachers can post to their class, or privately to students (e.g., for awarding grades). Also, there is a set of reinforcement badges that teachers can award for student work.

Twiducate

Twiducate is a recently developed social network (having begun in 2009), and it is more teacher friendly than the others (www.twiducate.com/). In this network, the teacher does all the initial work and gives students a simple code to punch in to establish their account. This network also provides more control for teachers than other free social networks.

Ning

Ning is a fee-based service that is currently being used by many educators (List & Bryant 2010). Ning is the world's largest platform for creating social networks (www.ning.com), and was originally designed for business. It includes all of the options offered by Facebook, and it is relatively cheap to use. In particular, Ning Mini (see the website above) is a simple option for small social networks such as an individual teacher's class, and originally cost $2.95 monthly. However, in 2010 Pearson Education, a large curriculum company, announced that they would partner with Ning to make these social networks free for teacher use. Those Ning Mini sites are limited to 150 persons, which should be enough for a teacher, her class, some administrators, and parents to join the network. Teachers need to visit the Pearson sign-up page to create a free Ning network (www.pearsoned.com/pearsonto-sponsor-free-access-for-educators-on-ning/#.UYP5_ZPD9jo).

To begin using a social network in your math class, you should initially consult your administrator about any school policies that bear on this question. Also, check with the instructional technology person at school about any firewalls that may be in place. However, once those issues are worked out, it is not difficult to begin using this tool in the math class. Teaching Tip 6.1 provides some guidelines on how teachers might establish a Facebook page for their math class.

Teaching Tip 6.1   Setting Up a Facebook Page for the Math Class

Select a Networking Platform

You should consider using Facebook, if possible, since many older students already have Facebook accounts. Again check with school authorities, and make it clear that this social networking page will focus exclusively on mathematics content. Also, to put everyone's mind at ease, you may wish to invite your administrator or another teacher to join in the discussions, or at least follow them. Also, either Edmodo or Ning options can be considered, if Facebook is not an option.

Investigate Potential Firewall Problems at School

In some cases, schools have established firewalls, or electronic blocks, that are intended to prohibit access to specific sites by school computers, including websites with inappropriate sexual content or vulgar language. Even in schools that do not prohibit the use of Facebook in the classroom, teachers have found that there may be a firewall prohibiting such usage.

(Continued)

(Continued)

While protecting students is certainly a worthy goal, I advocate that schools institute a policy of "acceptable uses" of the Internet, and have all students sign a pledge to abide by that policy. Such "acceptable use policies" can do more to prohibit students from getting into content that is inappropriate than firewalls typically do. While blocking some specific sites (e.g., sexual content sites, dating sites) may be appropriate in schools, the problem with firewalls is that they don't work very well. I often tell administrators, "You show me a firewall, and I'll find a middle school student in your school that can (and probably already has) gotten past it!" I think we do our students a better service when we stress appropriate Internet usage, rather than block locations that many teachers are finding to be effective instructional tools.

Inform Parents

Parents have many fears associated with Internet usage, and educators must be quite sensitive to those fears. I suggest that you have the administrator in the school send a letter to all of the parents in the math class informing them of the math class Facebook page. The parents should be assured that all communications on the Facebook class site will be instructional in nature, and that the teacher and school administrators will carefully monitor all communications at that Facebook account. Inviting parents to participate can go a long way to alleviating parental concerns.

Set Up Your Teacher Account

At this point, teachers should go to the Facebook website (or other network website) and complete the application process. The Facebook website requires an e-mail address, and instructions for establishing the account are fully explained at the site. The process for establishing Ning or Edomodo accounts is similar.

Invite Students (and Parents) to Participate

The next step is to invite students to join you on Facebook by sending each student a "friend" request. That process is straightforward and virtually any student who is familiar with Facebook can assist in that regard.

Create Initial Content

Once a Facebook (or Ning, or Edmodo) page is established, you should upload some content that might excite the class about the math topics to be covered. Teachers might write a brief paragraph on the unit under study and, if appropriate, ask students their opinions on one of the mathematic topics within that unit. This initial question can often begin an exciting, in-depth discussion of that issue or topic. You could post a math problem, or an example of where the mathematics under study are used in the real world. Also, you can invite students to find other "real world" examples. While teachers can post content to the Facebook page, I suggest that a better use of these networking options is to ask a question and have students do postings relative to that question. Also, don't post too much content on Facebook. While Facebook is an excellent way to heighten student interest, it is not the most appropriate format for presenting large chunks of information or multiple video examples at one time. A better format for that type of content is a class wiki, as discussed in the previous chapter.

Also, teachers using Facebook for the math class should make a determined effort to compliment students frequently on work they have completed successfully. Remember that parents often follow along on Facebook, and complimenting students on work well done certainly assists teachers in building successful relationships with both parents and students!

Post Daily

While some students check their Facebook status daily in most cases, others check it multiple times each day. I suggest that teachers do a daily post (on weekdays), if they choose to use Facebook in the classroom. These may be compliments on work, as noted above, or simple reminders of homework that is due, or quizzes that are planned for the class. You can post notes on news stories that involved mathematics, or interesting topics for students to explore. You can post brief notes for students to review. Because so many students enjoy Facebook, and participate on Facebook for many hours weekly, it is likely that a Facebook page for your class will dramatically increase the interest and engagement of your students (Watters, 2011c). Daily posts will help them feel much more comfortable in math.

Differentiating instruction in the context of a network is not difficult, since networks such as Facebook allow for private messaging. Thus, teachers can post private comments exclusively for particular students, suggesting different study strategies based on their learning profiles, or recommend particular items to consider related to the math content.

Also, differentiation is accomplished, in many cases, by what a student chooses to post. When students are creating comments or other content on their own, the students' selection of tasks is typically based on their own learning preferences, and thus, student postings often result in a high degree of differentiation. For example, visually oriented students are more likely to share graphics, videos, and so on, whereas linguistically talented students might share comments, charted data, or text. In this tech-based format, like many others, students tend to differentiate themselves by their selection of what they create and share with their teacher and classmates.

Twitter in the Classroom

Another option for socially, learning-focused networking with students today is the use of Twitter in the classroom (www.twitter.com). This book discussed blogging for the math class in Chapter 5. Twitter is a special type of blog, known as a "micro-blog," in which the size of each blog entry is strictly limited. In Twitter, each post (called "tweets") is specifically limited to 140 characters. However, even with that restriction on message length, there are still many uses of Twitter in the teaching and learning process, and Twitter is being used by many teachers today (Brumley, 2010; B. Ferriter, 2011). Twitter allows teachers and students to send and read brief blog-like messages, and each tweet posted on the author's (the teacher's) Twitter page will also be posted on the pages of persons following that teacher (in this case, the students).

> *Twitter is a micro-blogging service in which each posting is specifically limited to 140 characters.*

Twitter has been one of the fastest-growing social networks since 2008 (Richardson & Mancabelli, 2011). Further, educators are using Twitter in at least two ways, including both in instructional applications and professional development for teachers, and each is discussed below.

As a professional development tool, Twitter is a great source for brief descriptions of cutting-edge teaching ideas, recommendations for reading related to class instruction, or suggestions to follow specific blogs of other teachers. Instead of using Twitter as a "social network" many educators, including this author, are using Twitter exclusively to share educational ideas and suggestions for teachers.

In fact, here is an invitation for you personally! If you like, you can join me, the author of this book! You can "follow" me on Twitter by setting up a free Twitter account and then merely choosing to follow my comments (twitter.com/williambender1). I use that account exclusively as a way to share educational, classroom-focused information on interesting articles, brief videos, or websites that may be useful for educators; I typically post a few ideas three to five times each week. I'd also suggest that you add other local educators, including administrators in your own district, to keep up with what is going on locally. You might also want to follow the tweets from professional development organizations as well and from other teachers teaching the same mathematics content.

The terms "learning network" or "personal learning networks" have been used to distinguish this use of a social network from a purely *social* network (Richardson & Mancabelli, 2011). Thus, a personal learning network (PLN) is the social network of an individual that is dedicated almost exclusively to the study and discussion of one general topic.

Another educational use for Twitter is actual use as a teaching tool (B. Ferriter, 2011; Richardson & Mancabelli, 2011). One teacher in California required students to bring their own Internet-capable device to class (having students bring their own device is frequently called a BYOD initiative), and sign up for Twitter. He made school laptops or tablets available for students with no device. Then he required students to tweet his account during the actual lessons, and he used his laptop to transfer those tweets to the smart board in front of the class. Students could see each other's thoughts, and comment on them, throughout the class. Further, the teacher could see who was and who was not tweeting, and he could then prompt those students to participate more actively. In that class, Twitter increased the participation of all the students, and the students in that particular school considered those class discussions using Twitter to be among the most interesting activities during their entire school day!

> *A personal learning network (PLN) is the social network of an individual that is dedicated to the study and discussion of one general topic.*

Mathematics teachers can also use Twitter to remind students of quizzes or other class activities (e.g., "Remember, the quiz tomorrow on division of whole numbers and fractions. Study up!" or "Remember to review the Khan Academy video on long division with two- and three-digit numbers."). Teachers can use Twitter to highlight news stories related to mathematical content. (Election years are great times to talk about percentages in polling results!) Teachers can also encourage parents to sign up to follow the class tweets using Twitter. In fact, when some parents get a reminder such as the tweet above to study something for a quiz, they might be prompted to verbally remind their kids to study for that math quiz!

> *Twitter can also be used as a classroom teaching tool to make classes much more interactive.*

Twitter can also provide a relatively safe communication tool for one-to-one communications. Teachers might ask students to "tweet the most valuable point from class today!" and then teachers can determine whether or not to share that tweet (B. Ferriter, 2011). Students might be more comfortable requesting help from the teacher in this format, rather than raising their hand in front of the entire class, and this can result in a more open exchange of ideas.

Twitter is a great tool for taking quick polls within your class on various mathematics topics (Young, 2012). However, it can also help in student-to-student networking. Students can use Twitter as they complete homework assignments to request assistance from other students or from the teachers (List & Bryant, 2010). Other math instructional ideas involve using Twitter for a variety of instructional activities (List & Bryant, 2010; Young, 2012). These include

collecting data that can then be presented in bar graphs or pie charts,

polling the class,

having students tweet summaries of the math class discussion,

vocabulary reviews, and

questioning methods ("Everyone take a moment and tweet something that you think others might not be clear on!").

As these ideas suggest, there are many uses for this micro-blogging option in class, and teachers should experiment with it as a teaching tool.

Establishing a Twitter account is not difficult, and once students are using Twitter, figuring out which ways to use this in the classroom is relatively easy. Many teachers are already using Twitter as a personal, social networking tool, and I'd recommend that those teachers consider a separate Twitter account that should be used exclusively for their math class. In many ways, this is similar to Facebook, so I will not provide specific guidelines for setting up this account here.

Twitter can assist in differentiating the mathematics instruction in many ways. First of all, Twitter is fundamentally a social network communication option, with a private communication option built in. Many teachers find that they use the private tweet function within Twitter almost as frequently as they tweet to the entire class. Next, students will be empowered with this type of communication option, one that allows them to ask for help from the teacher and/or from others in the class. While Twitter does not present mathematics content, in the sense of Khan Academy, BrainPOP, or many other tech tools described in this text, it does represent 21st century communication skills, and lets students know that teachers are always available to help.

Finally, for students with lower motivation to participate in math class, Twitter is critical. In some sense, Twitter represents a forced interaction, since teachers can easily follow who is participating and who is not, and can then direct their instructional activities and/or questions appropriately. In that sense, Twitter is likely to lead to higher student participation, even from students who would not normally complete their class or their mathematics homework assignments (Young, 2012). These advantages make Twitter a powerful teaching tool for differentiating instruction in mathematics.

New Tech Tools for Mathematics Instruction

Each of the social networking tools described above can allow students to set up PLNs that focus on mathematics, or work collaboratively to solve math problems. Of course, many other tools can likewise support work in mathematics and/or facilitate collaborative or socially based learning. Still, even in classes where PLNs have been established, students may still struggle when completing mathematics homework alone. For that reason, various tech-based tools have been developed to assure that students are not left out in the cold when they hit a snag in their mathematics assignments at home. For example, IDEAL Web Math is an Android calculator app that can assist students working individually with the calculator (https://play.google.com/store/apps/details?id=in.co.accessiblenews.ideal.webmath). Unlike the many online calculators, this app not only calculates the mathematics problem for the students, but it also explains how that answer was derived. Thus, this is a true teaching tool, rather than merely one of many calculator apps currently available.

Several recently developed tech tools offer opportunities for math work that were not really possible only a few years ago. For example, WolframAlpha is a free interactive (www.wolframalpha.com/) search engine app that helps students find answers to questions in thousands of domains, including mathematics and science. Specifically, if one asks a mathematics question within this program, the program itself will search online, obtain data to address the question, compute the answer, and present it. For example, on the WolframAlpha site, a student might type in "Average inches of rainfall in the United States 1990–2000); this program will obtain that information and produce the answer in fractions of a second.

> Unlike the many online calculators, IDEAL Web Math not only calculates the mathematics problem for the students, but it also explains how that answer was derived.

The homework assistance program ASSISTments is another example of a recently developed instructional tool in mathematics. In Bangor, Maine, seventh-grade students are using this homework assistance program in mathematics to obtain automatic feedback from the online program (McCrea, 2012). This program has been available in a limited way for several years and is now being evaluated at many schools around the nation and internationally (McCrea, 2012).

In addition to these programs, a number of other programs are available to assist with collaborative work. While collaborative work has not been a hallmark of traditional instruction in mathematics, the technology today makes at-home collaboration possible. Many Web 2.0 tools foster collaborative instructional opportunities, and in such a collaborative setting, students

> *Many Web 2.0 tools foster collaborative instructional opportunities, and students are often more willing to participate and experiment with various answers to math problems, and even to learn from each other.*

are often willing to participate more, to experiment with various answers to math problems, and to learn from each other.

Imagine, for example, teaching a class in which four students, working on class computers, could be given the same mathematics problem at once, and truly work together on a solution. In essence, those students have formed a network for that specific time frame, and they could even work collaboratively on that problem at a scheduled time that evening, with each student working from a home computer. A variety of modern computer-based teaching tools allows for students to work on the same document at exactly the same time.

For example, Sync.in is one option for teachers to consider (http://sync.in/). If five students are online and working on a mathematics problem, each student's contributions to the work would be highlighted with a different color, and their work shows up on everyone's screens at the same time, with no cutting and pasting necessary. Students can even use the built-in chat function to ask questions or make comments to each other, as they work to solve the problem. However, sync.in is, in essence, a word processing program, and as such it handles text very well, but it is not a strong a platform for numeric expressions.

MixedInk is another free collaborative work option that allows students to work on the same document at the same point (www.mixedink.com). This platform is more user friendly, and tends to be a bit more geared to classroom situations than Sync.in, but once again this is a text-writing program. These may be used to have students brainstorm ideas on how to solve a word problem, but mathematical expressions present some problems for this app.

Regardless of the application or tech tools that teachers ultimately select to support students or to foster collaborative work in the mathematics class, it should be clear at this point, that 21st century collaboration will look quite different from anything seen in classrooms even 10 years ago. Much more collaborative work, and more work supported by various tech tools, will characterize the modern math class, and students are likely to benefit when assignments are presented in a collaborative framework in which students can serve as a resource for each other. In essence, that is the very definition of a personal learning network.

One Technology Caution

While the array of technology options for teaching mathematics today can be quite daunting, there is one fundamental caution teachers should note. It is clear from early research that technology alone is not a great teacher. (See Bender and Waller, 2013, for a review and an extended discussion of this point.) In short, *"**the box is not enough!**"* That is to say that research has shown that the computer or laptop (i.e., the box), by itself, does not lead to increased engagement or academic performance. Rather, teachers must use good pedagogy, good, research-proven instructional tactics, and embed the technology within these proven instructional practices in order to realize increased achievement. In short, teachers will need, as always, to focus on the desired learning, and present that content in the context of the individual strengths and learning profiles of the students in the class. Only within that context can teachers select appropriate teaching strategies for differentiation, and ultimately appropriate technologies that best fit the educational needs and preferences of the students.

The next section of this chapter focuses on specific strategies for older students in the elementary and middle school grades. One promising area for mathematics instruction is the concept of anchored instruction, as described below. Also, much of the research, for the last three decades, has been founded on various theories in the cognitive sciences and brain research, so a description of these perspectives is presented next. Then, an array of mathematics strategies is presented for older students.

> *Technology, by itself, does not lead to increased engagement or academic performance. Rather, teachers must use good, research-proven instructional tactics and embed the technology within these proven practices in order to realize increased achievement.*

ANCHORED INSTRUCTION IN MATHEMATICS

As recommended in the Common Core State Standards, as well as the growing emphasis on project-based learning (discussed in Chapter 3), mathematics instruction is most effective when problems are grounded in real-world experiences in which students apply mathematics to solve interesting problems. No instructional procedure in math has emphasized the critical importance of real-world applications of math as much as the anchored instructional approach (Bottge & Hasselbring, 1993; Bottge, Heinrichs, Chan, & Serlin, 2001; Bottge, Heinrichs, Mehta, & Hung, 2002; Bottge et al., 2007). In anchored instruction, applied mathematics from Grades 5 through 8 is "made concrete" by using real-world story problems coupled with video vignettes that present the problem in a challenging way. In the perspective of the proponents of anchored instruction, mathematics must be "anchored" in real-world problem solving, and this is accomplished most effectively by creative use of video technology.

> *In anchored instruction, applied mathematics from Grades 5 through 8 is "made concrete" by using real-world story problems coupled with video vignettes that present the problem in a challenging way.*

Anchored instruction originated at the Cognition and Learning Technology Center at Vanderbilt University in 1997 (Bottge et al., 2002; Bottge et al., 2007). A set of curriculum materials using video "anchors" (i.e., real-world math problem scenarios), called The Adventures of Jasper Woodbury, was published in 1997 and has recently been updated (Bottge 2007). This curriculum allows students to navigate CDs to review real-world scenarios and solve mathematics, geometry, and algebra problems involving concepts such as distance, rate, and time.

An Anchored Instruction Example

This curriculum uses 12 video vignettes as the video anchors for instruction in mathematics, geometry, and algebra. Each presents a series of real-world, problem-solving challenges in a believable scenario that is highly interesting to middle school students. Unlike the Khan Academy, discussed previously, these videos do not provide explanations of how to solve problems; rather, they present the problem in a contextual background that students typically find quite motivating. An accompanying computer-based program allows students to try out various problem solutions based on their initial calculations. Sample story problems are presented on the website, along with photos from the video vignettes. This commercially available series concentrates on middle school math applications using basic algebra and geometry skills and has been researched widely. The series is intended for Grades 5 through 8 but because of the publication date, this series was correlated with the standards of the National Council of Teachers of Mathematics (NCTM, 2000), rather than Common Core Standards.

"Kim's Komet" is one episode in this series. This episode is designed to help students master pre-algebraic concepts such as linear function, line of best fit, and calculating slope, rise, and run. Prerequisite skills include computation with whole numbers and decimals. This video anchor involves two girls who compete in a Grand Pentathlon that requires these competitors to calculate where they should release their cars on an inclined ramp in order to allow the car to completely navigate one of five different obstacles (e.g., a short jump, a long jump, a loop-the-loop, and so on). Students initially learn to calculate speeds when times and distances are known, using video examples of cars completing the obstacles (Bottge et al., 2007). Students then plot the speeds and release points and then draw a line of best fit. After this is completed on a computer program in the curriculum itself, community members actually build a full-size ramp (for handheld cars) and five obstacles similar to the ones shown in the video. Instructions for construction of the ramp are included within the curriculum (Bottge et al., 2007).

Efficacy of Anchored Instruction

The effect of using video anchors to present math problems can be both positive and quite profound for many students (Bottge et al., 2007). Further, this enhancement of instruction is directly tied to the emerging insights from brain-compatible instruction. For example, Chapter 1 discussed the emotional brain and the key role played by emotional involvement with and motivation to solve the math problem. Without emotional involvement, students will tend to be less motivated to work on math. In particular, story problems as they are traditionally taught are often rather boring, and most students are not highly motivated to engage in solving the problems.

Anchored instruction problems, however, are presented using video or CDs and the student is directly and repeatedly shown the real-world context in which the problem is based. The video anchors used in anchored instruction are highly motivating and provide some "emotional intensity," leading students into increased involvement with the problem and toward problem solution, and this positive

> *The effect of using video anchors to present math problems can be both positive and quite profound for many students.*

motivational impact of anchored instruction has been noted repeatedly by researchers using this teaching technique (Bottge et al., 2007). Students "get into" the story problems represented on the video, each of which presents a realistic scenario consisting of multiple subproblems in math (Bottge et al., 2002; Bottge et al., 2007). Further, these subproblems can offer options for tiering math instruction and adapting the level of difficulty to various subgroups of students—thus differentiating the instruction. Clearly, this innovation offers a brain-compatible instructional tool for teaching word problems in math in the higher elementary grades.

In addition, researchers have now coupled use of these video anchors with subsequent applied tasks based on the video story in an effort to increasingly motivate students to successfully complete the series of math problems (Bottge et al., 2001; Bottge et al., 2002). Bottge and his coworkers (2001, 2002, 2007) refer to this as *Enhanced Anchored Instruction*, or EAI. In short, by solving the math problems presented in the video examples, the students are concentrating on the mathematics, and this is followed by actually building the track shown in the video anchors based on those mathematical solutions. That is quite motivating, even for the most reluctant math learner. For example, in one EAI teaching exercise, students were exposed to video anchors for between 8 and 10 days. Then, with students working in pairs, they read building plans, using various calculations to figure out the most effective use of their building materials. This scenario was specifically constructed to involve a wide variety of math problems. The video anchor was, in and of itself, quite motivational, but the students' real motivation for this work was the opportunity.

In terms of differentiated instruction, the video anchors provide a variety of ways in which students may approach particular problems. With the guidance of both their teacher and their peer buddy—much of the anchored instruction research emphasizes the use of pairs of students working together—students begin to understand applied mathematics in much more concrete ways than in the traditional classroom. Also, for tear-out groups, such video-based instruction offers a wide variety of options for groups of students to work independently of the teacher.

Questions on Anchored Instruction

While research has documented the efficacy of the anchored instructional approach (Bottge et al., 2001; Bottge et al., 2002; Bottge et al., 2007; Woodward & Montague, 2002), this approach has not yet been widely implemented for several reasons (Woodward & Montague, 2002). First, this approach is recent and is still in development. Next, development of a wider variety of video curricula in a user-friendly format will be necessary prior to wide-scale implementation of these practices. Further, Woodward and Montague (2002) raise the concern that lessons from anchored instruction may not generalize as well as conceptual lessons that are not as heavily based in context. Woodward (2001) also indicated that some of the problems considered socially relevant by those developing the video scenarios were not as relevant to 12- and 13-year-olds as was hoped. Next, increased validation of these practices for students across the ability spectrum is necessary, since most of the research has been undertaken with learners who are struggling in math. Thus, several questions will have to be addressed prior to wholesale implementation of anchored instruction in math.

However, in spite of these concerns, several implications of this instructional approach are compelling. For example, in only a few years educators may use math curricula across the grade levels in which many math word problems are presented to the students in nonwritten form, and this will more closely represent real-world problem solving. This would also be a great advantage for students who struggle in mathematics because of their reading deficits. Using anchored instruction, problem-solving skills can now be taught using enhanced video technology. In turn, this would effectively increase the motivation of most students to undertake efforts toward serious solutions to the problems presented.

Next, almost every educator has been challenged by a student asking, "How is this problem important to me?" In anchored instruction, the "importance" or application of the problem is obvious and inherent in the video presentation of the problem, as well as the actual application of the problem solution (i.e., building the ramp!). While this emphasis on practical, authentic problems from real-world situations will not satisfy all such questions, such challenges will be considerably reduced should we move to math instruction founded on the anchored instructional principles.

These instructional aspects of anchored instruction closely parallel some of the instructional practices emphasized by project-based learning, including an emphasis on real-world problems, teamwork in problem solving, and so on (see discussion of PBL in Chapter 3). Therefore, some experts may consider these two innovations to be aspects of the same instructional paradigm. However, there are some obvious differences. For example, in PBL students participate in the generation of the problem, whereas in EAI the problem is presented to students. Nevertheless, PBL will, ultimately, provide an excellent instructional platform for using anchored instruction.

Finally, a shift in emphasis to anchored instruction will be realized only when appropriate curricula are widely available. Within the next several years, we may all expect the major publishing companies to produce video anchors, at first relatively rarely, but then more aggressively. As teachers are confronted with instructional demands for authenticity and practical applications of mathematics, as emphasized within the Common Core State Standards in Mathematics, the anchored instruction strategy will certainly be one of the most important influences in the development of new mathematics curricula. Because of the efficacy of presenting problem-solving curricula in this format, it is possible that, within a 10-year period, most problem-solving instruction will shift to this model.

> In anchored instruction, the "importance" or application of the problem is obvious and inherent in the video presentation of the problem.

Ultimately, this approach will offer a plethora of tear-out options to students in the differentiated class, and teachers moving into differentiated instruction should consider this instructional as one option. Today, teachers should consider applications of the existing programs, such as the program mentioned above, and should embed anchored instruction within their curriculum whenever possible.

TEACHING GAMES IN HIGHER GRADES

While the broader concept of tech-based gaming in the 21st century classroom was discussed previously, the selection of mathematics educational games is larger in the middle school grades and the high school grades (Helms, 2013; A. Miller, 2011a, 2011b; Takahashi, 2012). Further, in addition to tech-based games, there are many tried and true gaming situations for middle school mathematics that do not involve tech-based teaching, making these games very appropriate for differentiating mathematics instruction in non-Wi-Fi classrooms.

Of course, making mathematics both fun and challenging for some middle school and/or secondary school students can be quite daunting, since some older students have developed quite a dislike of mathematics. In some cases, middle or high school students may be totally unmotivated to attempt any math activity at all—a phenomenon that sometimes results from earlier failures in mathematics. For older students with these types of serious motivational problems, using math-based teaching games may be just the answer (Helms, 2013).

One example of a recently developed, online game for middle school mathematics is Lure of the Labyrinth. This game has received a great deal of attention from mathematics teachers because it has been developed by a powerful team of partners in educational gaming. Initially, this game was developed by the Massachusetts Institute of Technology Educational Arcade (educationarcade.org), in conjunction with FableVision (www.fablevision.com/). This online, team-play game is hosted by the website of Maryland Public Television (labyrinth.thinkport.org).

In Lure of the Labyrinth, students find themselves in a mysterious labyrinth, while they search for a lost dog. They are visited by an unearthly sprite, who takes the form of a young girl and offers help from time to time. Also, students communicate regularly with each other during the game, using mathematical procedures to make progress and solve various problems. The mathematical content in this game is focused on pre-algebra, with emphases on number sense, ratios, proportions, variables, and geometry. A one-minute intro on this game can be viewed on YouTube (www.youtube.com/watch?v=SXN9M4hFV8M), and a longer demo video is also available (www.youtube.com/watch?v=t-VEAVimafs). The game incorporates a variety of practical, task-based assessment strategies that are embedded within the game. This assessment approach will provide mathematics teachers with targeted data to track each student's progress.

Today, mathematics teachers are finding ways to use games for math instruction, including games that were not specifically developed as mathematics teaching tools. For example, many teachers from Grades 7 through high school have explored using the popular game Angry Birds as an instructional tool in algebra (Helms, 2013). In fact, a simple Google search will show an array of uses for the Angry Birds game in mathematics classes, and at least one website is now devoted to using Angry Birds for mathematics instruction across the grade levels (math .playangrybirdsgames.com/).

With the increased attention to online, or cloud-based gaming or ARGs, veteran teachers of mathematics will realize that games have been used for years to teach mathematics, though there does seem to be more emphasis today on gaming in mathematics than previously (Shaftel et al., 2005). Also, some of the newly developed games are board games, and do not involve technology, and this can be a critical concern for teachers in schools without Wi-Fi or computer access. For example, Shaftel and colleagues (2005) describe two board games similar to other board games in that players undertake various activities to assist them in progressing around the board. In the game titled That's Life, as students land on certain squares around the outside edge of the game, they engage in various adult-level financial activities such as buying a car, having to pay a $50 credit card bill, or going clothes shopping with $50. Of course, imponderables are present, such as a utilities bill of $100 to pay, or a roommate moving out, and thus doubling the required rent (this teaches multiplication with decimals). Games such as this are likely to engage attention for even the most reluctant math learner in middle and high school, while teaching financial planning skills, as well as other math skills (addition/subtraction of figures with two decimal places, etc.).

> *For older students with these types of serious motivational problems, using math-based teaching games may be just the answer.*

COGNITIVE STRATEGIES AND BRAIN RESEARCH

A number of instructional strategies in recent decades have been based, not in constructivist thought as discussed in the preceding chapter, in the cognitive sciences. This body of research has also been referred to as neurocognitive science or the metacognitive theory of learning. Because cognitive strategies are directed toward procedural completion of the required task as well as development of a deeper conceptual understanding of mathematics, there is an excellent fit between cognitive strategies and the emphases on deeper levels of understanding as recommended by the Common Core Mathematics Standards. In fact, for this reason, cognitive theories of learning have become one of the dominant influences in educational psychology in recent decades (E. D. Jones et al., 1997; Sousa, 2008).

Metacognition literally means "thinking about thinking"; it is also defined as planning and monitoring how one performs a task. Metacognitive theory evolved in the 1970s and 1980s, and represents a significant change from earlier behaviorally based theories of learning, which were the basis of the time delay instructional tactic, as described in Chapter 4.

> *Metacognition literally means "thinking about thinking"; it is also defined as planning and monitoring how one performs a task.*

Metacognitive theory stipulates that the thinking processes, which behavioral psychologists had always considered unobservable and therefore unimportant, are the basis for problem completion, and a simple example can help illustrate this point. Consider the problem below:

$$45$$

$$+87$$

Of course, even in the simplest math problems, a series of steps must be done sequentially in order to arrive at the correct answer. At a minimum, this problem requires a student to:

- Add the digits in the ones column (to get the sum of 12),
- Write the digit "2" under the ones column,
- Write the digit "1" at the top of the tens column,
- Add the three digits in the tens column (to get the sum of 13),
- Write both digits of that sum below the problem.

Of course, this series of sequenced steps can be very difficult for students struggling in math; in particular, students with learning disabilities have difficulty with organization and planning tasks such as this. Thus, specification of these steps for the student allows the student to "think about his or her thinking" or to plan a series of steps for completing the math problem, while monitoring his or her performance.

While modern brain research began in the late 1980s with the development of the MRI brain scan techniques, recent brain research has shown that students use a different part of their brain to monitor their own steps toward problem completion than they use when actually doing a mathematics problem (Sousa, 2008). Whereas mathematical thinking seems to be based in the right hemisphere and the visual cortex, much of the planning for completing a math problem (i.e., the metacognitive thought) is based in the forebrain areas of the left hemisphere of the cerebrum. Thus, for the problem above, the cognitive, planning processes—that is, the planning and monitoring of the steps toward problem completion—takes place in a different region of the brain than the actual addition functions. In doing math problems, students use their forebrain to "plan" the steps and use other brain areas to conduct the actual calculations. If we as math teachers can teach explicitly the exact steps that a student must engage in to complete a word problem or operations problem, the student will be better able to plan the steps in the problem and to monitor his or her progress in that problem. This will ultimately lead to higher math achievement.

> Students use a different part of their brain to monitor their own steps toward problem completion than they use when actually doing a mathematics problem.

Thus, this brain research has become one of the bases that underlie cognitive instruction. Again, other terms might be used for this instructional practice, including cognitive strategies, metacognitive strategies, and learning strategies. However, regardless of the terminology used, the emphasis is on helping the student think through the problem conceptually, and complete the steps sequentially, while simultaneously self-monitoring his or her progress.

In order to understand cognitive instruction better, it may help to consider the difference between a simple mnemonic technique to enhance memory and a cognitive strategy. Mnemonic techniques are typically used to assist students to remember the basic steps in a problem and are often one component of the broader learning strategy. For example, the long-used sentence, "Please excuse my dear Aunt Sally," has assisted students for decades to remember the order in which they should conduct operations in a multistep equation. In that sentence-based mnemonic, the first letters of each word correspond to the first letter in the terms that make up the correct order of operations (parentheses, exponents, multiplication, division, addition, and subtraction). Another acronym used to teach the same concept is PEMDAS. These should be considered mnemonics in that these are merely memory techniques and do not aim for or address deeper understandings such as "why" the various operations should be performed in this order. There are some mnemonics that involve movement for memorization of definitions, and others that assist memorization using chants, songs, and rhythms.

In contrast, a cognitive strategy is typically more complex than a mere acronym or memory-enhancing sentence, and does usually include some emphasis on why steps should be ordered in the fashion suggested. Thus, cognitive strategies tend to be more developed and require more time to complete than a memory-enhancing acronym.

COGNITIVE STRATEGIES FOR WORD PROBLEMS

To date, a number of researchers have developed specific cognitive strategies or tactics that specify the steps that a student should complete in working on a story problem (Woodward & Montague, 2002). These steps are typically represented by an acronym that would be committed to memory by the students and emphasize both memory of the steps and the conceptual basis for completing each step. Other strategies are not identified by an acronym, but do represent an attempt to have students think through the math problems more deeply. In general, teachers from Grades 4 and higher should have a variety of these tactics at their disposal, since these can be assigned to different tear-out groups as problem-solving strategies. Several are presented below.

> A cognitive strategy is typically more complex than a mere acronym or memory-enhancing sentence, and usually includes some emphasis on why steps should be ordered in the fashion suggested.

The RIDD Tactic

The Read, Imagine, Decide, and Do tactic (RIDD; Jackson, 2002) uses imagery to help students transform new information into meaningful visual, auditory, and kinesthetic units. In using this tactic, new material is transformed into a student's own mental database, which makes learning more efficient. RIDD was first developed to aid students reading math problems as well as directions within those problems, and has been used for students who were struggling in math across the grade levels. Moreover, this strategy is easily modeled for the class and thus less time is taken away from mathematics instruction to teach the tactic itself. Finally, some students view only the answer as important in math, so application of this strategy can teach these students that the process of doing the problem is an important consideration also. In short, there is a variety of reasons for students struggling with word problems to learn this cognitive strategy. Like many cognitive strategies, the RIDD strategy involves the use of an acronym, which specifies four metacognitive steps for the child to complete, as presented in Box 6.2.

BOX 6.2 THE RIDD STRATEGY

Read the problem. The R in RIDD stands for "Read the passage from the beginning to end." Students who are struggling in math tend to read a single line of text or a phrase suggestive of one operation and then stop rather than finish at the punctuation mark. Further, these students will also sometimes stop at an unknown word in the text, and this leads to incomplete understanding and incorrect answers. Consequently, this tactic involves teaching students to substitute a simple word, name, or nonsense word for the difficult word, and then to "keep on reading." Teaching students to substitute "their designated word" for unknown words aids in the release of memory processing resources and allows students to continue their process of constructing meaning from text. Such substitutions should even be made for long numbers in the text on the first reading. Then the student should be encouraged to read the problem again. In teaching this tactic, teachers should read a problem aloud using several substitutions and thus model the strategy. Students must be aware of why the teacher is substituting words.

Imagine the problem. Step 2 of RIDD is represented by an I, and encourages students to "Image the problem." RIDD's use of imagery helps students to transform new information into meaningful visual, auditory, and kinesthetic formats. Also, this imagery process activates various areas of the child's brain and involves more cognitive resources in problem solution.

The new conceptual material in the problem is then readily stored in the student's own knowledge base. The imagine step serves two metacognitive purposes: First, it helps students focus on concepts or operations in the problem, and second, it aids students in monitoring their performance of the steps in the problem.

Decide what to do. The first D in RIDD stands for "Decide how to do the problem." Students decide what to do to solve a problem by mentally reviewing what they comprehend from the text and the visual imagery they created for the problem. For young learners, the decide step may be facilitated by teacher questioning to guide students in deciding what procedures to choose to solve the problem.

Do the work. The final step is represented by the second D in RIDD and stands for "Do the work." Many students who struggle with word problems have a habit of reading through the problem only until they encounter the first suggested operation, and they then stop reading and begin the operation. Of course, this leads to errors, so the RIDD tactic emphasizes planning in several steps prior to doing any work. When beginning this final step, students use what they have already visualized and decisions they have already made about solving the problem in order to complete the work.

First, note how these cognitive tactics involve a number of techniques that were discussed in the previous chapter, such as use of visualization, imagery, and cognitive guiding questions. This tactic pulls together these highly effective teaching tactics into one overall strategy, making this an excellent choice for many students in the differentiated math class. In particular, students with a learning strength in visual learning may benefit more from this strategy since visualization is utilized. Teachers may further involve those visually oriented students by telling them that their differentiated group is going to learn a tactic that the mainline instructional group is not going to learn! This makes students in the differentiated, tear-out group more excited about this strategy.

Students often indicate that they like RIDD because the final step is the only step in which they "do any work." As teachers implement this tactic, they will sometimes hear students voice such thoughts. Of course, this indicates that students do not recognize that the planning or metacognitive processes in the first three steps are a critically important part of the whole problem-solving process. In short, using RIDD helps students realize that there are other steps involved between reading a problem and doing the math the problem requires.

When using strategies such as RIDD, teachers must understand that there is considerable difference between knowing a cognitive strategy acronym and successful use of the strategy in the differentiated math class. RIDD, like all cognitive strategies, must be repeatedly taught in several lessons over several weeks, and should ultimately become the basis for student's approach to all word problems.

> *When using strategies such as RIDD, teachers must understand that there is considerable difference between knowing a cognitive strategy acronym and successful use of the strategy in the differentiated math class.*

While various theorists provide different guidelines for teaching cognitive strategies, all emphasize repeated practice using the cognitive strategy over time. The steps presented in Teaching Tip 6.2 are common to the various cognitive strategy procedures and should be used with all of the cognitive strategies presented in this chapter. Again, for all such strategy instruction it is critically important that the strategy to be learned is practiced repeatedly each day, until the strategy itself is memorized and therefore available for immediate use by the student.

Teaching Tip 6.2   Teaching With a Cognitive Strategy

1. Explain the strategy and what it can be used for with some initial guided practice. Teach students to identify problems for which the strategy is appropriate and problems for which it is inappropriate. Make a poster of the strategy steps and keep it in front of the class.

2. Explain the differences between spoken language and thought. Be sure that students understand that strategies are ways of thinking that can assist them in solving mathematical problems for the rest of their lives. This makes the strategy valuable to students and increases their motivation to invest themselves in the strategy.

3. Introduce the strategy steps one at a time. Model each step separately and in combination with other steps. Reinforce each step and practice each step over a period of several days. Explicitly teach students to memorize the steps, to recognize the steps, and to identify the activities done in each step. Work with the students until each develops automaticity in strategy implementation.

4. Use direct instruction (as described in Chapter 2) to teach the steps themselves. Once the students say and write the steps independently, they can begin to use them to solve problems.

5. Aim for wide application and generalization to other problems. Once a strategy is learned, students should be provided with opportunities to practice the strategy daily for a period of time.

Another strategy that enables students to complete word problems is the STAR tactic (Foegen, 2008; Gagnon & Maccini, 2001). The STAR tactic emphasizes the translation of the word problem into a meaningful mathematical equation, enabling the student to think through the problem prior to attempting problem completion. This strategy also employees the CRA instructional procedure discussed previously (concrete, representational, abstract instruction; Foegen, 2008). The steps in the STAR strategy are presented in Box 6.3.

BOX 6.3 THE STAR STRATEGY

Search the word problem.

1. Read the problem carefully.

2. Ask, "What do I know, and what do I need to find?"

3. Write down the facts.

Translate the words into an equation in picture form.

1. Choose a variable to solve for.

2. Identify the operations necessary (using cue words).

(Continued)

(Continued)

3. If possible, represent the problem with counters/manipulatives.

4. Draw a picture of the equation, including known facts and operations.

Answer the problem.

1. Perform the necessary operations, solving for the unknowns.

Review the solution.

1. Reread the problem.

2. Ask, "Does the answer make sense? Why or why not?"

3. Check the answer.

Source: Adapted from Gagnon & Maccini, 2001.

Although both manipulatives and representational imagery are used in this process, the emphasis here is on linguistic translation of the word problem into an equation. Thus, in contrast to the RIDD strategy above, the STAR strategy is primarily a language-based linguistic tactic that would be appropriate for students with a learning strength in linguistic skills. By selecting strategies that utilize different learning strengths, teachers can easily differentiate their instruction using cognitive strategies.

Of course, as a teacher moves into cognitive strategy instruction, it is possible to present too many options for students and thus to confuse the issues associated with word problems. Therefore, if teachers note that certain cognitive strategies are intended to serve the same function for the same group of students, the teacher should select only one of these for presentation to a struggling student.

With that caution in mind, using different strategies for different members of the class in the differentiated math class can be a very effective instructional tactic. Again, in order to offer a wide diversity in the tactics and strategies used in the differentiated math class, teachers should have a variety of tactics at their disposal for use with various groups of students in the class. Presented below is one additional learning strategy for word problems, after which we will look at several other cognitive approaches to differentiated math instruction for the upper grades.

The SQRQCQ Tactic

Many mathematics concepts, in particular word problems, are taught by having the students read the problem, while carefully thinking it through. Therefore, a student's reading skills can, and often do, directly hinder his or her achievement in mathematics. Of course, teachers in all subjects must emphasize reading, but the skills associated with reading a word problem—where one term can change the entire meaning of the problem—are sometimes a bit more demanding than reading a passage in history or science. In fact, some students may have strength in mathematics that is not reflected in their math grades because they are unable to read and comprehend the directions or the words necessary to perform the mathematical functions in the word problems they encounter. Therefore, teachers of mathematics must also teach reading, and one way to do this is to provide students with a graphic organizer that will assist them in recognizing the terms for concepts and operations within the problem.

Barton, Heidema, and Jordan (2002) proposed a cognitive strategy to assist in reading the text of a word problem. The strategy is called the SQRQCQ method. Like the strategies discussed previously, this strategy is intended to assist students with thinking through exactly what the problem is and how they might begin to solve it. The steps are presented in Box 6.4.

BOX 6.4 STEPS IN THE SQRQCQ STRATEGY	
Survey	Read the problem quickly to get a general understanding of it.
Question	Ask what information the problem requires.
Read	Reread the problem to identify relevant information, facts, and details needed to solve it.
Question	Ask what must be done to solve the problem: "What operations must be performed and in what order?"
Computer	Do the computations and compute a solution.
Question	Ask whether the solution process seems correct and the answer reasonable.

In several ways, this tactic is a bit more detailed than the strategies described earlier. For example, in this tactic the student is explicitly told, in the third step, to reread the problem. Also, the order of operations is stressed in the fourth step. Finally, this tactic, like all cognitive strategies, should be taught over an extended time frame, and emphasized repeatedly.

The PASS Strategy

PASS is both a relatively new theory of intelligence and a cognitive strategy based on cognitive theory. This strategy will effectively assist

> *PASS is both a relatively new theory of intelligence and a cognitive strategy based on cognitive theory.*

elementary students, middle school students, and older students in developing understanding of their own cognitive processes as those processes interact to solve a math problem. The theory is based on the growing understanding of intelligence, as founded within the emerging studies of brain structures (Das, Naglieri, & Kirby, 1994; Naglieri & Gottling, 1997; Naglieri & Johnson, 2000).

PASS is intended to result in deep understanding of the algorithms, constructs, and problems under discussion, and is therefore consistent with the stated goals of the Common Core State Standards in Mathematics. The letters in the acronym PASS stand for:

P Planning

A Attention

S Simultaneous

S Successive

The items in the acronym are considered both as steps for students to go through, as well as mental functions for completing mathematics problems. The first mental function, planning, is a process that is composed of the development of strategies and plans necessary to complete the problem at hand (Naglieri & Gottling, 1997; Naglieri & Johnson, 2000). This takes place predominately in the forebrain of the cerebrum and involves self-monitoring, self-regulation, and utilization of the processes involved in completing the task. As in many other cognitive strategies, this step enhances the students' thought processes and encourages the understanding that planning for problem solution is as important as actual problem solving.

The next mental function, attention, refers to focused activity, resistance to distraction, and selective attention to the pertinent facts within the problem. Also, attention involves inhibition of irrelevant stimuli as well as an "appropriate level" of arousal in relation to the problem (e.g., what teacher has not experienced students who were either under- or overstimulated when a particular topic within a math problem was discussed?).

Next, the simultaneous processing function takes place in the occipital-parietal areas of the brain. This process allows a person to deal with many pieces of information at one time and to arrange the information in groups for use in solving the problem (Naglieri & Gottling, 1997; Naglieri & Johnson, 2000).

Finally, the successive mental function involves the integration of stimuli into a specific serial order. Thus, this activity allows a person to work with information in a specific order or series; students may then determine what information presented is needed at each particular step in problem solving (Naglieri & Johnson, 2000).

As is obvious from this description, this cognitive strategy tends to be more holistic than the more specific strategies offered earlier. As noted above, the steps in this strategy are specifically intended to closely parallel the very mental processes that are utilized in solving complex problems (Das et al., 1994). In fact, almost all students can benefit from personal, reflective consideration of their own mental processes in relation to the specific problem at hand. Using PASS, students who are struggling in mathematics are taught to think the problem through on the basis of their own mental processing skills, and then undertake problem completion.

Implementation of PASS

The implementation of the PASS strategy uses guided questioning and reflection and is implemented daily, in a 30-minute mathematics class (Naglieri & Gottling, 1997; Naglieri & Johnson, 2000). During the 30 minutes, students are required to complete math problems for the first 10 minutes, hold a discussion for the next 10 minutes, and complete math problems for the final 10 minutes. These phases of PASS instruction are described below.

During the initial problem work time frame (the first 10 minutes of class), students are given mathematics worksheets that present math problems on a subject that has already been taught to the students in the traditional fashion. Thus, the students have, at a minimum, at least seen these types of problems before. The students are given 10 minutes to complete as many problems correctly as possible, and are initially provided with no additional instruction. This period of work can be used to establish a pre-instruction score for the students.

As an aside, this aspect of PASS makes this strategy fit in nicely with the use of Khan Academy, or some similar resource in the flipped classroom. Students will have done some practice work on a specific type of problem prior to class, as well as viewed the video, and will thus be ready for this initial problem work.

> *The implementation of the PASS strategy uses guided questioning and reflection and is implemented daily, in a 30-minute mathematics class.*

Next, the students have a 10-minute discussion time. In PASS, the teacher should not lead this discussion; rather, the students should lead the discussion, and the discussion may involve any topic at all. During this discussion time, student work is displayed anonymously on the interactive whiteboard or an overhead projector. In most cases, this is enough encouragement and results in students' discussing the work presented. If, after several 30-minute math periods over a number of days, the students are not discussing their personal approach to problem solving, the teacher should step in and lead the discussion in that direction (Naglieri & Gottling, 1997; Naglieri & Johnson, 2000). This "freedom to choose" to discuss math is viewed as essential during the initial days of instruction, since students who realize they make such a choice are much more likely to be "brain involved" in the subsequent discussions.

When the discussion does turn to problem-solving strategies for the work displayed on the interactive whiteboard, the teacher should begin to participate more, using guided questions to focus on the students' mental processes during problem solving. The questions should challenge the students to do self-reflection in order to

- See how each student completed the problems,
- Have each student verbalize and discuss problem-solving ideas, and
- Encourage each student to explain which methods worked well and which methods did not work as well.

Teachers can use a series of probing questions to assist students to jump-start their thinking as soon as the discussion turns to the problems on display. This can be considered as Phase 1 of the teacher's probe questions. Some phase one probes suggested by Naglieri and Gottling (1997) are in Teaching Tip 6.3 below.

Teaching Tip 6.3   Probe Questions for the PASS Strategy

Phase 1 Probe Questions

Can anyone tell me anything about these problems?

Let's talk about how you did the worksheet.

Why did you do it that way?

How did you do the problems?

What could you have done to get more problems correct?

What did these problems teach you?

What else did you notice about how these problems were done?

What will you do next time?

I noticed that many of you did not do what you said was important.

What do you think of that?

Phase 2 Probe Questions

How did you decide what to pay attention to?

What numbers in the math problem did you have to use first? What numbers were used second? How did you decide when to use them?

Who can tell us how they thought through the problem before they started?

Does this problem have a partial answer?

Are there things that you have to remember when you do the final part of the problem? How can we "remember to remember" those things?

Remember that for this discussion the students have already been exposed to the types of problems on the worksheet prior to the PASS class, but they may need assistance in planning their methods of problem solving. These probe questions are intended to allow the students to verbalize their individual thinking about the methods used. Thus, the guided questions and verbalization phase is the critical step in PASS. Over time, teachers can eventually turn the probing questions more directly toward the planning, attention, simultaneous, and successive mental processes that are utilized in math, using a different type of question such as the Phase 2 probe questions shown in Teaching Tip 6.3. Again, having students discuss their own "brain thinking" during the mathematics problem is an excellent way to get students both involved and motivated. Also, the collaborative nature of these discussions on problem solving will facilitate students' ability to present his or her work, argue for that work, critique others' work, and communicate about mathematics, as stressed in the Common Core Math Practices (see Box 1.1 in Chapter 1, item number 3).

Unlike the earlier probe questions, these Phase 2 questions focus more directly on the mental processes emphasized within the PASS strategy. By using the PASS tactic repeatedly over time, students should learn to focus more directly on their own mental processes while completing a math problem, and will thus become more cognitively engaged in problem solution.

Finally, in the daily lesson, after the students have done initial problem work and completed the discussion of various problem-solving strategies, they are provided with an additional set of problems to complete. Students should be encouraged to implement some of the effective problem-solving ideas discussed previously, as well as to ask questions during this set of problems if they need a reminder for a particular strategy.

Using PASS, students eventually figure out what method works best for them, and the problems become easier. As new material is introduced, the students can discuss differences between the new problems and previous work. For some students the same solving strategy will work, while others may need to change their problem-solving strategies completely. The exchange of ideas allows students to discover possible ways to solve the current problems or new types of problems.

Eventually, students automatically try various ways to complete the mathematics problems presented online or on the worksheets and are quite likely to begin to discuss problem-solving ideas with each other during the 10-minute work sessions. Teachers should not only allow but encourage this exchange, as students are using that time meaningfully in building their PLN! Students will start new worksheets using past successful problem-solving strategies. If these strategies do not work, they will use methods that other students have mentioned in the discussion periods.

Although some teachers are reluctant to offer free-ranging discussing time to students during the first few days of the PASS strategy—particularly given the time pressures of today's emphasis on standards and accountability—research has shown that these few sessions of time will not be a major concern. In the various research studies done to date, students generally take around three days before the 10-minute discussion starts to revolve around various methods of completing the worksheets (Naglieri & Gottling, 1997; Naglieri & Johnson, 2000). Further, the freedom of choice that students are given is a critical motivating factor—they will pay more attention on subsequent days because of their choice to begin discussing the problem-solving strategies. Depending on the type of math problem (calculation, or word problem), student discussions would eventually have planning strategy exchanges. Here is one such exchange for students learning the higher times tables, or division facts.

> *I do the ones with the ones, zeros, and tens. They are easy.*
>
> *I do the fives, too.*
>
> *I move my seat when I am distracted.*
>
> *I do the problems row by row.*
>
> *I like to do one problem from the top of the sheet, and one from the bottom row, since I like working toward the middle.*

As these quotes suggest, students will share both effective and ineffective strategies, and the teacher should encourage discussion of all strategies.

This will develop deeper thinking about various problem solution options on the part of the students.

While this approach can also be used for almost any type of math problem, it is particularly useful for math problems involving multiplication and division. Students who use repetition of facts will probably memorize the facts more rapidly. Students are generally taught the multiplication facts in groups, and use of various memory strategies and ideas can be critical. For instance, to recall $7 \times 9 = 63$, a student might start with the easier fact of $7 \times 7 = 49$, and then "build up" to $7 \times 8 = 56$, and finally $7 \times 9 = 63$. When discussing this strategy, students will quickly discover that while this process works, it takes a much longer time to answer the problem than using automatic recall. PASS theory allows students to discuss these tactics among themselves with only minimal teacher guidance in the discussion.

In algebra, problems involve solving for "x" and often involve repetition of steps. PASS can assist in this higher level of cognitive planning. Also, giving a student a worksheet that presents these steps over and over again will allow the student to recall the steps later. In geometry, PASS can be used to train the student in all of the various formulas. These formulas could be anything from the area of a triangle to the area of a rhombus. Of course, complex problems take more time, so the more complex the type of problems on the worksheet, the fewer completed problems should be expected during a 10-minute work session.

Finally, PASS may offer one area in which math instruction can become a broader vehicle for improved cognitive understandings in other areas. The proponents of PASS suggest that these problem-solving approaches provide students with a problem-solving strategy that can be utilized in all areas of academic work and subsequently in various other areas as well (Naglieri & Gottling, 1997; Naglieri & Johnson, 2000). Ideally, students will eventually form the habit of asking others how they approached particular problems, and of sharing their own problem-solving strategies. Of course, these are exactly the types of collaborative learning skills that are demanded in the 21st century workplace.

Research has shown increased conceptual understanding of math, resulting from continued use of the PASS strategy (Das et al., 1994; Naglieri & Gottling, 1997; Naglieri & Johnson, 2000). Most of these studies researched this tactic on students who were in either elementary or middle school, and involved students with difficulties in math. Even with these "tough to teach" math students, the research consistently shows improvement in math achievement as a result of PASS. Further, students who were less adept at planning their problem-solving tactics typically demonstrated the greatest improvement. Students with good planning skills improved, but not as rapidly as the students with weaker planning skills. Thus, research has shown that PASS is effective for all students in the differentiated math class.

A SCHEMA-BASED STRATEGY FOR PROBLEM SOLVING

Another approach to problem solving involves use of graphic representations, or schemas, to represent the math problems (Allsopp, 1999; Garderen, 2007; Jitendra, 2002). In many ways, this is similar to both the visualization technique and the word problem map technique described previously. However, students using the schema (or graphic representations) are encouraged to draw their visualization of the math problem in a "hard copy" form using a predefined set of graphic organizers. Thus, this technique can greatly assist students with strength in visual-spatial thinking.

Research has shown increased conceptual understanding of math, resulting from continued use of the PASS strategy.

The use of schema-based instruction has a number of advantages (Garderen, 2007; Goldman, 1989; Jitendra, 2002; Jitendra, Hoff, & Beck, 1999). Using graphic representations, like many of the strategies discussed above, assists the students in forming a picture of the math problem. According to the brain-compatible learning perspective described in Chapter 1, this tactic will empower students to actively engage the visualization areas within their brain. Also, unlike the visualization tactic described above, students doing graphic representation are actually drawing or filling in a graphic picture of the problem, which provides a hard copy for later use as a student guide.

In this strategy, various types of math problems are represented by graphic organizers that are referred to as different "schemas." A schema may be defined as a mental diagram or concept for a particular aspect of the problem (Jitendra, 2002). As the story problem is presented, students try to determine which schematic diagram might represent that problem, or represent the different aspects of the problem (Jitendra, 2002). Several examples are presented in Box 6.5.

BOX 6.5   COMMON PROBLEM-SOLVING SCHEMA

Sample Schematic Diagrams for Word Problems

The Change Schema

One type of problem requires a change schema. These problems include a set of information that indicates change in other information in the problem.

John had some apples. Paul gave him 13 more apples. Now John has 17 apples. How many did John have in the beginning?

The change information (13 apples) must be subtracted from the total resultant set of information (17) in order to determine the start set. This change problem may be represented as follows.

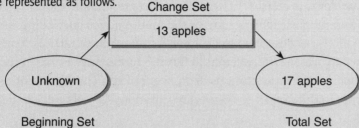

The Group Schema

In a group schema, items are grouped together from various sets. Consider the following problem:

Tiffany owns 13 blouses that she wears to school. Her twin sister, Tammy, owns 13 blouses. When these girls swap clothes for school, how many blouses can they choose from?

A group schema would be represented as follows.

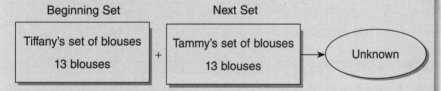

The Comparison Schema

Some word problems present "comparison" problems, which require the student to determine and subsequently compare values.

John has 6 computer games. He has 3 more than Paul. How many games does Paul have?

In order to solve this problem, the child must have a comparison schema or mental concept that includes three pieces of information: two reference quantities (the number of computer games that John has, and the difference) and a derived piece of information involving the comparison answer. Note also that the cue word more usually means that a child should add, but in this example it indicates subtraction.

A comparison schema would be represented as follows:

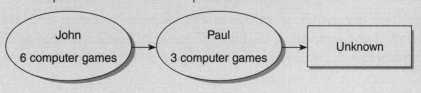

As with many strategies presented in this text, there are different cognitive levels of the graphic representation strategy, making it appropriate for different grade levels. Clearly the use of schema or graphic representations of problems is consistent with the efforts to include more concrete-representational-abstract teaching in the mathematics curriculum across the grade levels, as described in Chapter 3 (Mancl et al., 2012). Teachers may choose to present the schemas in Box 6.5 to students, or have students develop their own representations of story problems. Guidelines for teaching students to develop their own representations for solving schema are presented in Box 6.6.

BOX 6.6 GUIDELINES FOR DEVELOPING SCHEMAS

1. Find the problem pattern.

   a. Read the problem carefully.
   b. Ask whether the problem requires changing, grouping, or comparing (think about the overall schema of the problem).

2. Organize the problem within a diagram.

   a. Map the known information on the diagram (write it in!).
   b. Flag the unknown information using a question mark.

Solving the Problem

1. Plan to solve the problem.

   a. Find the total amount under the largest set of objects and write a "T" under the total.
   b. Select an operation based on known and unknown information. (When the total is not known, add to get the total; when the total is known, subtract to find the part.)

2. Solve the problem.

   a. Add or subtract.
   b. Check to see if the answer makes sense.
   c. Write the whole answer.

Source: Adapted from Jitendra, 2002.

For younger students or students who may be less mature in their mathematical understandings, teachers will merely tell students what type of problem each is, and then present a pre-drawn schema or representation for that type of problem. The students would then write the appropriate information from the problem on the graphic representation. Using the designs above can greatly assist struggling students in their comprehension of math prob-

> *A schema may be defined as a mental diagram or concept for a particular aspect of the problem.*

lems. For older, mathematically mature students, teachers should spend more time actually teaching students to recognize the different types of problem schemas.

Implementation of Schema-Based Instruction

Using schemas for math instruction is fairly straightforward once students are acquainted with the concept (Garderen, 2007; Jitendra, 2002). However, instruction will vary, based on the grade and skill level of the students. While simple schema may suffice in the lower grades, older students who struggle with math may face increasing difficulties as word problems become more sophisticated. For example, some complex problems involve mathematics operations to derive information that is used in subsequent operations to solve for the answer. Even for the complex word problems that are often found in the upper elementary grades—problems that involve multiple operations—students can be taught to map critical features of math word problems into schematic diagrams as well as identify and solve for missing information (Goldman, 1989; Jitendra, 2002). Schema-based instruction for higher-level math involves the following:

> *Instruction in recognition of the various schemas presented in complex word problems,*

> *Identification of the primary question posed by the word problem, and*

> *Identification of any secondary schema that may be required.*

The various types of schemas for simple word problems presented above help the student translate multistep math problems into smaller, step-by-step problems. However, students can be directly taught strategies for solving two-step word problems, and those techniques are demonstrated below (Goldman, 1989; Jitendra, 2002). In application of the schema or graphic representation tactic in problem solving, teachers should plan on using this specific tactic over a period of several weeks in order for students to internalize these deeper understandings.

Phases in Schema-Based Instruction

As students become more advanced, they should be taught to distinguish between various schemas and eventually to develop diagrams themselves. Thus, students will learn how to identify and map problem elements onto the schema diagrams after teacher demonstration and facilitative questioning help them identify critical elements. The phases of instruction focus on finding specific information in the text of a word problem, and subsequently translating this information into a schematic map. This process involves a number of steps (Goldman, 1989; Jitendra, 2002), which are presented below.

Distinguishing the Features of Various Schemas

First, teach the students how to distinguish the features of each schema, focusing initially on problems that do not have any missing information. Students should be taught how to map features of the story with the help of explicit and overt modeling. Teachers should scaffold this instruction by providing schema diagrams, and then gradually wean students from them so that students eventually develop their own diagrams. Also, teachers must encourage frequent student exchanges to help all students identify the crucial elements of the word problem and map them on the schema diagrams.

In order to differentiate their instruction, math teachers should consider using a peer tutoring approach for this step, since students can use their interpersonal skills and generally will master this technique when it is demonstrated by their peers.

Teaching Change Problems

The purpose of this step is to emphasize the change schema problems, those in which students find the total amount by focusing on specific information in the text and using either addition or subtraction. Students should be taught that "change" problems start with a beginning set where objects and their respective values are defined. Next, a "change" occurs that causes the beginning set to change—by either adding or subtracting—into the ending set. Students should also be taught to examine the semantics of the problem, as well as to search for cue words in the text. In the following story problem, a change occurs.

Marty had 31 marbles on Friday. He lost 7 of them when he went to school one morning. How many does Marty have when he arrives at school?

The ending set here is less than the beginning set because Marty "lost" some of his marbles. The "change" resulted in fewer marbles at the end, and thus, change problems are time dependent. Students should begin to see that the beginning set number and ending set number cannot both be accurate at the same time because a "change" occurred in the problem. Students eventually should be able to recognize that in change problems where the problem ends up with more than at the beginning, the ending amount represents the total amount or the highest number in the problem. If the problem ends with less, however, the beginning amount to be used in the problem solution is the higher number of the two.

Teaching Group Problems

In "group" problems, time does not affect values like it does in "change" problems. In group problems, the smaller groups are combined to form a larger group or total set. In some cases, the total set provides the answer to the primary question in the problem, but in other cases one is solving to identify one of the small sets. Consider this example.

Maryanne has 50 flowers in her flowerbeds. Of these, 28 are daffodils and the remaining are pansies. How many pansies does she have?

As you can see, "group" problem types involve the understanding of parts of a whole. They emphasize common attributes, flowers in this case, and distinctions within that broader group (pansies vs. daffodils). Students should come to understand that the whole is equal to the sum of its parts in "group" problems. Once students have the concept and have identified the missing information, they can solve for the correct answer.

Teaching Comparison Problems

"More than" and "less than" concepts are the focus of all comparison schema problems. Thus, in "comparison" problems, students should be taught to focus on two sets: one of smaller and another of larger value. Students should learn to identify one set as the comparison set and one set as the referent set. Consider this problem:

Thomas has 46 baseball cards and William has 63. How many more cards does William have than Thomas?

In this example, the referent set is 63, and the comparison set is 46. It is critical for students to learn to identify the difference in value by comparing the two sets. This determination is made by evaluating the difference statement (using cue words and concepts such as *more than*) from the word problem.

Teaching Decision Rules

There are several rules of identification of the correct operations to be used in schema-based problem solving. For example, students should be taught to determine the correct operation for problem solving by determining whether or not the unknown value is the total (or the larger) set in the problem. Next, students should be taught that in a "change" problem, if the problem results in more, then the ending amount is the total, but if the problem ends up with less, then the beginning amount is the total. In "group" problems, the larger group is always the total. In "compare" problems, students must determine the total by examining the difference statement. Jitendra (2002) presented the following decision rules for using schemas, shown in Box 6.7. Teachers may wish to

---

BOX 6.7 DECISION RULES IN SCHEMA-BASED INSTRUCTION

Decision Rules in Schema-Based Instruction

1. Change Problems

   If the problem ends with more than it started with, the ending set is the total. If the problem ends up with less than it started with, then the beginning set is the total.

2. Group Problems

   The larger set is always the total.

3. Comparison Problems

   The larger set (compared or reference set) in the comparison of difference statement is the total.

Identifying the Operations

   When the total is unknown, add to find the total.
   When the total is known, subtract to find the unknown.

Source: Adapted from Jitendra, 2002.

develop a large poster of this information as an organizer for students to be displayed at the front of the room.

Teaching Missing Elements

Next, the teacher should have the students review the problem schema and search for missing information. Teachers may lead demonstrations of various problems and encourage questioning to aid students in identifying and mapping the problem's critical elements onto schema diagrams. The students should search for and flag (i.e., highlight) the missing elements with a single question mark on the schema diagram. Have several students read the same problem, develop a schema diagram for it, and compare these, while the teacher clears up any misconceptions about critical and/or missing information.

Teaching Multi-Schema Problems

After students master one-schema problems, they should be taught problems involving several schemas. For example, the following two-step problem involves both a change schema and a comparison schema. Students must determine the primary question and identify any missing information that will be necessary to solve for the answer to the primary question. General suggestions for two-step problems are presented in Teaching Tip 6.4.

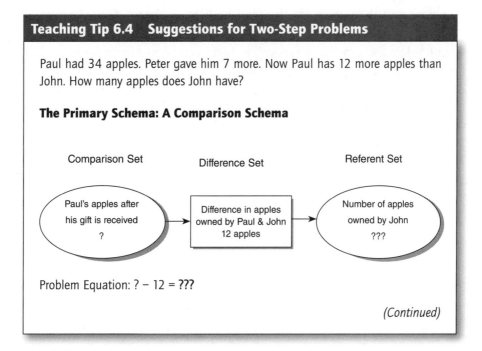

Teaching Tip 6.4   Suggestions for Two-Step Problems

Paul had 34 apples. Peter gave him 7 more. Now Paul has 12 more apples than John. How many apples does John have?

The Primary Schema: A Comparison Schema

Comparison Set   Difference Set   Referent Set

Paul's apples after his gift is received ?   Difference in apples owned by Paul & John 12 apples   Number of apples owned by John ???

Problem Equation: ? − 12 = ???

(Continued)

(Continued)

The Secondary Schema: A Change Schema

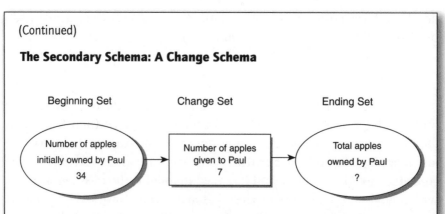

Problem Equation: 34 + 7 = ? This is the PA (partial answer) in the problem.

Note the use of the term primary schema to identify the ultimate answer to the problem question above. Also, using three question marks, in bold (**???**), identifies this unknown information as the final answer to the problem. The terms secondary schema and PA or partial answer as well as a single question mark (?) identify unknowns that must be solved for in order to answer the final problem. Teachers should explicitly teach these identification terms and markings in order to encourage students to specifically identify the unknowns in the problem as well as the final answer.

Instruction on the use of schemas to solve two-step word problems focuses on backward chaining of two different schemas. Backward chaining is used to show the students how to first search for the unknowns in the problem and then solve for the final problem solution. Thus, backward chaining requires students to focus on the primary question asked and identify key facts in the surrounding text, as well as key unknowns that must be solved for, prior to solving for the final answer. Students should be taught to write PA or "partial answer" by the answer to the secondary schema. They may use this notation in the primary schema to represent the missing information that will be provided by solving the secondary schema.

The change schema in the problem above involves addition (34 + 7) and then a comparison schema involving subtraction (41 – 12). Students would be taught to identify the primary problem question (i.e., the number of apples John has, which is provided via a comparison of apples owned by Paul and John) and the secondary problem or partial answer (PA, which represents the change problem concerning how many apples Paul has).

Differentiated Math Instruction With Schemas

Schema diagrams can be modified to help students who have more difficulty with identifying and mapping the critical elements in math word problems. In the differentiated class, some of the diagram elements on the schema diagrams can be provided to certain students; other students should develop their own diagrams and identify all of the elements themselves. Further, the number of elements already provided for certain students can be phased out as students become more adept at identifying the critical elements needed for their diagrams.

The number of required operations offers another way to differentiate using schemas. For example, a teacher may challenge some tear-out groups with a word problem with multiple schemas involved, whereas for other groups one-schema problems may be used. With four or five tear-out groups working on different problems to determine the schema involved, the teacher will have ample opportunity to tier the work of the tear-out groups to the students. This would be a good instructional activity for the second day on word problem schema. The lesson on that day should proceed as described in Teaching Tip 6.5.

Teaching Tip 6.5   Differentiated Lesson Using Problem-Solving Schemas

Step 1. Orient the students to the idea of schemas, and remind them of the concepts discussed previously. Tell them, "Today, we will learn to identify schemas word problems."

Step 2. Specify the tear-out groups of students and assign either single-schema or multiple-schema problems to those groups for analysis. Give the groups 10 minutes to discuss the problem, make some notes on their work, and select the word problem schema for that problem.

Step 3. Group work. The teacher should provide a map of all possible story problem schemas to assist groups of lower-functioning students in identification of the schema in their problem. The teacher should visit each group during the 10 minutes in order to assure that the discussions are moving in the correct general direction.

Step 4. Have each group report back to the class and identify the story schema involved in that word problem.

Research on Schema-Based Instruction

Results of a number of studies indicate that this schema instructional tactic can enable students who are struggling in math to learn to solve math word problems, including complex, two-step word problems (Goldman, 1989; Jitendra, 2002; Jitendra et al., 1999). Students in these studies who were having difficulties in math showed increases in math achievement for both single-schema and multiple-schema problems. Further, the use of the schema facilitated more correct choices of operations during problem solution. It also aided students to decrease calculation errors in two-step problems. The research has shown schema-based instruction to be effective from Grade 3 through high school. Clearly, teachers in the differentiated math class should consider using this tactic for struggling students across the grade levels.

TEACHING EXPANDED NOTATION AND PARTIALING

Algorithms involve a combination of basic facts and more complex computations. Lock (1996) presented several ideas to give students alternatives to the typical method for solving simple problems in addition, subtraction, and multiplication. These include expanded notation and partial sums/products, or partialing. Using these ideas in tear-out groups can provide students with a novel, more interesting method of problem solution, and will help students unlock the deeper meanings of algorithms. This strategy is presented in Box 6.8.

BOX 6.8   EXPANDED NOTATION AND PARTIALING

Expanded notation involves identification of steps in transforming a complex math problem into a series of simpler math problems. This concept can be used in various operations such as addition and subtraction. Consider the problem 29 + 43 = _____. The expanded notation for this problem is presented below.

```
  29                                     2 tens and 9 ones
+ 43                                   + 4 tens and 3 ones
```

The problems would be completed as follows:

Add the ones and tens:	6 tens	+	12 ones
Regroup the ones, if necessary:	6 tens	+	(1 ten and 2 ones)
Put the tens together:	(6 tens and 1 ten)	+	2 ones
Write the tens and ones in simple way:	7	+	2
Write the answer:	72		

Partialing can assist some students in their approach to mathematics operations, and it leads to a deeper understanding of what the operations represent. A partial sum in addition would involve summing the ones column, summing the tens column, and then summing the sums, as follows:

```
  37          First, add the ones (7 + 4 = 11)
+ 64          Next, add the tens (30 + 60 = 90)
─────         Next, add the partial sums above (90 + 11 = 101)
```

An example of a partial product would be a bit more complicated, but it does have the advantage of demonstrating for the student what the multiplication process really involves. Consider the problem below. The partial product solution goes like this:

23   First, multiply each top digit by the 2.

×12 $2 \times 3 = 6$

_____ $2 \times 20 = 40$

Next, multiply each top digit by 10, since the 1 in the tens column represents 1 set of 10.

$$10 \times 3 = 30$$
$$10 \times 20 = 200$$

Finally, add the partial products.

$$(6 + 40 + 30 + 200 = 276)$$

Note the use of the smaller multiplication sign (i.e., "×") in the ones place and the larger multiplication sign ("×") in the tens place. This can help students remember that multiplying by tens results in much larger numbers.

Source: Adapted from Lock, 1996.

When the strategies and tactics presented up to this point in this text are employed in the differentiated math class as either tear-out instructional options or for mainline instruction, teachers should be able to construct a variety of differentiated instructional activities for students with a wide range of abilities in every grade level. The array of activities, including CRA, tech-based instruction, games, cognitive strategies, scaffolding tactics, and many others, offers an exciting set of instructional choices for teachers to use. Further, continued use of these innovative tactics can assist in the gradual progression into higher-level math in the middle school and even into secondary school.

E. D. Jones and colleagues (1997) provided some guidelines for how teachers may design practice activities that will be involving for middle school and secondary learners who have difficulty in mathematics. In general, for learners who have difficulty in math the teacher's challenge is to present complex math in a way that does not embarrass the students, but that does include appropriate scaffolding to support the students' learning during the practice phases of instruction. Technology and collaborative instruction can greatly assist in this process. Also, this may involve many of the strategies presented in earlier chapters, such as use of representations of mathematical problems, concrete examples, scaffolding, guided questions, and process mnemonics.

These guiding principles, delineated by E. D. Jones and coworkers (1997) and modified for the differentiated classroom, are presented in Teaching Tip 6.6. With these ideas in hand, and the plethora of tactics described previously, teachers should be able to construct a highly differentiated math class that increases success in math for all learners.

Teaching Tip 6.6 Differentiation Guidelines for Higher-Level Students

1. Avoid memory overload by assigning manageable amounts of practice work as skills are learned. Present the practice work in a variety of ways that are intended to involve as many of the multiple intelligences as possible over the course of an instructional unit, including use of the high-impact learning tactics represented by SHEMR (presented in Chapter 1). Let students know at the beginning of each instructional unit what the planned activities are and which multiple intelligences will be stressed, so that each student can anticipate an interesting learning experience when his or her intelligence strength is emphasized on a particular day within the unit.

2. Build retention by providing review within a day or so of the initial learning of difficult skills. Provide supervised practice to prevent students from practicing misconceptions and misrules. Use peer buddy plans to assist in practice. Employ novelty to assist in memory exercises, and process mnemonics activities whenever possible. Movement, songs, and chants are great for reviewing content across the grade levels, assuming the content can be represented in a coherent and relatively complete fashion.

3. Reduce interference between concepts or applications of rules and strategies by separating practice opportunities until the discriminations between them are learned. After the discriminations are mastered, emphasize the decisions students must make in determining which concepts seem to conflict with each other.

4. Make new learning meaningful by relating the practice of subskills to the performance of the whole task. Discuss the whole task and subskills with the students, and have the students reflectively consider what they learned about mathematics.

5. Give credit for partial answers in two-step problems, and offer graphic representations of them.

6. Reduce processing demands by preteaching component skills of algorithms and strategies, and by teaching easier knowledge and skills before teaching difficult knowledge and skills.

7. Require fluent responses. Offer a variety of methods for presenting responses, such as oral, group work, written work, pictorial work, and so on.

8. Ensure that skills to be practiced can be completed independently with high levels of success before moving on to new skills. Use peers to do periodic review activities.

WHAT'S NEXT?

While previous chapters presented actual differentiated instructional plans for teachers in the primary and mid-elementary grades, no such plan is presented here, as schools vary widely in terms of how mathematics instruction is managed in the upper elementary and middle school grades. In some cases a fifth-, sixth-, or even seventh-grade teacher may be teaching all subjects, including math, to a single group of students all day, and those teachers will developed a plan that is quite different from a middle school sixth-grade math teacher that sees one class for a 50-minute period. However, the ideas and recommendations presented in the differentiation plans in Chapters 4 and 5 can be considered as a basis for teachers in varied instructional situations, and should be used in developing your own plan for differentiated instruction.

This chapter has presented an array of instructional strategies that can facilitate differentiated instruction in the upper elementary and middle school grades. Strategies such as Facebook, Twitter, or Ning can help move mathematics instruction to much higher levels of student engagement, since most students expect application of 21st century learning tools in today's math classes. Many other tech tools described in this and previous chapters can also make mathematics much more engaging for students today, and teachers are rushing to embrace these new instructional tools.

However, as discussed in various chapters, the mere application of technology alone will not result in higher levels of student engagement or achievement in the middle-elementary and higher grades. Rather, these strategies must be implemented within the framework of sound, proven instructional practices, and a wide variety of these were likewise presented here, including cognitive strategy instruction, schema-based instruction, and educational games for older students.

Further, in addition to sound, differentiated instructional practices, teachers must implement sound, differentiated assessment practices in order to determine where students are in their varied levels of understanding. The next chapter presents an array of differentiated instructional practices that will assist mathematics teachers in understanding exactly where students are, and what their students might need in the way of differentiated instruction in math.

Differentiated Assessments and Response to Intervention

7

ASSESSMENT IS A CHANGIN' SOON!

In assessment, as in instruction generally, change is coming! Chapter 1 of this book began with a discussion of changes in mathematics instruction anticipated over the next 5 to 10 years, and this chapter begins by discussion of concomitant changes in mathematics assessment practices. In fact, as this book is being revised in 2013, it is quite difficult to coherently describe the changes teachers are likely to experience in mathematics assessment over the next few years, because so much is currently unknown. While change seems to be a constant in education, there are certain times when there seems to be even more transition than normal. Today, it seems that everything in math assessment is changing at the same time, and this book is riding atop that wave!

In *The Teaching Revolution: RTI, Technology, and Differentiation Transform Teaching for the 21st Century* (Bender & Waller, 2012), I and my coauthor, Laura Waller, recently summarized this drastic transition. With the advent of increased technology in the classroom, implementation of the Common Core Mathematics Standards, as well as the RTI initiative in mathematics, it is not inaccurate to say that virtually everything will be impacted in mathematics instruction and assessment education over the next five years, and, as we argued in that book, the whole of the coming changes is likely to be greater than the sum of the parts! It is very difficult to say exactly what mathematics instruction and assessment might look like in 5 to 10 years.

Of course, many teachers have already developed a variety of ways to differentiate their assessment practices in math, while they were developing a wider array of differentiated teaching strategies. Still, major changes in assessment practices at the state level are most assuredly coming, and teachers are well advised to get abreast of these changes as soon as possible.

As reported in Chapter 1, 45 states and the District of Columbia are implementing the Common Core Standards in Mathematics, and presently, two different assessment systems for the Common Core are being developed, by two federally funded consortia. The Partnership for Assessment of Readiness for College and Careers is a coalition of 23 states and the District of Columbia that is developing an assessment associated with implementation of the Common Core, and the assessment should be in place for the 2014–2015 academic year (parcconline.org/). This assessment will test students' ability to read complex texts, complete research projects, excel at classroom speaking and listening assignments, and work with digital media. This assessment will also replace the one end-of-year high-stakes accountability test with a series of tests throughout the year that will be averaged into one score, reducing the weight given to a single test.

> *Virtually everything will be impacted in mathematics instruction and assessment education over the next five years, and the whole of the coming changes is likely to be greater than the sum of the parts!*

The Smarter Balanced Assessment Consortium is a similar group of 21 states (four additional states are participating in an advisory capacity), likewise funded by the federal government to develop assessments associated with the Common Core (www.smarterbalanced.org/). This assessment will measure student performance using computer-adaptive technology that will ask individual students tailored questions based on their previous answers. In addition to an end-of-year assessment in mathematics, these will be a series of interim tests used.

While these Common Core Mathematics assessments are likely to be used by nearly 80% of students in the United States, it is still too early to ascertain the exact implications for differentiated instruction and assessment in the classroom. However, several things do seem clear. First, these new assessments in mathematics will be quite comprehensive, assessing a balance of math skills centered around conceptual understanding, procedural fluency, and application/problem solving.

Next, the days of the single-item Scantron answer sheet to assess mathematics performance are soon to be over. Rather, the assessments associated with the Common Core are going to be computer-based, practically focused assessment items that assess across multiple skills, multiple levels, multiple standards, or even multiple grade levels within a single item. Students will be expected to prove or justify their answers on these assessments, and those justifications will impact the student's overall assessment score.

Finally, these Common Core assessments will contrast significantly with the types of progress-monitoring assessments used within the RTI paradigm. RTI assessments are quite likely to focus, very specifically, on highly discrete mathematical skills, since this RTI model stems from behavioral thought, which has historically stressed measurement of highly defined, observable, and discrete behaviors.

Of course, one might argue that major assessment changes at the state assessment level, of the school by school level, do not directly impact the assessment practices used by individual teachers for progress monitoring within the RTI model. However, at a minimum, any description of assessment practices, whether in-class assessments—the major focus of this chapter—or statewide assessments, must present these anticipated transitions in assessment as a backdrop, and at least at some level the assessment practices of virtually all mathematics teachers in the states participating in the Common Core will be impacted.

These Common Core Mathematics assessments are likely to be used by nearly 80% of students in the United States.

Coupled with the wholesale transition to differentiated instruction in classrooms over the last decade, there has been a parallel shift toward differentiated assessment practices (Bender, 2012a; Chapman & King, 2005). Teachers in virtually all subjects are increasingly using grading and assessment practices that provide a deeper, richer understanding of a student's knowledge than merely a paper-and-pencil test, and while this trend may be somewhat less obvious in mathematics, there is still a significant shift to a broader array of assessments—and more transition is coming in the near future.

In order to place the current and upcoming transitions in context, this chapter initially presents an array of assessment options that allow teachers to differentiate assessment in the general education class. Some of these are assessment options that have been developed over a few decades, while others are much more recent. Later, the RTI initiative is discussed at length, as the assessment practices built into that initiative are likely to impact virtually every mathematics teacher (Bender & Crane, 2011; Koellner, Colsman, & Risley, 2011). Finally, two RTI case studies are included to illustrate how teachers are assessing mathematics today.

DIFFERENTIATED ASSESSMENT OPTIONS FOR MATH

In general education classrooms in the United States, Canada, and around the world, teachers are finding various options by which they can differentiate the assessments that they undertake with particular students (Bender & Crane, 2011). While the initial literature on differentiated instruction did not emphasize differentiated assessments a great deal (Tomlinson, 1999), more recently there has been an increased emphasis on finding the right assessment for particular students with varied learning styles and preferences (Chapman & King, 2005; Sousa & Tomlinson, 2011), and thus differentiated assessments are critically important for all mathematics teachers in general education today (Bender & Crane, 2011).

Assessment innovations such as standards-based assessment, authentic assessment, dynamic assessment, portfolio assessment, curriculum-based measurement (CBM), and digital portfolio assessment have received increasing emphasis as assessment paradigms that provide a clearer picture of what students have mastered in the general education class at the Tier 1 level (Chapman & King, 2005; Larmer & Mergendoller, 2010; Niguidula, 2011). These all represent assessments for the 21st century

> *Assessment innovations discussed herein have received increasing emphasis as assessment paradigms that provide a clearer picture of what students have mastered in the general education class at the Tier 1 level.*

that should be used in virtually all general education math classes at the Tier 1 instructional level. Some of these assessments may also meet the requirements for universal screening within the RTI paradigm.

Standards-Based Assessment and Criterion-Referenced Assessment

Many teachers are familiar with standards-based assessments that involve comparing a student's performance with a list of educational standards rather than with the performance of other students. While the term standards-based assessment is frequently used today, the original term for this assessment practice was criterion-referenced assessment. In fact, criterion-referenced assessments were among the first of the diagnostic assessment tools to be developed, and this type of measure has been around for at least 40 years. Further, over the years criterion-referenced assessment has served as the basis for, or as a component of, many other types of assessment, such as standards-based assessment, curriculum-based assessment, and portfolio assessment, discussed later in this chapter (Bender, 2009; C. J. Jones, 2001). However, this assessment emphasis has been relabeled, as is so often the case in education, and has received recent attention as the standards-based assessment initiative.

> *Standards-based assessments involve comparing a student's performance with a list of educational standards rather than with the performance of other students.*

While most statewide assessments in the 1980s and 1990s compared a student's performance with the academic performances of his or her peers by virtue of a global summary score such as a standardized score or a grade equivalent score (a practice that is often referred to as norm-based assessment), standards-based assessment essentially assesses a student's performance relative to a specific list of educational standards. These may be Common Core State Standards in reading and mathematics or other state-specific standards. Of course, states such as Virginia, Texas, and Alaska have chosen not to adopt the Common Core State Standards, and those states will retain their own state standards, but even in those non–Common Core states, the state-specific standards will serve as the basis for a standards-based assessment.

In the simplest terms, standards-based assessment typically involves a list of sequenced skills or education standards in mathematics and items that represent each of those discrete skills. Thus, the student's performance references how well that student does on those targeted skills. As one example, consider the sequenced skills involved in whole-number addition. An assessment for whole-number addition is presented in Box 7.1, and each separate line involves a discrete addition skill. For example, line 1 presents single-digit addition with sums less than 10. Line three represents double-digit addition with no regrouping, and so on. Each line of items is directly tied to a specific criterion/skill in the broader area of whole-number addition.

> *Standards-based assessment typically involves a list of sequenced skills or education standards in mathematics and items that represent each of those discrete skills.*

BOX 7.1   CRT ASSESSMENT FOR WHOLE-NUMBER ADDITION

1.	5	7	4	2	8	
	+2	+2	+4	+6	+6	Percentage Score _____

2.	6	3	8	2	9	
	+8	+9	+4	+4	+2	Percentage Score _____

3.	35	47	54	25	83	
	+42	+32	+24	+13	+22	Percentage Score _____

4.	27	27	37	28	39	
	+46	+25	+34	+13	+22	Percentage Score _____

5.	64	87	98	79	78	
	+36	+35	+24	+14	+22	Percentage Score _____

6.	73	87	98	76	81	
	+36	+35	+21	+13	+22	Percentage Score _____

Source: Bender (2009).

With the results from a student's performance on this assessment in hand, teachers can easily determine the specific skill on which a student needs assistance. Also, using this assessment, the teacher can determine exactly what instruction to offer. For example, if a student completed the first three rows of problems at 90% or 100% accuracy, and then achieved only 20% accuracy on the fourth row of problems, the student clearly has mastered single- and double-digit addition without regrouping, but has a difficult understanding the concept of regrouping in general or place value in double-digit operations because that is the exact difference between the problems completed successfully and those that were not completed successfully. That student would require intensive instruction on place value and regrouping, and intensive instruction would begin with the problems involving double-digit addition with regrouping in the tens and hundreds place.

While standards-based assessment is the newest iteration of criterion-referenced assessment, the standards-based assessment initiative does stress several concerns that were not components of criterion-referenced assessment originally. First, the standards-based assessment movement stresses alignment between the school curriculum and the newer standards stressed on the assessment, a process which is ongoing in many states currently.

Next, in many standards-based assessments, cut scores are used to delineate levels of performance. Typically, terms such as "Above Standard," "Meets Standard," and "Below Standard" are used. These levels are typically used in a benchmarking process to describe individual students' performance, and may even be utilized several times during a given year, specifically for benchmarking purposes. Standards-based tests may be holistically graded, rather than graded correct or incorrect among multiple choices.

Curriculum-Based Measurement

Curriculum-based measurement (CBM) is best understood as another example of criterion-referenced assessment. Historically, traditional assessments sometimes emphasized measurement of cognitive ability deficits such as auditory perception, visual memory, or other cognitive skills that might hamper learning (Deno, 2003; C. J. Jones, 2001). In contrast, many educators in the 1980s and 1990s began to stress academic or specific curriculum-based performance measures that involve direct assessment of specific academic skills. Thus, curriculum-based measurements, or CBM, evolved over recent decades as one progress-monitoring system that allows teachers to focus specifically on highly discrete skills in the curriculum and to differentiate their instruction to emphasize the specific skills a child has not mastered (Deno, 2003; C. J. Jones, 2001; Koellner et al., 2011). In fact, the assessment presented in Box 7.1 is an example of a CBM measure as well as an example of criterion-referenced assessment.

Scholars agree that through repeatedly measuring a child's progress on a particular set of academic skills, mathematics teachers can obtain information that is highly useful for planning the next instructional task for specific students (Deno, 2003; McMaster, Du, & Petursdottir, 2009). For this reason, assessment based directly on the skills in the child's curriculum, measured on a repeated and frequent basis, seems to be the option of choice for differentiating instruction at the Tier 1 level for all students within general education classes. However, CBM has also been stressed as the most effective option for measuring progress in Tiers 2 and 3 of the RTI procedure as well (Koellner et al., 2011).

> *CBM has been stressed as the most effective option for measuring progress in Tiers 2 and 3 of the RTI procedure.*

While frequent measurement of students' performance can help teachers target their instruction, scholars disagree on the frequency with which a student's performance should be assessed. For example, some theorists argue that a teacher-made assessment administered weekly or every other week is sufficient (D. Fuchs & Fuchs, 2005), whereas others have suggested that student progress should be assessed every day in the RTI process. (See Bender and Shores, 2007, for a review).

Finally, CBM assessment data from those repeated measures are often summarized in some readily interpretable form, such as X/Y axis charts of an individual student's performance. The information in that format can easily serve as both universal screening data from the general education math class, or as progress monitoring data in a subsequent Tier 2 or Tier 3 interventions. Several data charts of this nature are presented in the RTI case studies later in this chapter.

However, in addition to charting data for one student, teachers may choose to provide charted data for the entire class, or each individual within the class. Such data charted for each student in a class can not only target a student for supplemental Tier 2 intervention in math, but would also specifically target discrete mathematics skills for further emphasis in the math class. Clearly charted CBM assessment data represent the best possible example of assessment for instruction throughout the general education class, as well as all of the RTI intervention tiers.

> *Charted CBM assessment data represent the best possible example of assessment for instruction.*

For these reasons, curriculum-based measurement is fairly widely accepted as the basis for much of the assessment in RTI, as described later in this chapter. Therefore, most math teachers in elementary and middle school grades are soon likely to become quite familiar with this assessment option, if they are not already using CBM. Several websites are available where teachers can obtain help in developing CBMs or purchase CBMs for mathematics skills, as presented in Box 7.2.

BOX 7.2   COMMONLY USED CBM OPTIONS

Aimsweb is a fee-based assessment and data aggregation service that includes CBM assessments in reading, math, spelling, and writing (www.aimsweb.com). Because this covers both subjects that are, in most schools, the curricular areas stressed in RTI (reading and math), this service is one of the most popular in schools today. In math, the assessments include early math fluency, math computation, and concepts and applications probes. Aimsweb also allows for printing sets of assessments materials, computer and software tools for efficient data capture, and web-based management of CBM data.

(Continued)

(Continued)

EasyCBM contains an array of reading and math CBM assessments and is free for individual teacher use (www.easycbm.com). Schools and districts are required to pay a per-student, yearly fee. The site includes K–8 math assessments tied to Focal Point Standards in Mathematics from the National Council of Teachers of Mathematics rather than Common Core Math. These assessments are described by the developers as testing "conceptual understanding" rather than basic computational fluency (see the website). This program allows teachers to generate progress-monitoring charts and aggregate students' performance across the class.

Intervention Central is a very helpful website that provides a wide variety of instructional strategies and assessment options in mathematics and reading (www.interventioncentral.org/). This is a great help in developing RTI progress-monitoring options for RTI in math. The site provides a CBM worksheet generator teachers can use to create CBMs in whole number operations for primary and elementary students, as well as many pre-prepared CBM tools. Many different instructional interventions are also described in sufficient detail to allow teachers to implement them to assist students in Tiers 2 and 3 math interventions.

Edcheckup is a web-based service that provides commercial measures of reading, writing, and math, as well as student data management (www.edcheckup.com). Math assessment probes measure performance on computation, using a "cloze math" format. This also offers schools the option of entering their student CBM data online and generating screening and progress-monitoring reports and graphs.

Authentic Assessment

Authentic assessment is based on the concept that students should produce actual products that are similar to products that would be produced in the "real world." In this approach, evaluation of the students' conceptual understanding should be based on those products or their performance in producing those products (Bender, 2012a; Boss & Krauss, 2007; Larmer & Mergendoller, 2010). Authentic tasks require that the student perform tasks in as realistic a fashion as possible, based on the context of the real world (Larmer & Mergendoller, 2010). Further, some authentic tasks may be quite extensive and involve participation of groups of students rather than merely an individual student.

Authentic assessment practices may involve a variety of evaluation mechanisms, as the examples below indicate. Students may:

> Perform a piece of music, and then describes in math terms, the musical relationships (e.g., representing chord structure of a piece with the circle of fifths); develop a video about Pythagoras doing his work in mathematics; or creating a graph to summarize aggregated data.

Today, authentic assessment is most frequently tied with the project-based learning approach to differentiating instruction as discussed in Chapter 3, since both stress real-world products as the basis for assessment. Further, because of the recent resurgence of interest in project-based learning, there has been an increased emphasis on authentic assessment in the last decade. Also, while authentic assessment represents an excellent option for evaluation in general education, it does not provide a realistic option for evaluation of students' individual performance on specific targeted skills over time (e.g., operations with whole numbers and fractions), so this assessment innovation is much more likely to be used in general education classes than in Tier 2 or Tier 3 progress monitoring in RTI.

> *Today, authentic assessment is most frequently tied with the project-based learning approach to differentiating instruction since both stress real-world products as the basis for assessment.*

Portfolio Assessment

Portfolio assessment involves collecting a portfolio of a student's mathematics work over time, and this has been discussed as one differentiated assessment option over the last decade (Bender, 2009; Chapman & King, 2005). A portfolio is an indexed compilation of selected work by the student that demonstrates the academic growth of the student over time and provides evidence of student accomplishment on particular skills. Portfolios tend to de-emphasize one overall score as a summary of a student's work, and thereby encourages increased student ownership of the responsibility for the work. This tactic also makes the teacher and the student joint collaborators in the student's progress in mathematics.

A portfolio is an indexed compilation of selected work by the student that demonstrates the academic growth of the student over time and provides evidence of student accomplishment on particular skills.

The portfolio should include math work that the teacher and the student believe reflects the student's accomplishments most accurately. Students may include work that they are particularly proud of (a great score on a math quiz), work that represents their most challenging task, or work that represents ongoing studies in progress. For example, the badges earned in Khan Academy, or documentation of similar achievement from other computer-based curricula, should be noted in the portfolio. Also, each portfolio should include two critical components:

1. An index prepared by the student describing each item included, and

2. A description of the items, their importance, and what they represent.

The index is included to let readers (future teachers of the student, parents, and the student) know what the portfolio contains, and the time frame associated with the work enclosed. The reflective essay might detail why the student believes that the selected work represents his or her most important efforts. That reflective essay should show the relationship between the work projects in the portfolio and describe that relationship in terms of student growth over time. Further, both of these items, the portfolio index and the reflective essay, may be developed as an ongoing project within the portfolio itself. Of course, both should be completed prior to assigning a grade for the entire portfolio.

The portfolio should include mathematics work from a student over a period of time. In some cases, work of problem solving, as one example, from the first of the academic year may be compared directly with problem-solving work from the end of the year. However, some portfolios are completed in more limited time frames (e.g., a single grading period). All of the portfolio materials should be gathered and placed in some type of folder, and while some teachers use an actual portfolio folder—hence the name—others may use small boxes, file drawers, or other containers to keep the work together and organized.

With the increased use of digital media, many teachers now have students create digital portfolios as a differentiated assessment tool in mathematics (Niguidula, 2011; Stiggins, 2005). In digital portfolios work is developed, presented, and stored digitally, and in most cases, the index for the work in the portfolio is, likewise, digital in nature. This is particularly effective when students are doing computerized mathematics work, and many modern computerized programs create various charts that can be included in digital portfolios.

Niguidula (2011) recommends structuring the index for a student's digital portfolio around specific standards (e.g., from the Common Core State Standards) for student performance. In that sense, when a student, the student's parent, or a teacher wishes to show that the student demonstrated competence relative to a specific Common Core Math standard, that teacher could get into the student's digital portfolio, select a specific standard, and the portfolio itself would present work completed by the student that demonstrated the student's competence relative to that standard (Niguidula, 2011).

Both the content of the portfolio and the hard-copy reports developed by students can, with today's technology, be scanned into digital form, and any presentations or digital photo/video products may likewise be put into digital portfolios. While digital portfolios were originally housed on school computers (Niguidula, 2011), technology applications (e.g., Google Apps) now present the option of housing digital portfolios "on the cloud," thus making these portfolios of student work available to teachers working with specific students in the future, as well as to the students and their parents for many years to come.

Rubric-Based Assessment

As teachers develop strategies for differentiating assessments, many teachers have become familiar with using scoring rubrics to evaluate students' work. A rubric is an attempt to communicate expectations of quality around an assignment by giving specific descriptions for various assignment components and/or criteria for earning specific grades on an assignment. A good rubric will perform several functions. It will serve as a guide for planning students' work, as well as a gauge for measuring progress and maintaining focus on project goals. Finally, a rubric can serve as an instrument for assessing the effectiveness of a project.

In many cases, scoring rubrics are used to delineate consistent criteria for grading, and also assist students in completing the assignments. Because the grading criteria are public and presented on the rubric, a scoring rubric allows teachers and students alike to evaluate students' work, including evaluations that are quite complex or even subjective in nature. A scoring rubric can also provide a basis for self-evaluation,

A rubric is an attempt to communicate expectations of quality around an assignment by giving specific descriptions for various assignment components and/or criteria for earning specific grades on an assignment.

reflection, and peer review. It is aimed at accurate and fair assessment, fostering understanding, and indicating a way to proceed with subsequent learning/teaching.

Box 7.3 presents a sample of a rubric associated with one artifact from a PBL project described in Chapter 3 (Box 3.3 When Can I Buy a Car?). The first artifact from that project, presented below, involved creation of data in a spreadsheet.

Artifact 1—Excel Budget Sheets: You will develop a personal budget in Excel or other database. It must cover at least a two-month time frame, and must include:

- a total of all the funds you earn in that two months;
- a total of all of your personal funds you spend in that two months; and
- a total of the excess funds that you can save for your car purchase in that two months.

BOX 7.3   SAMPLE SCORING RUBRIC FOR SPREADSHEET ARTIFACT

Artifact Assignment

Excel Budget Sheets: *You will develop a personal budget in Excel or other database. It must cover at least a two-month time frame, and must include*

- a total of all the funds you earn in that two months;
- a total of all of your personal funds you spend in that two months; and
- a total of the excess funds that you can save for your car purchase in that two months.

Scoring Rubric	
Item Descriptions	*Score Earned*
Spreadsheet included	*C*

- all earned funds listed individually, and then totaled for two months
- all expenditures listed individually, and then totaled for two months
- generally clearly written notes on anticipated monthly savings

Scoring Rubric	
Item Descriptions	Score Earned
Spreadsheet included	B
• all earned funds listed individually, and then totaled month by month over a two-month period • all expenditures listed individually, and then totaled month by month over a two-month period • averages computed correctly for earned funds and expenditures • written notes, referencing exact figures from spreadsheet data and projected monthly savings	
Spreadsheet included	A
• all earned funds listed individually, and then totaled month by month over a three-month period or longer • all expenditures listed individually, and then totaled month by month over a three-month period or longer • averages computed correctly for earned funds and expenditures • explicit written notes, referencing exact figures from spreadsheet data and projected monthly savings • evidence in written notes suggesting consideration of unexpected expenses	

As this rubric shows, the relationship between the assignment for the artifact and the information to be evaluated is clear within the rubric itself. Thus, this rubric will make the assignment clearer to the students as they complete this work. Also, various levels of work are delineated, making this school work a bit more authentic in the sense that, in many jobs, employees can determine the level of effort to put into various tasks, based on the importance of those tasks. Finally, a rubric of this nature forces students to consider their own desires for a specific grade.

Rubrics may be as extensive as necessary but should stipulate the specific components of the performance assessment project as well as the relative grading "weight" for each required assignment or artifact. In that fashion, students quickly realize what is required for assignment completion as well as what aspects of the assignment to emphasize (Bender, 2012a). Scoring rubrics also help students become thoughtful evaluators of their own work and the work of others, which can be a key concern in project-based learning, as well as in other differentiated instructional approaches.

Rubrics should stipulate the specific components of the performance assessment project as well as the relative grading "weight" for each required assignment or artifact.

There is one other advantage of using a rubric: Evaluation work using a rubric can be completed by students as well as by teachers. In fact, rubrics may reduce the amount of time teachers spend evaluating student work, by having students complete the evaluations on each other or on themselves with all such work subject to later teacher review. However, like many of the other assessment innovations described previously, rubrics are probably more useful in general instruction rather than in the higher RTI tiers, since they seem to be more global in nature and are not typically targeted to highly discrete academic skills.

While many online sources provide ready-made rubrics in mathematics, several websites are available to assist teachers in developing their own. If you would like to explore developing rubrics, you might consider Rubistar (rubistar.4teachers.org/), a free option.

Fundamentals of Differentiated Assessment Within RTI

Most schools in the United States adopted a three-tier model of RTI as was briefly described in Chapter 1. Tier 1 of that model represents instruction in the general education mathematics class, and it is expected that that instruction meets the needs for perhaps 80% of the students in the class. However, some students will require a more intensive, supplemental instructional intervention to succeed in math. Thus, in this model, Tier 2 represents a more intensive supplemental intervention, typically required by perhaps 20% of the students, while Tier 3 depicts very intensive supplemental instruction, which is typically required by perhaps 5% of the class. Of course, assessment in various levels determines which students might require specific tiers of intensive instruction. This three-tier RTI pyramid is presented in Box 7.4.

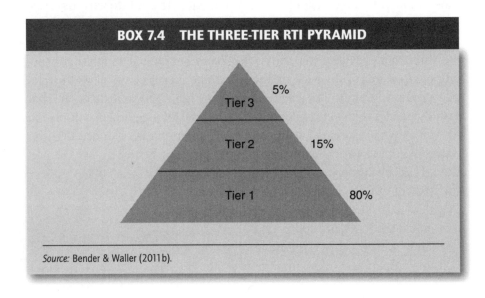

BOX 7.4   THE THREE-TIER RTI PYRAMID

Tier 3 — 5%

Tier 2 — 15%

Tier 1 — 80%

Source: Bender & Waller (2011b).

Teachers in mathematics should exercise some caution in their interpretation of this general RTI model. For example, these data on which percentages of students should have their needs met at various tiers stem from data on elementary reading instruction, not mathematics performance (Bender & Crane, 2011). In fact, there may be fewer students who are succeeding in mathematics than in reading at some grade levels, in particular schools, and these percentages should be interpreted as general guidelines rather than school-specific data.

As described in Chapter 1, Tier 1 instruction in the RTI model is instruction provided in the general education mathematics class for all students in the class. Because differentiated assessment is now recommended for all general education mathematics classes, all of the assessment options described above may be used for Tier 1 instruction. However, when struggling students require more targeted, intensive interventions in mathematics, the assessment practices likewise become more targeted, more intensive, and more frequent.

The initial research descriptions of the RTI process presented two purposes for formative assessments—screening and progress monitoring. Both of these types of assessments are frequently required from almost all mathematics teachers in primary, elementary, and middle school grades (Bender & Crane, 2011).

Universal screening is defined as screening every child in the general education class on an individually administered screening assessment two or three times each year in order to benchmark that student's performance (i.e., to document whether or not each individual student was meeting required growth expectations in mathematics skills). This level of assessment is actually referred to as "benchmarking" in some states. These universal screening data are used to determine if students are meeting expectations, or if some students need supplemental instructional interventions on particular skills in mathematics.

> *Universal screening involves screening every child on an individually administered assessment two or three times each year in order to document whether or not each individual student is meeting benchmarks in mathematics.*

Progress monitoring, in contrast, may be defined as frequent repeated assessments during specific targeted RTI interventions that are typically completed each week or every other week, during supplemental Tier 2 and Tier 3 RTI interventions. These assessments are intended to document the impact of the intervention and to assist in planning the student's ongoing educational intervention program.

> *Progress monitoring, in contrast, may be defined as frequent repeated assessments during specific targeted RTI interventions that are typically completed each week or every other week, during supplemental Tier 2 and Tier 3 RTI interventions.*

Thus, in the simplest terms, universal screening is a Tier 1 function, because it applies to every student in the class, whereas progress monitoring is a function of Tier 2 and Tier 3 RTI procedures, and only applies to students in those supplemental interventions. While this may seem to be a simple distinction, there is much confusion on this point. That is because some assessments commonly used for universal screening in mathematics may also serve as progress-monitoring tools as well. Further, many states have required specific assessments for either universal screening or progress monitoring within the RTI paradigm. Thus, all mathematics teachers should check the website of their state education agency to see if specific assessments are required for either of these purposes.

As the definitions above indicate, RTI has its roots in a variety of innovation practices such as CBM, criterion-referenced testing, and more general performance monitoring initiatives (Deno, 2003; Koellner et al., 2011). In RTI as well as the more recent literature on in-class assessment, differentiated assessment is seen as a tool to enable the teacher and student, working in concert, to specifically target the student's weaknesses and design instruction to address those specific weaknesses (Chapman & King, 2005; Niguidula, 2011; Sousa & Tomlinson, 2011). Thus, assessment and instruction are not seen as separated endeavors but rather as techniques that are mutually supportive. Again, this emphasis—the merger of instruction and assessment—has carried into the RTI initiative.

Of course, the tools described herein do not represent all of the assessment needs within a differentiated classroom, but they do represent the recent influence of the RTI initiative in mathematics. Teachers should understand the relationship between RTI and previously discussed innovations in assessment because each of these types of assessments within RTI draws on a long tradition of formative assessment for instruction (Bender & Crane, 2011; Chapman & King, 2005; Deno, 2003).

Tier 1 RTI Interventions in Mathematics

While most educators in primary and elementary grades are now familiar with the RTI three-level pyramid model, and may use that model for reading instruction, RTI in mathematics is a somewhat more recent emphasis in most schools. Understanding how various instructional and assessment tools fit within the three-tier RTI model in order to foster differentiated instruction may be new to some.

First, the general education mathematics teacher is responsible for both instruction and universal screening in mathematics, as in reading. Any of the instructional strategies presented in Chapters 4, 5, and 6 of this book provide excellent instructional options, and many of those same strategies can be used as interventions in Tier 2 or Tier 3 RTI procedures.

Next, many differentiated assessment strategies have been presented earlier in this chapter for Tier 1 instruction, in contrast with assessment in Tiers 2 and 3, where virtually all assessment is based on CBM. Also, the RTI literature presents the expectation that primary and elementary-level general education teachers will use universal screening assessments three times each year in reading and mathematics in order to check that all students have met certain benchmarks, and to identify those students who need a more intensive supplemental intervention at the Tier 2 level (Bender & Crane, 2011; Bender & Waller, 2011a).

There are many ways that elementary and middle school math teachers may complete these universal screenings. First, the CBMs discussed in Box 7.2 provide universal screening options. Next, teachers may use screening instruments that are built into their curriculum. In addition, several new assessments have become available specifically for diagnostic work in mathematics. These are presented in Box 7.5.

BOX 7.5   NEW ASSESSMENT TOOLS FOR RTI IN MATHEMATICS

Dibels Math

This recently developed universal screening tool for mathematics was developed and published by the same company that publishes the widely used DIBELS Next assessment in reading, which may be the most widely used tool for universal screening in elementary reading. For that reason, it is likely that DIBELS Math will receive considerable attention as RTI procedures for mathematics are developed around the country. This tool provides a universal screening and progress-monitoring tool for teachers to use that measures mathematics skills in a series of 1- to 2-minute timed predictive measures that assess mathematics proficiency in kindergarten and Grade 1. It can suggest targeted interventions and track student growth. The website provides additional information (dibels.org/dibelsmath.html).

SMI (Scholastic Math Inventory)

This recently developed, computer-based mathematics inventory was published by Scholastic in 2011 (teacher.scholastic.com/math-assessment/scholastic-math-inventory/). SMI is a research-based, computer-adaptive math assessment program for students in Grades 2 through 8 that measures mathematical understanding on the Quantile framework. This provides a fast, reliable assessment to guide instruction in the RTI process and is aligned to the Common Core State Standards.

Finally, in an RTI procedure, the general education teacher delivers mathematics instruction at the Tier 1 level, and perhaps in Tier 2 level as well. He or she also conducts universal screenings in mathematics three times each year. This means that the general education teacher is, typically, the first person to collect hard data on students' performance within the RTI procedure (Bender & Crane, 2011).

Tier 2 and Tier 3 Instructional and Assessment Responsibilities

In the area of reading, universal screening data generally indicate that 20% of students are not succeeding in Tier 1 instruction (Bender & Crane 2011; Bender & Waller, 2011b). However, that figure may be somewhat higher in mathematics (Bender & Crane, 2011), because evidence indicates that more students have deficits in mathematics than in reading by the end of Grade 8 (NMAP, 2008). Thus, 20% or more students in most primary and elementary grades will probably require some type of Tier 2 supplemental mathematics intervention. That intervention is required in order to attain mastery of the content, and such interventions usually involve a teacher working some extra time (usually 20 or 30 minutes three times weekly) with four to six kids in the classroom on mathematics. These Tier 2 interventions should be highly targeted and focused on the exact mathematics skills that individual students need. In many cases, this can, most effectively, be addressed by a computerized, individualized mathematics software program, and several such programs are described in Appendix A.

In addition to delivering Tier 2 instruction, the general education mathematics teacher is likewise expected to monitor the progress of each student in that group. Again, this can be done in a computerized program, or via CBM developed for progress monitoring by the teacher. Thus, RTI represents an increased role for general education teachers in mathematics, at least in terms of the universal screening and Tier 2 instructional expectations.

> *RTI represents an increased role for general education teachers in mathematics, at least in terms of the universal screening and Tier 2 instructional expectations.*

However, the RTI model suggests that some students may not have their needs for intensive, supplemental mathematics instruction meet by Tier 2 interventions (Bender & Crane, 2011), and these few students may require a much more intensive Tier 3 intervention. Today in most elementary schools that have implemented RTI in mathematics, the daily Tier 3 instruction is typically undertaken by someone other than the general education teacher. For example a mathematics coach, lead teacher, or intervention specialist may assume this role, conducting highly intensive, supplemental mathematics instruction and monitoring each student's progress. Typically, these Tier 3 interventions involve daily instruction for 30 to 45 minutes in very small instructional groups (e.g., one teacher and no more than three students), in order to assure that students get the intensive instruction they require in mathematics (Bender & Crane, 2011).

CASE STUDY ONE: AN RTI PROCEDURE IN ELEMENTARY MATH

An example of how assessment and intervention support each other in an RTI procedure should illustrate how these RTI assessment procedures are utilized. Let's imagine a male student, Kenny, in Grade 3. Kenny is having some difficulty learning his multiplication math facts. Specifically, he is not meeting the Operations and Algebraic Standard in Grade 3 from the Common Core State Standards in Mathematics (Standard, 3.0A.1):

> *Represent and solve problems involving multiplication and division.*
>
> *1. Interpret products of whole numbers, e.g., interpret 5 × 7 as the total number of objects in 5 groups of 7 objects each. For example, describe a context in which a total number of objects can be expressed as 5 × 7.*

His teacher, Ms. Fox, used a CBM measure as a universal screening for everyone in the class in October of the year, after students had been taught the times tables. That measure was merely a series of simple times tables problems, with five problems from each fact family (i.e., each number of 10 facts is a separate fact family; 4 Xs, 6 Xs, 8 Xs, etc.). Kenny got every problem correct on the ones, twos, threes, and fives times tables, but not the other fact families. Also, Kenny's quiz grades after the class moved beyond the times tables indicated ongoing problems for Kenny.

Ms. Fox also noted that Kenny has experienced earlier problems in mathematics, as shown by his second-grade statewide assessment score, which indicated a grade equivalency of 1.4 on operations. Ms. Fox talked with Kenny's second-grade teacher, who likewise indicated that Kenny was having some difficulties in mathematics, specifically in place value operations involving regrouping.

At that point, Ms. Fox determined that Kenny was not progressing in mathematics in a manner that will allow him to succeed in Grade 3. Therefore, she discussed Kenny's performance and the data above with the lead teacher for Grade 3, Ms. Lovorn, and they jointly decided that Kenny would require a supplemental Tier 2 intervention in math. While place value and addition/subtraction were a concern, these two decided that multiplication facts were more critical for Kenny, in that much of the third-grade curriculum (fractions, division, etc.) were dependent on multiplication math facts. Thus the Tier 2 intervention would focus on that specific set of skills. That meeting left Ms. Fox with two tasks: (1) Write up a summary of these data and the decisions of this meeting with Ms. Lovorn, and (2) plan and write a description of a supplemental Tier 2 intervention for Kenny.

Ms. Fox also noted there were five other students who, like Kenny, were having difficulty on multiplication math facts, so she collected the same type of data on each of them, and let Ms. Lovorn know that she proposed to do a Tier 2 intervention for each of those students at the same time. Therefore, Ms. Fox would make time to do this supplemental intervention at some point in the day outside of the mathematics instructional time, and she would work with that small group of Kenny and five other students. In order to make this work in her classroom, Ms. Fox planned to have the other students complete group work assignments in social studies while she conducted this Tier 2 math intervention three times each week for a minimum of 25 minutes each time.

> *In most school districts, notes on students' individual performance are collected in a file using some type of RTI form or folder.*

In most school districts, those notes on Kenny's performance will be collected in Kenny's file (as they would be for the other students). Many districts use some type of RTI form or folder. Later in this chapter, a completed example of such an RTI is presented to show exactly how these data might be aggregated, as well as the steps in the RTI procedure in mathematics.

A Tier 2 Math Intervention

Ms. Fox decided to undertake this Tier 2 intervention by combining two research-proven intervention strategies that were described previously—reciprocal peer tutoring (see previous discussion of classwide peer tutoring, though in this instance Ms. Fox was not doing this classwide) and time delay. She wrote a paragraph-long description of that combined intervention and presented that to Ms. Lovorn, the third-grade lead teacher. She was specific in terms of doing the intervention three times each week for 25 minutes, and continuing that intervention for the next six-week grading period.

Ms. Fox already knew exactly which math fact families each student needed to work on from the CBM measure the class completed as the universal screener. Thus, she could specifically target each student's supplemental instruction to the multiplication fact families they needed help with. In order to be considered a valid Tier 2 intervention, the intervention must be specifically targeted to each student's individual deficit areas. This will increase the likelihood of strong positive effects. This is one major advantage in using CBM measures for the universal screening with all of the math class: These CBM measures help target specific skills for the intervention.

By pairing students together for peer tutoring, Ms. Fox could quickly teach these six third-graders to "call out the times tables" to their peer buddy. Thus, each student was presented with the exact fact family they needed and was supposed to either provide the answer immediately, or wait until the tutor provided the answer, and then repeat it. Students were trained to mark each student's response on a time delay chart like the one presented in Chapter 4 (Box 4.7). After 10 minutes of practice for one student, the students changed roles, and the tutor became the tutee. In that way, each of the six students served as both tutor and tutee each day, and each was presented with work on the exact fact family he or she needed. After only two days, all of the students had learned the reciprocal tutoring procedure, and at that point, all Ms. Fox had to do was monitor the students as they completed their work and create a data chart for each student, collecting and charting the number of "correct anticipations" for each student.

> After 10 minutes of practice for one student, the students changed roles, and the tutor became the tutee.

Once the intervention was planned, Ms. Fox shared it with Ms. Lovorn once again. She then sent a letter to each parent of the six students informing them of the need for the supplemental intervention, and her plans for that intervention. While parental agreement is not necessary prior to beginning a Tier 2 intervention, it is always a good idea to inform parents on their child's performance (Bender & Crane, 2011). Then, Ms. Fox began the Tier 2 intervention for this group of six students.

Tier 2 Progress-Monitoring Results

As mentioned above, it took Ms. Fox only two days to teach the reciprocal peer tutoring procedure to the six students. As Ms. Fox progressed through this intervention over the next few weeks, she compiled daily progress-monitoring data for each student and charted that data. Notice in this procedure that the instructional procedure itself— reciprocal peer tutoring coupled with time delay—essentially combined instruction and assessment. Thus this intervention procedure generated direct CBM progress-monitoring data that simply needed to be compiled and charted. After only four weeks, the CBM progress-monitoring chart, presented in Box 7.6, showed that Kenny was making some progress, but that his growth was not fast enough for him to catch up with the other third-graders.

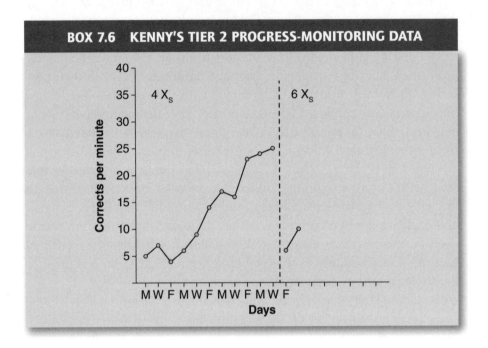

BOX 7.6   KENNY'S TIER 2 PROGRESS-MONITORING DATA

Ms. Fox shared these data, based on four weeks of intervention with Ms. Lovorn, and they discussed Kenny's progress. While four of the other five students in the intervention were making high levels of progress, Kenny and one other student were not. Because both Ms. Fox and Ms. Lovorn felt that Kenny's progress, though substantial, did not show sufficient growth, they approached Mr. Johnson, the chairperson of the Student Support Team (SST) in their school, and requested a team meeting focused specifically on Kenny's academic progress.

The student support team in most schools is not the same as the child study team, in that the student support team does not determine student eligibility for special education. Rather the SST's job is to help teachers find alternative teaching ideas for students with significant deficits, and one aspect of that responsibility often involves reviewing progress monitoring data for students who may require a more intensive, supplemental, Tier 3 intervention.

The student support team in most schools is not the same as the child study team, in that the student support team does not determine student eligibility for special education.

Tier 3 Intervention Planning

The SST in this school included the school's mathematics coach, Ms. Jensen, who typically implemented all Tier 3 interventions in the school. She taught in a room called the instructional lab, and was provided with a number of computers with appropriate mathematics software, as well as a paraprofessional to assist in those Tier 3 responsibilities. With that support, she could conduct very intensive interventions for various students individually on the computer.

Ms. Jensen indicated that she would work with Kenny daily for 40 minutes, and place him in an individualized computerized mathematics program called SuccessMaker Math (see a review of that program in Appendix A). That program involves individual diagnostic work and targeted intervention to address each student's deficit areas. The team also decided that Ms. Fox should continue to work with Kenny in the ongoing Tier 2 intervention in the general education classroom.

Tier 3 interventions should always be clearly more intensive than Tier 2 interventions, and both must be tied directly to an individual student's deficit areas, rather than merely another small-group intervention in which all students complete the same tasks.

Note that the planned Tier 3 supplemental intervention, like the previous Tier 2 intervention, was directly tied to specific deficit areas for Kenny. Also the Tier 3 intervention was much more intensive than the Tier 2 intervention, because Tier 3 involved a daily intervention and was conducted 40 minutes each day, on an individualized basis. Tier 3 interventions should always be clearly more intensive than Tier 2 interventions, and both must be tied directly to an individual student's deficit areas, rather than merely another small-group intervention in which all students complete the same tasks (Bender & Crane, 2011).

Tier 3 Progress Monitoring

After an additional six-week period, both Ms. Fox and Ms. Jensen were ready to present the Tier 3 progress-monitoring data to the student support team. An SST meeting was scheduled, at which those data were presented and discussed with the team. Box 7.7 presents the charted data from Ms. Fox's math facts intervention. Ms. Jensen presented a number of additional data charts, representing the outcome data charts from the SuccessMaker Math curriculum for Kenny, which showed essentially the same increased growth curve for Kenny as did Ms. Fox's data.

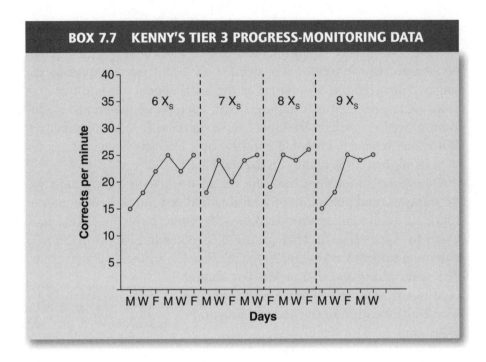

BOX 7.7   KENNY'S TIER 3 PROGRESS-MONITORING DATA

As these data show, the combined interventions conducted by Ms. Fox and Ms. Jensen did result in quick progress for Kenny. After the next grading period, the team reviewed these Tier 3 intervention data and determined that Kenny was making sufficient progress in third-grade mathematics skills, but that he would continue to need this level of intensive support. Thus, the team decided to discontinue the Tier 2 intervention, because Kenny had now mastered at 90% level all of the math fact families. However, the Tier 3 intervention in Ms. Jensen's class would be continued for Kenny, until he caught up with his classmates.

Critical Points for RTI in Math

There are several important points to consider when implementing a Tier 2 or Tier 3 intervention. First, note that in describing the interventions above, the teachers attended to the RTI expectation that higher tiers provide more intensive instruction in mathematics (Bender & Crane, 2011). The indicators of increased intensity were documented within the decision-making process, as noted above. These included such things as documenting the pupil-teacher ratio for each intervention, noting the duration and frequency of the intervention (how many minutes per day and days per week, over how many weeks, etc.), and noting the frequency of performance monitoring in each intervention tier. This level of detail should be included in every RTI procedure.

Next, in the RTI procedure described above, the general education teacher was responsible for the Tier 1 intervention in the general education class and also implemented the Tier 2 supplemental intervention. In some cases, the general education teacher may have to handle these activities without extensive support, and for that reason, finding the time for such interventions may be one of the biggest challenges to RTI. Undertaking a peer tutoring intervention at the Tier 2 level, and a computerized intervention at the Tier 3 level, certainly helped with these time concerns in this example.

> *Finding the time for such interventions may be one of the biggest challenges to RTI.*

Next, as this discussion shows, the RTI process is a data-driven process. In this instance, the data demonstrated that both the Tier 2 and Tier 3 interventions were successful, but a Tier 3 intervention was necessary in order to speed up Kenny's progress. In many cases, interventions work but don't result in the high levels of progress necessary, and in those examples a more intensive, Tier 3 intervention may be necessary, even when some success was shown on the Tier 2 intervention.

Next, as shown in this case, it is sometimes necessary to extend either the Tier 2 or Tier 3 intervention over a longer period of time. To put the matter bluntly, we do not undertake RTI simply to find students that need help; we undertake these interventions to find the exact level of intensity students need in order to succeed in mathematics. Once a successful level of intervention intensity is found, that intervention should be continued as long as necessary. This often means extending a Tier 2 or Tier 3 intervention in mathematics for a year or more (Bender & Crane, 2011).

> *Once a successful intervention is found, it should be continued as long as necessary, and this often means extending a Tier 2 or Tier 3 intervention for a year or more.*

Finally, note the extreme interplay between instruction and assessment in the RTI process. Both are components of each other and both inform each other, helping teachers make ongoing plans for each individual student's academic growth. Both differentiated instruction in the general education math class and these RTI procedures impact how the teacher plans and conducts lessons, and these two initiatives are mutually supporting (Bender & Crane, 2011).

CASE STUDY TWO: A MIDDLE SCHOOL RTI ON PROBLEM SOLVING

In order to demonstrate an RTI procedure in a higher grade level, the example in Box 7.8 is utilizing an RTI form that was originally recommended by

Bender and Shores (2007). This example involves helping a sixth-grade student on one and two step problem solving.

BOX 7.8   RTI ON PROBLEM SOLVING

Pupil Name: Nicole Tamian   **Age:** _12_   **Date:** 10/17/14

Teacher: _Ms. Renet Popham_   **School:** _Toccoa Middle School_   **Grade** 6

Statement of Academic/Behavioral Problem:

I've noticed since the beginning of the year that Nicole was having difficulty in the most basic one-step (one-operation) story problems in my first-period general mathematics class. While she struggles on some operations (both multiplication and division), her most pressing problem is a weakness in overall problem-solving skills. I've tutored her on several occasions, and assigned her a peer buddy to work with on story problems. She still doesn't get it, and her fifth-grade state assessment results (from last spring) indicated a weakness on problem solving. On that assessment, she scored 4.1 on mathematics applications, while scoring 6.8 on operations. It seems Nicole needs a more intensive intervention focused on solving story problems. I shared these concerns with Ms. Karzi, the department chair for Mathematics, and suggested a Tier 2 intervention on story problems for Nicole.

Signature: *Mrs. Renet Popham*   **Date:** *10/17/14*

Tier 2 Supplementary Intervention Plan

As the chairperson for Mathematics at Toccoa Middle, I consult with teachers on students who are struggling in mathematics, and I often complete any Tier 2 interventions that may be necessary. Also, our school holds a 30-minute intervention period four afternoons each week in which students may receive help in any of their subjects, or may participate in special enrichment classes taught by some faculty members.

After Mrs. Popham shared her concerns with me about Nicole Tamian, we determined that Nicole needed a Tier 2 intervention on story problems. Initially, I evaluated her using a short (six-problem) pretest on one- and two-step story problems, along with eight other students that needed assistance. On that assessment she missed two single-step story problems and all three two-step problems. I've recorded those scores as a pretest on story problems and will begin the intervention with instruction on single-step story problems using the STAR strategy [described previously in this book]. I will then move into multistep word problems.

To teach the STAR strategy, I plan on reviewing that strategy each day during the intervention, and then demonstrating it prior to having the students practice on a story problem individually. A poster representing that strategy will be posted on my wall for the students to refer to.

Nine students need a Tier 2 intervention of this nature during the next grading period, and each will come to my room during their schoolwide interventions period, Monday through Thursdays, weekly. Working in pairs for 20 minutes each day, they will complete a series of one- or two-step story problems using the STAR strategy. Nicole and the other students in this Tier 2 intervention will score each daily worksheet they and their peer buddy complete.

On Thursday of each week, at the end of the intervention period, I will provide the students with five single-step or two-step story problems selected from the school curricula, which they will complete individually. I will collect those scores, and chart the data for each individual student. We will continue this intervention for one grading period, and at the end of the grading period, we will re-evaluate Nicole's progress, along with the others. Nicole's mother was contacted via letter, and agreed that Nicole could participate in this Tier 2 intervention.

Signature: *Ms. Atem Karzi*   **Date:** *10/19/14*

Tier 2 Intervention Summary

The Student Support Team reviewed Nicole's progress on the Tier 2 intervention on story problems [presented in Box 7.9 below] The team noted that Nicole was able to master the STAR strategy within only two weeks of beginning the intervention, and that she quickly mastered one-step story problems. The data further indicate that she has now mastered two-step story problems. Also, Mrs. Popham recently indicated that Nicole is now much more enthusiastic in her mathematics class, and that she has seen an improvement in both her attitude and her daily work. Because the peer buddy idea worked so well with Nicole, Mrs. Popham has decided to implement that version of peer tutoring for her entire mathematics class.

Given Nicole's success, the Student Support Team believes that she will no longer require this Tier 2 intervention, and that, from this point, she can successfully complete the work in her mathematics class without Tier 2 support. Thus, this Tier 2 intervention was successful.

Signature: *Mrs. Toni Varella, Chair, Student Support Team*   **Date:** *11/12/14*

This RTI procedure for Nicole demonstrates many of the same issues as the previous case study. However, as this case study indicates most Tier 2 interventions are successful, and no Tier 3 intervention is required. Research has indicated that, in mathematics, about 60% of the students who begin a well-developed, targeted Tier 2 intervention do succeed, and thus, do not require a Tier 3 intervention (Bender & Crane, 2011). In this case, the RTI process ended sooner than in the previous case study, since no Tier 3 intervention was required in the example in Box 7.9.

Research has indicated that, in mathematics, about 60% of the students who begin a well-developed, targeted Tier 2 intervention do succeed, and thus, do not require a Tier 3 intervention.

Next, while most Tier 2 interventions involve one specifically targeted skill, some do involve two sequenced skills, as shown in this example (e.g., one step problems and two step problems). In such cases, the assessment data must depict a clear, interpretable distinction between the child's performance on each discrete skill.

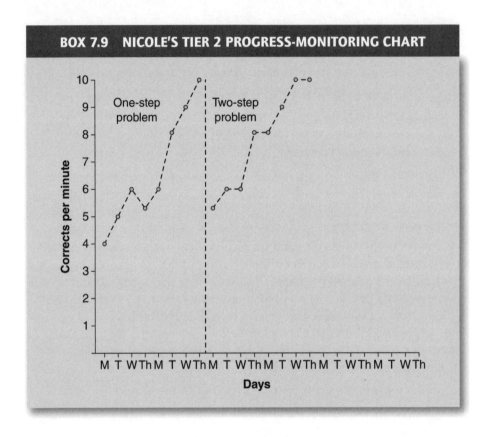

BOX 7.9   NICOLE'S TIER 2 PROGRESS-MONITORING CHART

Again, note the data-driven nature of the RTI process, as well as the team-based decision making. In some schools, a math teacher may initiate a Tier 2 intervention merely by documenting the need and sharing the planned intervention with a lead teacher or master teacher, as suggested in Case Study One above; in other cases, schools have made the decision that the full SST (or the similar team) should be involved prior to any Tier 2 intervention. In almost every case, elementary schools follow the same guidelines on when to involve the SST in an RTI/mathematics process, as that school does for RTI in reading.

Finally, the interdynamics of instruction and assessment in mathematics are shown in each of these case studies. Math teachers in the future can rest assured that there is likely to be a much closer relationship between math instruction and assessment, particularly when CBM is the assessment option utilized as the universal screening tool in the general education math class.

> *In the future there is likely to be a much closer relationship between math instruction and assessment, particularly when CBM is the assessment option utilized as the universal screening tool in the general education math class.*

CONCLUDING NOTES: AN EXCITING TIME FOR MATHEMATICS TEACHERS!

As suggested throughout this chapter, and indeed this entire book, both instruction and assessment in mathematics are changing drastically. Teachers may anticipate that these dynamic changes will impact their classes, and many teachers have already embraced many of the instructional options described herein. Across the nation, teachers of mathematics are flipping their classes, posting video demos of specific types of math problems on a class wiki, blogging on mathematics in the news with their students, finding or developing CBM measures to explicitly identify students' deficit areas, and then providing Tier 2 or Tier 3 interventions targeted to those areas.

Gone are the days when a teacher can sit in front of the class, using the whiteboard or smart board, while demonstrating one problem at a time for the entire class. The very definition of differentiated instruction mandates distinctions among the tasks that students are completing in the class. In fact, classes in the next decade will be much more student centered, with students undertaking peer tutoring, team-based PBL projects, or creating innovative ways to present mathematics content to other students.

Because of the various changes described herein, this is one of the most exciting times to be a mathematics teacher, and the "whole" of these changes will be much greater than the sum of the parts (Bender & Waller, 2011a). While technology, for example, will certainly impact how instruction is delivered, that impact will be magnified ten-fold when tech-based instruction is placed within the context of highly differentiated classes, coupled with RTI interventions, and flipped lessons. In fact, it may be difficult to envision exactly what teaching mathematics might look like in 10 or 15 years, but teachers may be certain of one thing: Mathematics instruction will look drastically different from instruction of the 1990s.

I sincerely hope this book helps in that exciting transition. It is, indeed, a great time to be a teacher!

Appendix A

Recently Developed or Widely Used Curricula in Mathematics

There are a plethora of innovative instructional, computer-based software programs and recently developed hard-copy mathematics curricula used in schools today. Many of these, like the Khan Academy, have been described in text, and some are free for teachers to use. This appendix presents several recently developed, broad-scale mathematics curricula that many mathematics teachers are currently using. Many of these tools allow for individual laptop or tablet-based instruction, and might well provide the option of flipping the classroom, as discussed in Chapter 3. Others have proven to be a great foundation for Tier 2 and 3 RTI interventions in mathematics as discussed in Chapter 7. While other curricula could have been included here, these were chosen for the reasons above, or because they are frequently used in schools today.

NUMBER WORLDS

Griffin (2003a, 2003b, 2004a, 2005) has provided another research-based structure that represents children's early understanding of numbers, Number Worlds. This research-supported resource for teaching young students mathematical concepts is a mathematics readiness/math curriculum that teaches foundational mathematics concepts and skills on a conceptual level and an application level (Griffin, 2003b, 2004a, 2005). This curriculum is intended for children from prekindergarten through Grade 1, and includes software, manipulatives, problem-solving scenarios, games, lesson plans, and hard-copy workbooks, all of which focus on developing a hands-on understanding of numbers and how numbers are used in the real world (Griffin, 2004b; Griffin et al., 2003). While predating the Common Core State Standards for Mathematics, this curriculum is nevertheless congruent with those standards, in that students are taught mathematics readiness and number sense in a manner that stresses deep conceptual understanding. Number Worlds is now published by Scholastic Research Associates (www.sranumberworlds.com).

SRA Number Worlds is based on five instructional principles. The program was developed to

Build on the student's current knowledge using multilevel activities;

Use natural learning paths that children typically employ to develop number sense;

Present new knowledge in a way that supports the common progression children use when learning numbers;

Teach computational fluency; and

Stress hands-on exploration, problem solving, and communication using numbers.

Each concept in the curriculum is discussed and utilized in various ways to assure flexibility in students' understandings of math constructs (Griffin, 2003b, 2004b). In addition to being recommended for average achievers, this program has been evaluated with children from low-income populations, as well as children with special needs, and has proven effective in enhancing number sense, computational fluency, and reasoning, as well as performance on traditional, standardized mathematics achievement tests (Griffin, 2004a, 2005). Positive results of this program were evident in some of these studies, up to one year after termination of the program (Griffin, 2004a, 2005).

Differentiated activities are relatively easy to develop using Number Worlds. Teachers can adjust the sequence of work to accommodate students with many different learning styles. Teachers will assess each student's level of ability and select specific activities for the individual children throughout the year (Griffin, 2004a, 2005).

SAS CURRICULUM PATHWAYS

One recently developed online curriculum for older students that is being used increasingly in schools is the SAS Curriculum Pathways (www .sascurriculumpathways.com). This curriculum is free for teachers worldwide and is used by more than 50,000 teachers in over 12,000 schools. This program provides an extensive, online curricula with materials and instructional activities in English, language arts, science, social studies, mathematics, and Spanish. The lesson activities are designed around the Common Core State Standards in math and are appropriate from grade levels 6–12. While the curriculum is free, teachers are required to login to access the material, and a brief tutorial video is available free of charge at the website above. The company behind this website designed the curriculum materials extremely carefully, with content experts in various subject areas consulting on all aspects of the curriculum. A wide variety of instructional activities are incorporated into this curriculum, as well as excellent graphics and short video demos that can be used in flipped classes. Every mathematics teacher in the middle grades should explore this free curriculum.

MATH IN FOCUS: SINGAPORE MATH

This comprehensive math curriculum, by Marshall Cavendish, is based on instructional practices developed for mathematics in the nation of Singapore in recent decades (www.hmheducation.com/singaporemath/index.php). This curriculum has been developed for students from kindergarten through Grade 8 using a concrete, pictorial, and abstract framework to cover mathematics concepts in depth. In the Math in Focus curriculum, beginning in kindergarten, students are exposed to mathematical concepts, covering less content overall but at a greater depth, with a strong emphasis on conceptual learning as well as mathematical procedures. Rather than covering a concept in two or three days, students in this curriculum may spend two to three weeks exploring mathematical content much more fully, and students achieve mastery prior to moving to the next big idea. Because of this emphasis on deep understanding, this curriculum was one of 15 mathematics curricula that were reviewed in the development of the Common Core State Standards in mathematics. For that reason, this curriculum has and will continue to receive increasing attention.

ACCELERATED MATH FOR INTERVENTION

This newly developed commercially available curriculum from Renaissance Learning utilizes the widely popular Accelerated Math curriculum that has been around for a while, but adds an overlay of assessment and progress-monitoring tools to make this very appropriate for use in RTI interventions (www.renlearn.com/am/RTI.aspx). Accelerated Math for Interventions enables monitored, differentiated math practice, and is recognized as a mastery measure by the National Center on Response to Intervention. Reports from this curriculum provide daily information about student progress toward math mastery (TOPS report), skill by skill, and a variety of other reports (e.g., Status of the Class Report) are available to allow teachers to see student performance or compare students' performance. Because Accelerated Math has been widely used for years, and with the growing emphasis on specific targeted interventions in mathematics for students with mathematics deficits, teachers should expect to see this curriculum more frequently across the elementary grade levels.

IXL

IXL is a subscription-based site that presents mathematics exercises for grades kindergarten through middle school (www.ixl.com). Students completed activities online, answering simple questions on various topics, and their progress is tracked online. IXL assesses students' understanding as they practice, and then generates detailed performance reports that can be used for instruction and/or progress monitoring in an RTI framework. The various reports include data on grade-level proficiency, trouble spots, and even progress toward mathematics mastery.

VMATH

Vmath was developed by the Voyagers company, a company known for the Voyagers reading program (www.voyagerlearning.com/curriculum/math-solutions/vmath). Note: Be careful to not confuse Vmath with Vedic Math!). Vmath is a supplemental curriculum and benchmarking tool, supported by a number of case study applications (found at the website above) that is aimed at students who are struggling in math from Grade 2 through 8. Vmath presents a balance of teacher-led, explicit instruction, printed materials, assessment options, and student work online and is intended to fill gaps in student knowledge across the grade levels. In the daily lessons, teachers model the skills, facilitate both group and individual practice, and provide corrective feedback as students experience difficulty. Each lesson addresses conceptual understanding, skills practice, and problem solving. The program is founded on mathematics standard from the National Council of Teachers of Mathematics and uses CBM as one of the assessment tools. The program aligns well with RTI require-ments, and can be used either in Tier 1 instruction or in Tiers 2 and 3 for specific targeted interventions. Also, intensive training and support are provided once a school undertakes implementation of this program.

STUDY ISLAND

Study Island, from Archipelago Learning, is a supplemental web-based instructional program offering instructional practice in almost every sub-ject area, including math. This is tied specifically to each state's standards of learning (making this particularly useful for states that have not adopted the Common Core State Standards) as well as the Common Core. Study Island is also tied to each state's testing program (visit www.study-island.com for more information). By basing this curriculum exclusively online, the Study Island developers have made these instructional and assessment materials available to licensed users, including teachers and students, both at school and at home, and this can be a significant advan-tage. Some students will undertake these instructional activities in the home environment, and software programs that are loaded exclusively on computers at school do not have that option.

Instructional activities are flexible, and teachers can either allow stu-dents to select topics on which to work, or they can assign specific topics that are based on the exact learning needs and styles of the individual student. The student will then be presented with various computer-based work or educational gaming activities.

Based on adaptive assessment technology within the program, the curriculum adjusts itself according to the learning curve of particular students, either moving students through the reading content faster or moving students into a slower track with more practice on various con-tent items. Once students have mastered a particular lesson and assess-ment, they receive a blue ribbon and are able to move to the next lesson. However, should a student receive a low score, the program may prompt the student to continue working on the same skills until he or she devel-ops proficiency. Thus, students receive instructional feedback each time they answer a question. This can be implemented as either a stand-alone instructional program or as a supplemental program in conjunction with other instruction. Thus, this program can also be used as the basis for RTI procedures either as Tier 1 instruction or as a Tier 2 or Tier 3 interven-tion in mathematics across grade levels. The stand-alone nature makes this curriculum intervention and assessment program ideal for RTI implementation in elementary, middle, or even secondary schools. Like more modern computerized programs, reports can be generated either for individual students or the entire class.

Study Island has only limited anecdotal research support, and that research was prepared by an independent firm under contract with the company. The supporting research can be found on the Study Island website (www.studyisland.com). The Study Island website does present a variety of reports suggesting how Study Island can be implemented in the context of RTI, which will help schools considering RTI implementation in the future. A number of schools around the nation are using Study Island, with some success, in the RTI context.

TRANSMATH

TransMath (http://www.voyagerlearning.com/cs/Satellite/transmath) is a higher-level, hard-copy supplementary mathematics curriculum developed by John Woodward and Mary Stroh that focuses on moving students from elementary mathematics skill levels up to algebra readiness. This curriculum is intended for students functioning at or below the 40th percentile in Grades 5 through 9, but the content covers a wider range of skills, reaching from number sense to algebraic expression. This curriculum covers fewer overall topics than most core mathematics curricula but covers those topics in much more conceptual depth, making it consistent in intent with the Common Core Standards in Mathematics. This program progresses in three levels that focus on specific mathematics areas: number sense, rational numbers, and algebraic expressions.

Three placement assessments (one for each of the levels mentioned) come with the curriculum, and each instructional unit within each level also includes two performance assessments. Together, these assessments allow for frequent progress monitoring, making this a useful curriculum in the RTI context. There is limited research support for this curriculum. This curriculum has been implemented by many elementary, middle, and high schools in their RTI efforts, and given the transitional nature of this curriculum, a focus that is virtually unique in the mathematics area, this curriculum is likely to be implemented in many more schools.

THE SUCCESSMAKER MATH CURRICULUM

SuccessMaker Math is one component of the broader SuccessMaker curriculum from Pearson Learning. It is an instructional software core curriculum that is available for school or school district purchase. This curriculum provides individualized instruction for elementary and middle schools students in a variety of areas including mathematics (www.pearsonschool .com/index.cfm?locator=PSZk99). SuccessMaker is currently being used in many RTI intervention programs in math. Students take an initial assessment when they begin, and those data are used to place each student in specific levels in mathematics. As students complete the lessons, the levels and questions get increasingly complex to move students toward mastery. In addition, SuccessMaker Math generates a variety of progress-monitoring reports for teachers that make it possible to review student growth individually, in subgroups, or for the entire class. This is excellent data for RTI implementation, and the teachers can closely monitor students' growth. This program can be used with the entire class, or students needing a Tier 2 or Tier 3 intervention are able to work with SuccessMaker on an individual basis, at their own pace, with a customized program.

References

Allsopp, D. H. (1997). Using classwide peer tutoring to teach beginning algebra problem-solving skills in heterogeneous classrooms. *Remedial and Special Education, 18*(6), 367–379.

Allsopp, D. H. (1999). Using modeling, manipulatives, and mnemonics with eighth-grade math students. *Teaching Exceptional Children, 32*(2), 74–81.

Allsopp, D. H., Kyger, M. M., Lovin, L., Gerretson, H., Carson, K. L., & Ray, S. (2008). Mathematics dynamic assessment: Informal assessment that responds to the needs of struggling learners in mathematics. *Teaching Exceptional Children, 40*(3), 6–17.

Alsup, J. K. (2003). New classroom rules to promote preservice elementary teachers' mathematics learning education. *ChulaVista, 123*(3), 609–615.

Annenberg Learner. (2013). *Inductive and deductive reasoning.* Retrieved from http://www.learner.org/courses/teachingmath/grades6_8/session_04/section_03_b.html

Ash, K. (2011). Games and simulations help children access science. *Education Week, 30*(27), 12.

Baird, P. (2012, July 24). Many students now learning while having fun with video games. *StarNews Online.* Retrieved from http://www.starnewsonline.com/article/20120724/ARTICLES/120729863/-1/news300?p=3$tc=pg

Baker, S., Gersten, R., & Lee, D. S. (2002). A synthesis of empirical research on teaching mathematics to low-achieving students. *Elementary School Journal, 103,* 51–73.

Barton, M. L., Heidema, C., & Jordan, D. (2002). Teaching reading in mathematics and science. *Educational Leadership, 60*(3), 24–28.

Behrend, J. (2003). Learning-disabled students make sense of mathematics. *Teaching Children Mathematics, 9*(5), 269–274.

Belland, B. R., French, B. F., & Ertmer, P. A. (2009). Validity and problem-based learning research: A review of instruments used to assess intended learning outcomes. *Interdisciplinary Journal of Problem-based Learning, 3*(1), 59–89.

Bender, W. N. (2009). *Differentiating math instruction* (2nd ed.). Thousand Oaks, CA: Corwin.

Bender, W. N. (2012a). *Differentiated instruction for students with learning disabilities: New best practices for general and special educators* (3rd ed.). Thousand Oaks, CA: Corwin.

Bender, W. N. (2012b). Project-based learning: Differentiating instruction for the 21st century. Thousand Oaks, CA: Corwin.

Bender, W. N., & Crane, D. (2011). *RTI in math.* Bloomington, IN: Solution Tree Press.

Bender, W. N., & Shores, C. (2007). *Response to intervention: A practical guide for teachers.* Thousand Oaks, CA: Corwin.

Bender, W. N., & Waller, L. (2011a). *The teaching revolution: RTI, technology, and differentiation transform teaching for the 21st century.* Thousand Oaks, CA: Corwin.

Bender, W. N., & Waller, L. (2011b). *RTI and differentiated reading in the K–8 classroom.* Bloomington, IN: Solution Tree Press.

Bender, W. N., & Waller, L. (2012). *The teaching revolution: RTI, technology, and differentiation transform teaching for the 21st century.* Thousand Oaks, CA: Corwin.

Bender, W. N., & Waller, L. (2013). *Cool tech tools for lower tech teachers.* Thousand Oaks, CA: Corwin.

Bergmann, J., & Sams, A. (2012). Why flipped classrooms are here to stay. *Education Week.* Retrieved from http://www.edweek.org/tm/articles/2012/06/12/fp_bergmann_sams.html?tkn=WPCC1Rxu4%2FbCFsj3iEU3%2Bqk97aMS3xc0jkgq@cmp=cip-sb-ascd

Berkeley, S., Bender, W. N., Peaster, L. G., & Saunders, L. (2009). Implementation of responsiveness to intervention: A snapshot of progress. *Journal of Learning Disabilities, 42*(1), 85–95.

Boss, S., & Krauss, J. (2007). *Reinventing project-based learning: Your field guide to real-world projects in the digital age.* Washington, DC: International Society for Technology in Education.

Bottge, B. A., & Hasselbring, T. (1993). A comparison of two approaches for teaching complex authentic mathematics problems to adolescents in remedial math classes. *Exceptional Children, 59,* 545–556.

Bottge, B. A., Heinrichs, M., Chan, S., & Serlin, R. C. (2001). Anchoring adolescents' understanding of math concepts in rich problem-solving environments. *Remedial and Special Education, 22*(5), 299–314.

Bottge, B. A., Heinrichs, M., Mehta, Z. D., & Hung, Y. (2002). Weighing the benefits of anchored math instruction for students with disabilities in general education classes. *Journal of Special Education, 35*(4), 186–200.

Bottge, B. A., Rueda, E., LaRoque, P. T., Serlin, R. C., & Kwon, J. (2007). Integrating reform-oriented math instruction in special education settings. *Learning Disabilities Research and Practice, 22*(2), 96–109.

Bruer, J. T. (1999, May). In search of . . . brain-based education. *Phi Delta Kappan, 80,* 645–657.

Bruer, J. T. (2006, Summer). Points of view: On the implications of neuroscience research for science teaching and learning: Are there any? *CBE-Life Sciences Education, 5,* 104–110.

Brumley, M. (2010). Twitter. Teacher experience exchange. Retrieved from http://h30411.www.hp.com/discussions/68996?mcid=Twitter

Bui, L. (2012, October 28). Wheaton H.S. to model project-based learning for Montgomery County schools. *The Washington Post.* Retrieved from http://www

.washingtonpost.com/local/education/wheaton-high-to-model-project-based-learning-for-montgomery-county-schools/2012/10/28/b945602a-1a05-11e2-bd10-5ff056538b7c_story.html

Carpenter, T. P., Fennema, E., & Franke, M. L. (1996). Cognitively guided instruction: A knowledge base for reform in primary mathematics instruction. *Elementary School Journal, 97*(1), 3–20.

Carter, C. S., Cohen, S., Keyes, M., Kusimo, P. S., & Lunsford, C. (2002). Hands-on math projects (Vol. 2). Retrieved from http://www.edvantia.org/products/index.cfm?&t=products&c=math

Chapman, C., & King, R. (2005). *Differentiated assessment strategies: One tool doesn't fit all.* Thousand Oaks, CA: Corwin.

Checkley, K. (1999). Math in the early grades: Laying a foundation for later learning. *Association of School Curriculum Development.* Available online at http://www.ascd.org/readingroom/cupcake/1999/1sum.html

Clarkson, L. M. C., Fawcett, G., Shannon-Smith, E., & Goldman, N. I. (2007). Attitude adjustments. *Educational Leadership, 65*(3), 72–77.

Cook, J. (2012). Project-based learning math projects. Retrieved from http://www.ehow.com/list_6498504_project-based-learning-math-projects.html#ixzz2BMhw6UHG

Cook, G. (2011). From desktop to desk: A compelling way to teach math—"flipping" the classroom. Retrieved from http://www.boston.com/bostonglobe/editorial_opinion/oped/articles/2011/09/18/flipping_for_math/

Das, J. P., Naglieri, J. A., & Kirby, J. R. (1994). *Assessment of cognitive processes: The PASS theory of intelligence.* New York, NY: Allyn & Bacon.

Dehaene, S. (2010). The calculating brain. In D. A. Sousa (Ed.), *Mind, brain, & education.* Bloomington, IN: Solution Tree Press.

Deno, S. L. (2003). Development in curriculum-based measurement. *Journal of Special Education, 37*(3), 184–192.

Devlin, K. (2010). The mathematical brain. In D. A. Sousa (Ed.), *Mind, brain, & education.* Bloomington, IN: Solution Tree Press.

Doabler, C. T., Cary, M. S., Jungjohann, K., Clarke, B., Fien, H., Baker, S., . . . Chard, D. (2012). Enhancing core mathematics instruction for students at risk for mathematics disabilities. *Teaching Exceptional Children, 44*(4), 48–57.

Doidge, N. (2007). *The brain that changes itself.* New York, NY: Penguin Books.

Dvorak, T. (2013, February 28). Grant helps Idaho schools plug into online classes. *Associated Press.* Retrieved from http://www.kboi2.com/news/local/Grant-helps-Idaho-schools-plug-into-online-classes-194088691.html

Edick, H. (2012). 8 crucial resources for flipped classrooms. Retrieved from http://edudemic.com/2012/03/8-crucial-resources-for-flipped-classrooms/

eSchool News. (2011, August 29). Press Release: Detroit schools choose movie maker to fuel creativity and boost test scores. *eSchool News.* Retrieved from http://www.eschoolnews.com/2011/08/29/detroit-schools-choose-movie-maker-to-fuel-creativity-and-boost-test-scores/

eSchool News. (2012a). Georgia district implements virtual world technology: Forsyth County Schools will use ed tech to engage students with immersive experiences. Retrieved from http://www.eschoolnews.com/2012/03/28/Georgia-district-implements-virtual-world-technology/

eSchool News. (2012b). Researchers debate gaming's effects on the brain: Scientists caution that more research is needed to prove benefits of video games in education. Retrieved from http://www.eschoolnews.com/2012/01/11/researchers-debate-gamings-effects-on-the-brain/

Fahsl, A. J. (2007). Mathematics accommodations for all students. *Intervention in School and Clinic, 42*(4), 190–203.

Ferriter, B. (2011). Using Twitter in high school classrooms. Retrieved from http://teacherleaders.typepad.com/the_tempered_radical/2011/10/using-twitter-with-teens-.html

Ferriter, W. M., & Garry, A. (2010). *Teaching the iGeneration: 5 easy ways to introduce essential skills with Web 2.0 tools.* Bloomington, IN: Solution Tree Press.

Foegen, A. (2008). Algebra progress monitoring and interventions for students with learning disabilities. *Learning Disability Quarterly, 31*(2), 65–78.

Frontline. (2010, February 8). Digital nation. A broadcast on Public Television. Also available online at http://www.pbs.org/wgbh/pages/frontline

Fuchs, D., & Fuchs, L. S. (2005). Responsiveness to intervention: A blueprint for practitioners, policymakers, and parents. *Teaching Exceptional Children, 18*(1), 57–61.

Fuchs, L. S., Fuchs, D., Compton, D. L., Bryant, J. D., Hamlett, C. L., & Seehaler, P. M. (2007). Mathematics screening and progress monitoring in first grade: Implications for responsiveness to intervention. *Exceptional Children, 73*(3), 311–330.

Fuchs, L. S., Fuchs, D., Powell, S. R., Seehaler, P. M., Cirino, P. T., & Fletcher, J. M. (2008). Intensive interventions for students with mathematics disabilities: Seven principles of effective practice. *Learning Disability Quarterly, 31*(2), 79–92.

Fuson, K. C., & Wearne, D. (1997). Children's conceptual structures for multidigit numbers and methods of multidigit addition and subtraction. *Journal of Research in Mathematics Education, 28*(2), 130–163.

Gagnon, J. C., & Maccini, P. (2001). Preparing students with disabilities in algebra. *Teaching Exceptional Children, 34*(1), 8–15.

Garderen, D. V. (2007). Teaching students with LD to use diagrams to solve mathematics word problems. *Journal of Learning Disabilities, 41*(6), 341–353.

Garelick, B. (2012, November 20). A new kind of problem: The Common Core Math Standards. *The Atlantic.* Retrieved from http://www.theatlantic.com/national/archive/2012/11/a-new-kind-of-problem-the-common-core-mathe-standards/265444/

Gardner, H. (1983). *Frames of mind.* New York, NY: Basic Books.

Gardner, H. (1993). *Multiple intelligences: The theory in practice.* New York, NY: Basic Books.

Gardner, H. (2006). *Multiple intelligences: New horizons.* New York, NY: Basic Books.

Geller, C. H., & Smith, K. S. (2002, October). *Improving the teaching of math from textbook concepts to real-world application.* Paper presented at the annual meeting of the Council for Learning Disabilities, Denver, CO.

Gersten, R., & Chard, D. (1999). Number sense: Rethinking arithmetic instruction for students with learning disabilities. *Journal of Special Education, 44,* 18–28.

Gersten, R., Chard, D., Baker, S., & Lee, D. (2002, October). *Instructional approaches for teaching mathematics to students with learning disabilities: Findings from a synthesis of experimental research.* Paper presented at the annual meeting of the Council for Learning Disabilities, Denver, CO.

Goldman, S. (1989). Strategy instruction in mathematics. *Learning Disability Quarterly, 12,* 43–55.

Goleman, D. (2006, September). The socially intelligent leader. *Educational Leadership, 64,* 76–81.

Green, G. (2012). *My view: Flipped classrooms give every student a chance to succeed.* Retrieved from http://schoolsofthought.blogs.cnn.com/2012/01/18/my-view-flipped-classrooms-give-every-student-a-chance-to-succeed/?htp=hp_bn1

Greenwood, C. R., Delquadri, J. C., & Hall, R. V. (1989). Longitudinal effects of classwide peer tutoring. *Journal of Educational Psychology, 81,* 371–383.

Griffin, S. (2003a). Laying the foundations for computational fluency in early childhood. *Teaching Children Mathematics,* February 2003, 306–309.

Griffin, S. (2003b). Number Worlds: A research-based mathematics program for young children. In D. H. Clements & A. DiBiase (Eds.), *Engaging young children in mathematics: Findings of the 2000 national conference on standards for pre-school and kindergarten mathematics education* (pp. 325–342). Hillsdale, NJ: Erlbaum Associates, Inc.

Griffin, S. (2004a). Building number sense with number worlds. *Early Childhood Research Quarterly, 19*(1), 173–180.

Griffin, S. (2004b). Teaching number sense. *Educational Leadership, 61*(6), 39–42.

Griffin, S. (2005). Teaching mathematics in the primary grades: Fostering the development of whole number sense. In J. Bransford & S. Donovan (Eds.), *How students learn: History, mathematics and science in the classroom* (pp. 250–302). Washington, DC: National Academies Press (http://www.nap.edu).

Griffin, S., Sarama, J., & Clements, D. (2003). Laying the foundations for computational fluency in early childhood. *Teaching Children Mathematics, 81,* 371–383.

Grobecker, B. (1999). Mathematics reform and learning differences. *Learning Disability Quarterly, 22*(1), 43–58.

Gurganus, S. (2004). Promote number sense. *Intervention in School and Clinic, 40*(1), 55–58.

Harniss, M. K., Carnine, D. W., Silbert, J., & Dixon, R. C. (2002). Effective strategies for teaching mathematics. In E. J. Kame'enui, D. W. Carnine, R. C. Dixon, D. C. Simmons, & M. D. Coyne (Eds.), *Effective teaching strategies that accommodate diverse learners.* Upper Saddle River, NJ: Merrill/Prentice Hall.

Harris, C. A., Miller, S. P., & Mercer, C. D. (1995). Teaching initial multiplication skills to students with disabilities in general education classrooms. *Learning Disabilities Research and Practice, 10*(3), 180–195.

Hearne, D., & Stone, S. (1995). Multiple intelligences and underachievement: Lessons from individuals with learning disabilities. *Journal of Learning Disabilities, 28*(7), 439–448.

Helms, A. D. (2013, January 7). Education and video games are no longer enemies: Educators say some games develop skills. *Charlotte Observer*. Retrieved from http://www.charlotteobserver.com/2013/01/07/3768358/education-and-video-games-are.html

Hess, B. (2012). *The fate of the Common Core: The view from 2022. Education Week.* Retrieved from http://blogs.edweek.org/edweek/rick_hess_straight_up/2012/03/the_fate_of_the_common_core_the_view_from_2022.html?utm_source-twitterfeed$utm_medium-twitter&utm_campaign=Walt+Gardner+Reality+Check

Higbee, K. L. (1987). Process mnemonics: Principles, prospects, and problems. In M. A. McDaniel & M. Pressley (Eds.), *Imagery and related mnemonic processes: Theories, individual differences and applications* (pp. 407–427). New York, NY: Springer.

Hudson, H. (2012). *The teacher report: 6 ways teachers are using video games in the classroom.* Retrieved from http://www.weareteachers.com/community/weareteachers-blog/blog-wat/2012/11/06/the-teacher-report-6-ways-teachers-are-using-video-games-in-the-classroom

International Society for Technology in Education (ISTE). (2010). Topic: Student learning. Retrieved from http://caret.iste.org/index.cfm?fuseaction=evidence&answerID=12&words=Attention

Jackson, F. (2002). Crossing content: A strategy for students with learning disabilities. *Intervention in School and Clinic, 37*(5), 279–283.

Jitendra, A. (2002). Teaching students math problem solving through graphic representations. *Teaching Exceptional Children, 91,* 345–356.

Jitendra, A. K., Hoff, K., & Beck, M. M. (1999). Teaching middle school student with learning disabilities to solve word problems using a schema-based approach. *Remedial and Special Education, 20*(1), 50–64.

Jones, C. J. (2001). CBAs that work: Assessing students' math content-reading levels. *Teaching Exception Children, 34*(1), 24–29.

Jones, E. D., Wilson, R., & Bhojwani, S. (1997). Mathematics instruction for secondary students with learning disabilities. *Journal of Learning Disabilities, 30*(2), 151–163.

Jordan, N. C. (2007). The need for number sense. *Educational Leadership, 65*(2), 63–68.

Jordan, N. C., Kaplan, D., Locuniak, M. N., & Ramineni, C. (2007). Predicting first-grade math achievement from developmental number sense trajectories. *Learning Disabilities Research and Practice, 22*(1), 36–46.

Jordan, L., Miller, M., & Mercer, C. (1998). The effects of concrete to semi-concrete to abstract instruction in acquisition and retention of fraction concepts and skills. *Learning Disabilities: A Multidisciplinary Journal, 9*(3), 115–122.

Joseph, L. M., & Hunter, A. D. (2001). Differential application of cue card strategy for solving fraction problems: Exploring instructional utility of the cognitive assessment system. *Child Study Journal, 31*(2), 123–136.

Karp, K. S., & Voltz, D. L. (2000). Weaving mathematical instructional strategies into inclusive settings. *Intervention in School and Clinic, 35*(4), 206–215.

Katz, J., Mirenda, P., & Auerbach, S. (2002). Instructional strategies and educational outcomes for students with developmental disabilities in inclusive "multiple intelligences" and typical inclusive classrooms. *Research and Practice for Persons with Severe Disabilities, 27*(4), 227–238.

Keller, K., & Menon, V. (2009). Gender differences in the functional and structural neuroanatomy of mathematical cognition. *NeuroImage, 47*, 342–352.

Kessler, S. (2011). *5 best practices for educators on Facebook.* Retrieved from http://mashable.com/2011/12/05/educators-on-facebook/

King, K., & Gurian, M. (2006). Teaching to the minds of boys. *Educational Leadership, 64*(1), 56–61.

Koellner, K., Colsman, M., & Risley, R. (2011). Multidimensional assessment: Guiding response to intervention in mathematics. *Teaching Exceptional Children, 44*(2), 48–57.

Kortering, L. J., deBottencourt, L. U., & Braziel, P. M. (2005). Improving performance in high school algebra: What students with learning disabilities are saying. *Learning Disability Quarterly, 28*(3), 191–204.

Koscinski, S., & Gast, D. (1993). Use of constant time delay in teaching multiplication facts to students with learning disabilities. *Journal of Learning Disabilities, 26*(8), 533–544, 567.

Kroeger, S. D., & Kouche, B. (2006). Using peer-assisted learning strategies to increase response to intervention in inclusive middle math settings. *Teaching Exceptional Children, 38*(5), 6–13.

Kunsch, C. A., Jitendra, A. K., & Wood, S. (2007). The effects of peer-meditated instruction in mathematics for students with learning problems: A research synthesis. *Learning Disabilities Research and Practice, 22*(1), 1–12.

Larmer, J., & Mergendoller, J. R. (2010). 7 essentials for project-based learning. *Educational Leadership, 68*(1), 34–37.

Larmer, J., Ross, D., & Mergendoller, J. R. (2009). *PBL starter kit: To-the-point advice, tools, and tips for your first project in middle or high school.* San Rafael, CA: Unicorn Printing Specialists.

List, J. S., & Bryant, B. (2010). Integrating interactive online content at an early college high school: An exploration of Moodle, Ning, and Twitter. *Meridian Middle School Computer Technologies Journal, 12*(1). Retrieved from http://www.ncsu.edu/meridian/winter2009/

Lock, R. H. (1996). Adapting mathematics instruction in the general education classroom for students with mathematics disabilities. *LD Forum, 21*(2), 19–23. (ERIC Document Reproduction Service No. EJ529409).

Loveless, T. (2012). *How well are American students learning?* Retrieved from http://www.brookings.edu/~/media/Newsletters/0216_brown_education_loveless.PDF

Mabbott, D. J., & Bisanz, J. (2008). Computational skills, working memory, and conceptual knowledge in older children with mathematical learning disabilities. *Journal of Learning Disabilities, 41*(1), 5–28.

Magee, M. (2013, February 25). Revamping the "core" of education: New Common Core Standards will focus on critical thinking over memorization.

Retrieved from http://www.utsandiego.com/news/2013/feb/25/revamping-the-core-of-education/

Mancl, D. B., Miller, S. P., & Kennedy, M. (2012). Using the concrete-representational-abstract sequence with integrated strategy instruction to teach subtraction with regrouping to students with learning disabilities. *Learning Disabilities Research and Practice, 27*(4), 152–166.

Manolo, E. (1991). The incorporation of process mnemonic instruction in teaching computational skills: A case report on a mathematics learning disabled individual. *Focus on Learning Problems in Mathematics, 13*(4), 21–34.

Manolo, E., Bunnell, J. K., & Stillman, J. A. (2000). The use of process mnemonics in teaching students with mathematics learning disabilities. *Learning Disability Quarterly, 23*(2), 137–156.

Marsh, L. G., & Cooke, N. L. (1996). The effects of using manipulatives in teaching math problem solving to students with learning disabilities. *Learning Disabilities Research and Practice, 11*(1), 58–65.

Maton, N. (2011). *Can an online game crack the code to language learning?* Retrieved from http://mindshift.kqed.org/2011/11/can-an-online-game-crack-the-code-to-language-learning/

McCrea, N. (2012, December 20). Maine schools experimenting with web-based math homework. *Bangor Daily News.* Retrieved from http://bangordailynews.com/2012/12/20/education/maine-schools-experimenting-with-web-based-math-homework/

McMaster, K. L., Du, X., & Petursdottir, A. L. (2009). Technical features of curriculum-based measures for beginning writers. *Journal of Learning Disabilities, 42*(1), 41–60.

Mergendoller, J. R., Maxwell, N., & Bellisimo, Y. (2007). The effectiveness of problem based instruction: A comprehensive study of instructional methods and student characteristics. *Interdisciplinary Journal of Problem-Based Learning 1*(2), 49–69.

Merzenich, M. M. (2001). Cortical plasticity contributing to childhood development. In J. L. McClelland & R. S. Siegler (Eds.), *Mechanisms of cognitive development: Behavioral and neural perspectives.* Mahwah, NJ: Lawrence Erlbaum Associates.

Merzenich, M. M., Tallal, P., Peterson, B., Miller, S., & Jenkins, W. M. (1999). Some neurological principles relevant to the origins of—and the cortical plasticity-based remediation of—developmental language impairments. In J. Grafman & Y. Christen (Eds.), *Neuronal plasticity: Building a bridge from the laboratory to the clinic.* Berlin, Germany: Springer-Verlag.

Miller, A. (2011a). *Game-based learning units for the everyday teacher.* Retrieved from http://www.edutopia.org/blog/video-game-model-unit-andrew-miller

Miller, A. (2011b). *Get your game on: How to build curricula units using the video game model.* Retrieved from http://www.edutopia.org/blog/gamification-game-based-learning-unit-andrew-miller

Miller, A. (2012). *A new community and resources for games for learning.* Retrieved from http://www.edutopia.org/blog/games-for-learning-community-resources-andrew-miller/

Miller, S. P., & Hudson, P. (2007). Helping students with disabilities understand what mathematics means. *Teaching Exceptional Children, 39*(1), 28–35.

Montague, M. (1997). Student perception, mathematical problem solving, and learning disabilities. *Remedial and Special Education, 18*(1), 46–53.

Mortweet, S. L., Utley, C. A., Walker, D., Dawson, H. L., Delquadri, J. C., Reddy, S. S. et al. (1999). Classwide peer tutoring: Teaching students with mild mental retardation in inclusive classrooms. *Exceptional Children, 65*(4), 524–536.

Naglieri, J. A., & Gottling, S. H. (1997). Mathematics instruction and PASS cognitive processes: An intervention study. *Journal of Learning Disabilities, 30*(5), 513–520.

Naglieri, J. A., & Johnson, D. (2000). Effectiveness of a cognitive strategy intervention in improving arithmetic computation based on the PASS theory. *Journal of Learning Disabilities, 33*(6), 591–597.

National Council of Teachers of Mathematics (NCTM). (2000). *Principles and standards for school mathematics.* Available at http://standards.nctm.org

National Mathematics Advisory Panel (NMAP). (2008). *Foundations for success: The final report of the National Mathematics Advisory Panel:* Washington, DC: U.S. Department of Education.

Niguidula, D. (2011). Digital portfolios and curriculum maps: Linking teacher and student work. In H. H. Jacobs (Ed.), *Curriculum 21: Essential education for a changing world.* Alexandria, VA: Association for Supervision and Curriculum Development.

O'Meara, J. (2010). *Beyond differentiated instruction.* Thousand Oaks, CA: Corwin.

Ostad, S. A., & Sorensen, P. M. (2007). Private-speech and strategy use patters: Bidirectional comparisons of children with and without mathematical difficulties in a developmental perspective. *Journal of Learning Disabilities, 40*(1), 2–14.

Phillips, L. F. (2011, December 22). 5 tips for teachers to navigate Facebook's features and risks. Retrieved from http://www.schoolbook.org/2011/12/22/5-tips-for-teachers-to-navigate-facebooks-features-and-risks

Richardson, W. (2010). *Blogs, wikis, podcasts, and other powerful tools for educators.* Thousand Oaks, CA: Corwin.

Richardson, W. (2012). Preparing students to learn without us. *Educational Leadership.* Retrieved from http://www.ascd.org/publications/educational-leadership/feb12/vol69/num05/Preparing-Students-to-Learn-Without-Us.aspx

Richardson, W., & Mancabelli, R. (2011). *Personal learning networks: Using the power of connections to transform education.* Bloomington, IN: Solution Tree Press.

Richtel, M. (2012; January 20). Blogs vs. term papers. *The New York Times.* Retrieved from http://www.nytimes.com/2012/01/22/education/edlife/musclinig-in-on-the-term-paper-tradition.html?_r=1

Sawchuk, S. (2012). Universities, districts to partner on Common-Core Secondary Math. *Education Week.* Retrieved from http://blogs.edweek.org/edweek/teacherbeat/2012/05/_there_has_been_quite.html

Schlemmer, P., & Schlemmer, D. (2008). *Teaching beyond the test: Differentiated project-based learning in a standards-based age.* Minneapolis, MN: Free Spirit.

Schuster, J. W., Stevens, K. B., & Doak, P. K. (1990). Using constant time delay to teach word definitions. *Journal of Special Education, 24*, 306–317.

Seethaler, P. M., & Fuchs, L. S. (2006). The cognitive correlates of computational estimation skill among third grade students. *Learning Disabilities Research and Practice, 21*(4), 233–243.

Shaftel, J., Pass. L., & Schnabel, S. (2005). Math games for adolescents. *Teaching Exceptional Children, 37*(3), 25–31.

Shah, N. (2012). Special educators borrow from brain studies. *Education Week, 31*(17), 10.

Shaughnessy, J. M. (2011). *Assessment and the Common Core State Standards: Let's stay on top of it!* Retrieved from http://www.nctm.org/about/content.aspx?id=30169

Shaw-Jing, C., Stigler, J. W., & Woodward, J. A. (2000). The effects of physical materials on kindergartners' learning of number concepts. *Cognition & Instruction, 18*(3), 32–64.

Sheehy, K. (2011). *High school teachers make gaming academic.* Retrieved from http://www.usnews.com/education/high-schools/articles/2011/11/01/high-school-teachers-make-gaming-academic

Silver, H. F., & Perini, M. J. (2010). The eight Cs of engagement: How learning styles and instructional design increase student commitment to learning. In R. Marzano (Ed.), *On excellence in teaching.* Bloomington, IN: Solution Tree Press.

Silver, H. F., Strong, R. W., & Perini, M. J. (2000). *So each may learn: Integrating learning styles and multiple intelligences.* Alexandria, VA: Association for Supervision and Curriculum Development.

Sousa, D. A. (2001). *How the special needs brain learns.* Thousand Oaks, CA: Corwin.

Sousa, D. A. (2006). *How the special needs brain learns* (3rd ed.). Thousand Oaks, CA: Corwin.

Sousa, D. A. (2008). *How the brain learns mathematics.* Thousand Oaks, CA: Corwin.

Sousa, D. A. (Ed.). (2010). *Mind, brain, & education.* Bloomington, IN: Solution Tree Press.

Sousa, D. A., & Tomlinson, C. A. (2011). *Differentiation and the brain: How neuroscience supports the learner-friendly classroom.* Bloomington, IN: Solution Tree Press.

Sparks, S. D. (2011). Schools "flip" for lesson model promoted by Khan Academy. *Education Today, 31*(5), 1–14.

Stading, M., Williams, R. L., & McLaughlin, T. F. (1996). Effects of a copy, cover, and compare procedure on multiplication facts mastery with a third grade girl with learning disabilities in a home setting. *Education and Treatment of Children, 19*, 425–434.

Stansbury, M. (2012a). A first-hand look inside a flipped classroom. *eSchool News.* Retrieved from http://www.eschoolnews.com/2012/02/09/a-first-hand-look-inside-a-flipped-classroom/

Stansbury, M. (2012b). *Six ed-tech resources for ELL/ESL instruction. eSchool News.* Retrieved from http://www.eschoolnews.com/2012/02/10/six-ed-tech-resources-for-ellesl-instruction/2/?

Strauss, V. (2003, December 2). Trying to figure out why math is so hard for some; theories abound: Genetics, gender, how it's taught. *The Washington Post*, p. A13.

Stern, C. (1949). *Children discover arithmetic.* New York, NY: Harper.

Sternberg, R. (1985). *Beyond IQ: A triarchic theory of human intelligence.* New York, NY: Cambridge University Press.

Sternberg, R. J. (2006). Recognizing neglected strengths. *Educational Leadership, 64*(1), 30–35.

Stiggins, R. (2005, December). From formative assessment to assessment for learning: A path to success in standards-based schools. *Phi Delta Kappan, 87*(4), 324–328.

Takahashi, P. (2012, February 8). *Schools seeing improvement in math scores as students play video game. Las Vegas Sun.* Retrieved from http://m.lasvegassun.com/news/2012/feb/08/school-district-seeing-improvement-math-scores-stu/

Tate, M. L. (2005). *Reading and language arts worksheets don't grow dendrites.* Thousand Oaks, CA: Corwin.

Tomlinson, C. A. (1999). *The differentiated classroom: Responding to the needs of all learners.* Alexandria, VA: Association for Supervision and Curriculum Development.

Tomlinson, C. A. (2001). *How to differentiate instruction in mixed-ability classrooms* (2nd ed.). Alexandria, VA: Association for Supervision and Curriculum Development.

Tomlinson, C. A. (2003). *Differentiation in practice: A resource guide for differentiating curriculum: Grades K–5.* Alexandria, VA: Association for Supervision and Curriculum Development.

Tomlinson, C. A., (2010). Differentiating instruction in response to academically diverse student populations. In R. Marzano (Ed.), *On excellence in teaching.* Bloomington, IN: Solution Tree Press.

Tomlinson, C. A., Brimijoin, K., & Narvaez, L. (2008). *The differentiated school: Making revolution changes in teaching and learning.* Alexandria, VA: Association for Supervision and Curriculum Development.

Toppo, G. (2011, October 6). "Flipped" classrooms take advantage of technology. *USA Today.* Retrieved from http://usatoday30.usatoday.com/news/education/story/2011-10-06/flipped-classrooms-virtual-teaching/50681482/1

Toppo, G. (2012, May 2). Common Core Standards drive wedge in education circles. *USA Today.* Retrieved from http://www.usatoday.com/news/education/story/2012-04-28/common-core-education/54583192/1

Ujifusa, A. (2012). ALEC's Common Core vote now under public microscope. *Education Week.* Retrieved from http://blogs.edweek.org/edweek/state_edwatch/2012/05/alec_common_core_vote_now_under_public_micro scope.html

Varlas, L. (2010). Responding to the research: Harvey Silver and Matthew Perini address learning styles. *Education Update, 52*(5). Retrieved from http://www

.ascd.org/publications/newsletters/education-update/may10/vol52/num05/Responding-to-the-Research.aspx

Watters, A. (2011a). *Khan Academy expands to art history, Sal Khan no longer its only faculty member.* Retrieved from http://www.hackeducation.com/2011/10/19/khan-academy-expands-to-art-history-sal-khan-no-longer-its-only-faculty-member/

Watters, A. (2011b). *Why wikis still matter.* Retrieved from http://www.edutopia.org/blog/wiki-classroom-audrey-watters

Watters, A. (2011c). *Distractions begone! Facebook as a study tool.* Retrieved from http://mindshift.kqed.org/2011/09/distractions-set-aside-facebook-as-a-study-tool/

Wetzel, D. R. (2009). *Project based learning in mathematics.* Retrieved from http://suite101.com/article/project-based-learning-in-mathematics-a142678

Wetzel, D. R. (2012). *Using wikis in math classes.* Retrieved from http://suite101.com/article/using-wikis-in-math-classes-a67900

Whitenack, J. W., Knipping, N., Loesing, J., Kim, O. K., & Beetsma, A. (2002). Supporting first graders' development of number sense. *Teaching Children Mathematics, 9*(1), 26–33.

Witzel, B. S., Riccomini, P. J., & Schneider, E. (2008). Implementing CRA with secondary students with learning disabilities in math. *Intervention in School and Clinic, 43*(5), 270–276.

Wolery, M., Bailey, D. B., & Sugai, G. M. (1988). *Effective teaching: Principles and procedures of applied behavior analysis with exceptional students.* Boston, MA: Allyn & Bacon.

Wolery, M., Cybriwsky, C. A., Gast, D. L., & Boyle-Gast, K. (1991). Use of constant time delay and attentional responses with adolescents. *Exceptional Children, 57*, 462–474.

Woodward, J. (2001). Constructivism and the role of skills in mathematics instruction for academically at-risk secondary students. *Special Services in the Schools, 17*(1), 15–32.

Woodward, J. (2006). Developing automaticity in multiplication facts: Integrating strategy instruction with timed practice drills. *Learning Disability Quarterly 29*(4), 269–290.

Woodward, J., & Montague, M. (2002). Meeting the challenge of mathematics reform for students with LD. *Journal of Special Education, 36*(2), 89–102.

Wurman, Z., & Wilson, W. S. (2012). The Common Core Math Standards: Are they a step forward or backward? *Education Next, 12*(3). Retrieved from http://educationnext.org/the-common-core-math-standards/

Young, F. (2012, December 14). *How I use Twitter in my classroom.* Retrieved from http://edudemic.com/2012/12/how-i-use-twitter-in-my-classroom/

Index

CORWIN
A SAGE Company

The Corwin logo—a raven striding across an open book—represents the union of courage and learning. Corwin is committed to improving education for all learners by publishing books and other professional development resources for those serving the field of PreK–12 education. By providing practical, hands-on materials, Corwin continues to carry out the promise of its motto: **"Helping Educators Do Their Work Better."**